# THE MINISTRY OF PREACHING

**PREACHING THROUGH ETERNITY —
FAITHFULNESS TO GOD'S WORD IN THE LAST
DAYS**

Aaron Michael Roberts

© The Ministry of Preaching

© November 11, 2025, Aaron Michael Roberts/Victory Life Ministries Press

All rights reserved.

No part of this publication may be reproduced, stored in a retrieval system, or transmitted in any form or by any means—electronic, mechanical, photocopying, recording, or otherwise—without prior written permission from the publisher, except for brief quotations in reviews, sermons, academic research, or educational use.

All Scripture quotations are taken from the King James Version (KJV) of the Holy Bible, public domain. All Hebrew, Greek, Aramaic, and transliterated terms are used under fair academic use for educational and theological purposes. All references to ancient sources—including but not limited to the Dead Sea Scrolls, Targumim, Midrashim, Torah, Talmud, Septuagint (LXX), Josephus, Philo, Apostolic Fathers, and early Christian writers—are cited for educational use and fall within Fair Use. They are referenced within SBL 2nd edition standards and remain the property of their respective publishers.

Printed in the United States of America.

Victory Life Ministries Press
Email: victorylifemissions@gmail.com

ISBN: 979-8-218-89015-5
Library of Congress Control Number: 2025926885
First Edition
Internal production reference: FFS-03-TMP-6X9-PB

**LIBRARY OF CONGRESS CIP DATA**

    Library of Congress Cataloging-in-Publication Data
    Names: Roberts, Aaron Michael, 1973 – author.
    Title: The Ministry of Preaching: Preaching Through Eternity — Faithfulness to God's Word in the Last Days/Aaron Michael Roberts.
    Description: First edition. | Pounding Mill, VA: Victory Life Ministries Press, 2025. | Includes bibliographical references and index.
    Identifiers:
    LCCN 2025 – 2025926885
    ISBN 979-8-218-89015-5 (paperback)
    Subjects: LCSH: Preaching. | Bible—Homiletical use. | Clergy—Religious life. | Holy Spirit—Role in preaching. | Bible—Study and teaching. | Eschatology. | Revival—Christianity.
    Classification: LCC BV4211. R63 2025 | DDC 251—dc23
    LC record available at https://lccn.loc.gov/
    Cataloging-in-Publication Data is prepared by the Library of Congress.

# Dedication

To my sons, Daniel and Ezekiel: Your lives stirred this work into motion, and the hand of God in your lives assures its continuation in the fivefold ranks. May these pages bear witness to the desire and legacy you carry.

To my friend and former pastor, Jerry Fletcher: Your unwavering encouragement over fifteen years of shared overseas preaching urged this publication to completion. True friends inspire deeper love for Scripture and its exposition, and you are one in a lifetime.

To the memory of my father, Gary M., who pastored one congregation for nearly fifty years with unshakable devotion. You modeled exposition and the year study in Romans no one will ever forget. Thank you for your holy example - your midnight pursuits of truth, the saying "Put the Book on it," your prayerful resilience, and placing Thiessen and Hodge in my fifteen-year-old hands from your fabulous library. I will see you soon.

To emerging end-time preachers—men and women heralding the everlasting gospel: May this strengthen your hands and steady your hearts.

Finally, thanks to God for the grace to complete it. Christ and His Word remain the wonder of my life.

# Pre-publication Voices from the Global Church

"Inspiring truth, marked by bold honesty—a must-read for every pastor."

— **Bishop Dr. Samuel Kasango, Germany/Uganda**

"Ministry of Preaching is a revelational survey of the ministry of preaching from the Old Testament to its blossom and fulfillment in the work of Jesus Christ in the New Testament through the Holy Spirit."

— **Dr. Thomas Lubari, South Sudan**

"What resonated most was the book's insistence that faithfulness in the last days is not maintained by strategy or relevance, but by sustained intimacy with God's presence—where holiness, courage, and obedience are forged before pressure ever comes. This volume equips pastors by re-centering their calling in the prophetic stream of Scripture, reminding them that suffering, opposition, and marginalization have always been the normal environment for faithful proclamation—and that God meets His servants with fire precisely there. If you want your preaching and leadership to be anchored not in survival but in faithfulness, not in popularity but in the presence of God, this book will steady your heart and strengthen your voice."

— **Reverend Benjamin Dupte, India**

"This book is a timely and essential resource that equips shepherds to lead their flocks with courage, wisdom, and perseverance in uncertain times."

— **Bishop Boniface Gitau, Kenya**

"This is a must read for every minister, leader, pastor or bishop for insight, guidance and understanding of spiritual momentum on the call of God on your life through the thin and thick or through the light and darkest moments of life in your ministry journey teaching, enlighting and aligning us to God ' heart of love and full purpose in our lives."

— **Pastor Richard Abaliwano, Uganda**

# Preface and Methodological Statement

## Why Preaching Matters at the End of the Age

The widespread crisis in modern homiletics is there is a divorce in the ministry of preaching—our human act on Sunday morning—from the sovereign ministry of the Word of God to us—His cosmic, canonical, redemptive work. The central aim of this book is to demonstrate that faithful preaching is simply the process of aligning the ministry of preaching with the eternal, fivefold rhythm of the ministry of the Word of God to mankind.

There are moments in history when the earth grows quiet, not because God has withdrawn, but because His people have forgotten how to listen. Scripture calls it "a famine... of hearing the words of the LORD" (Amos 8:11), a sobering phrase because the famine does not begin in the heavens—it begins in the heart.

We are living in such an hour again—not a famine of resources, access, or information, but a famine of the living Word spoken with clarity, purity, authority, and the anointing of the Holy Spirit.

Before every major movement of God, He restores His voice to His people. Before Samuel, the lamp flickered low. Before John the Baptist, four hundred years of silence hung over Israel. Before the Reformation, Scripture lay hidden from the common people. Before every revival, a deep hunger stirred in ordinary hearts. What God restores first is never a program or institution—He restores preaching. He restores His covenant voice.

This book was born from that conviction, and from years of carrying a growing sense that the Church approaches a decisive turning point: a moment when God will again awaken the preaching gift—not only in ordained pulpits, but across the entire Body of Christ. Pastors, teachers, evangelists, prophets, and apostles—each called, each graced, each shaped by the Spirit—will rise with a unified voice to proclaim Christ with truth and fire.

This is why preaching matters at the end of the age: truth must be heard again in a world drowning in confusion.

The Spirit must burn again in a Church tempted by comfort.

Nations will need a clear gospel amid shaking; the Bride must be made ready for the return of the Lord.

This book is neither a theory of ministry nor a commentary on preaching styles. It is a scriptural journey through longing, covenant, history, revival, and the fivefold gifts, designed to renew the heart of every preacher God is raising today.

Throughout church history, revival preaching has often carried eschatological sobriety. Peter quoted Joel at Pentecost. The Reformers wrote as though the world trembled on the edge of the reformation. Wesley and Whitefield preached as if Christ might return before morning. Martyn Lloyd-Jones spoke of revival as the church's urgent hope "in the last days."

This continuity reveals a shared conviction—that faithful proclamation is always offered in the awareness that "the judge standeth before the door" (James 5:9). It is in this same spirit—not as speculation, but as pastoral seriousness—that I believe we stand near a decisive global turning and a fresh awakening of the fivefold voice.

To my Reformed brothers and sisters, I write this not as a departure, but as a continuation. What previous generations proclaimed instinctively, I now seek to articulate theologically.

### Methodological Statement: A Canonical-Theological and Homiletical-Praxis Approach

Christian preaching must rest upon a clearly articulated hermeneutical and theological method. Because preaching stands at the intersection of Scripture, theology, Spirit-empowered proclamation, and ecclesial formation, it cannot be reduced to private devotion or individual technique. This work therefore employs a canonical-theological and homiletical-praxis approach, rooted in three foundational convictions:

1. Scripture is a coherent canonical whole whose authority is encountered when the church submits to its shape, structure, and Christological center (Luke 24:27; Heb 1:1–2).

2. Authentic preaching reflects the inseparable unity of Word and Spirit that permeates the canon itself.

3. Preaching is transformational divine speech that forms the people of God for holiness and mission.

Though this volume is written from a renewal-oriented conviction that the ascension-gift ministries of Ephesians 4 continue today, it gladly stands in the debt of broad homiletical tradition. The call to expository fidelity, the importance of a controlling idea, and the pastoral aim of life transformation owe much to Reformed and evangelical voices such as Ray Stedman (whose body-life emphasis and expository series through entire books shaped a generation), Bryan Chapell (Christ-Centered Preaching), John Piper (The Supremacy of God in Preaching), Haddon Robinson, and countless faithful cessationist expositors who have modeled Scripture-first preaching across the centuries. In similar fashion, contemporary academic homiletics has sharpened our understanding of how the preached Word engages hearers in today's cultural moment.

While the methodological convictions and presuppositions of this work inevitably lead in a different direction at points, these voices are embraced as respected dialogue partners. Readers from every tradition are warmly invited into this discussion—not to abandon their theological commitments, but to weigh what is offered here against the canonical witness we hold in common.

In this spirit of shared pursuit, the homiletical-praxis method developed in this volume unfolds through five interwoven movements:

1. Longing – Cultivating holy desire that prepares the heart to hear (the divine ache and its human echo).

2. Revelation – Canonical exegesis and Christological interpretation that open the Scriptures.

3. Witness – Listening to the historic testimony of Israel, the apostles, the fathers, the Reformers, revivalists, and the global church.

4. Response – Calling hearers to embodied obedience, repentance, justice, mercy, and mission.

5. Renewal – Participating in the Spirit's ongoing work of individual and corporate transformation toward the eschatological future (Acts 3:19–21).

---

These movements do not function as a rigid formula but as a theological rhythm flowing from Scripture's own pattern—God longs and awakens human longing; God reveals, and we bear witness; God calls, and we respond, God renews, and we are transformed.

In this way, the rhythm is not an addition to the preaching tradition but a renewed articulation of what faithful voices have practiced across time.

The theological rhythm rings aloud- derived from Scripture's own pattern: God longs → awakens human longing → speaks → forms a people → sends them with His voice.

Theologically, preaching is positioned as
- canonical – arising from the whole witness of Scripture.
- Christological – centered on the Living Word.
- pneumatological – animated by the Spirit's presence and power.
- ecclesial – forming the covenant community.
- missional – joining God's sending of the church into the world.

This methodological framework governs every chapter. It invites the reader—whether pastor, scholar, student, or lay preacher—to engage the sacred task of proclamation with scholarly integrity, pastoral reverence, and expectant faith that the same Spirit who brooded over the waters, walked in the garden, thundered at Sinai, and breathed at Pentecost still speaks today.

Aaron Michael Roberts
November 11, 2025
Tazewell, VA

## Invitational Prologue

Every generation discovers that God speaks not only in words but in patterns—a holy rhythm woven through Scripture from the brooding Spirit over the void to the fire at Pentecost.

While writing this book that rhythm surfaced again and again, gentle yet unmistakable, like the heartbeat of the Shepherd Himself.

To the reader — receive these pages not as a new system to master, but as a lens to see Scriptural patterns of communication.

To the teacher and preacher — consider this a companion, not a constraint. Nothing here is meant to replace the sacred uniqueness God has forged in you through midnight wrestlings with God, your experiences and mercy upon mercy. Instead, may these rhythms awaken what is already alive in your ministry and remind you that you stand in a lineage stretching from Torah to the Upper Room.

Slow down. Breathe. Step inside expecting the Shepherd to speak.

You are not about to learn a method—you are about to trace a rhythm older than Sinai and gentler than the whisper in the cave of Elijah.

Welcome to the journey.

---

# TABLE OF CONTENTS

**Dedication**

**Author's Preface & Methodological Vision**

**Invitational Prologue**

---

**PART I — GENESIS: PASTORAL STREAM - THE SHEPHERD'S CALL**

1. The Shepherd's Ache - The Heart of a Pastor     3
2. The Call of God Echoed in the Heart of a Preacher     19
3. The Five-Fold Voice - Torah as the Canonical Foundation.     37

---

**PART II — EXODUS: PRIESTLY STREAM - TEACHING THE TRUTH IN COVENANT**

    4. The Ministry of the Priest     71

---

**PART III — LEVITICUS: PROPHETIC STREAM - THE LIVING WORD**

    5. Prophetic Preaching: Declaration of the Living Word     97

---

**PART IV — NUMBERS: EVANGELISTIC STREAM – HERALDING THE GOOD NEWS**

    6. Evangelistic Preaching: Proclaiming God's Kingdom     123

---

**PART V — DEUTERONOMY: APOSTOLIC STREAM – DIVINE COMMISSIONING**

    7. Apostolic Preaching: God's Divine Continuum     153

---

**PART VI — MINISTRY OF PREACHING: ONE VOICE OF THE PEOPLE OF GOD**

    8. The Fivefold Voice in One Preaching People     179

    Epilogue — The Rhythm Endures: Preaching into Eternity     201

## APPENDICES

| | |
|---|---|
| Appendix A — The Canonical Architecture of Ascension Gifts | 203 |
| Appendix B — Implementation: A Pastoral Practice Workbook | 217 |
| A Conceptual Guide to the Key Theological Terms in this book | 229 |
| The Ministry of Preaching: A Formative Movement | 235 |
| Appendix C — Master Original Language Lexicon | 249 |
| Appendix D — Second Temple Preaching Forms | 259 |
| Appendix E — The Preacher and the Sacred Trust | 269 |
| Appendix F — Historical Witness on Preaching | 273 |
| Appendix G — Dead Sea Scrolls, Midrash, and Targum Sources | 281 |
| Appendix H — The Preacher's Prayer Manual | 291 |
| Appendix I – Preaching Through Centuries | 301 |
| Addendum: A Response to Warfield, Gaffin, and MacArthur | 311 |
| Master Glossary (A–Z) | 321 |
| Scripture Index | 327 |
| Subject Index | 331 |
| Ancient Sources Index | 349 |
| Bibliography & Works Cited (SBL 2nd Edition) | 351 |
| Intellectual Stewardship Policy | 365 |
| Stewardship Statement | 371 |
| About the Series/About the Author | 373 |

# Genesis:
# Pastoral Stream –
# The Shepherd's Call

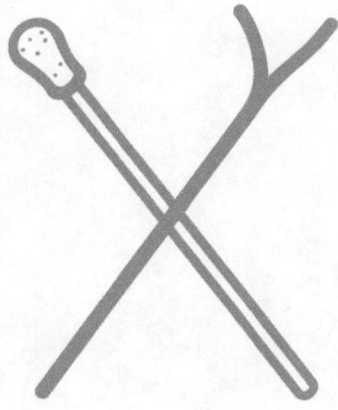

# CHAPTER ONE

## THE SHEPHERD'S ACHE & HEART OF A PASTOR

**When the Shepherd's Ache First Stirred the World**

Before there was preaching, before there were prophets, before covenant or altar or law, there was an ache the longing of God our Father. The Spirit hovered over a world "without form, and void" (Gen 1:2 KJV), and Scripture allows us to glimpse something deeper than mere observation—a divine yearning. The Spirit "moved upon the face of the waters," brooding, guarding, warming the darkness with presence. The Hebrew verb rachaph (רָחַף), used here for "hovering," appears again in Deuteronomy to describe an eagle stirring her nest, fluttering over her young, sheltering them with fierce devotion.[1] Already, at the dawn of time, God reveals Himself not first as King, nor Judge, nor Warrior, but as Shepherd—the One who sees before He speaks, who discerns before He commands, who longs before He forms.

This ache is not weakness; it is the pulse of divine insight and love. Let us look carefully together at Genesis 1. Before God says, "Let there be light," the text implies observation-God was there watching and longing. The next passage is speech and then it says, "And God saw…" (Gen 1:4).[2] The Shepherd had surveyed His flock of unformed matter, comprehending its emptiness, perceiving its potential. Rabbinic tradition reads Genesis 1 not only as cosmic architecture but as the tenderness of a Shepherd longing to bring His creation into wholeness.[3] This longing—holy, watchful, discerning—is the first movement of ministry. It is the soil from which preaching will one day rise.

**Genesis – The Call of God and Protection of the Rod**

In Genesis, the call of God does not arise from divine deficiency but from covenant intention. The ache that accompanies the call is not emotional lack; it is resolve—the weight of God's purpose seeking relationship - a people who will walk with Him and bear His voice in the world.

Before law, before office, before authority is exercised-- God addresses humanity as a shepherd, addresses those He intends to guide. The rod signifies this first movement of calling: direction before discipline, initiative before instruction. The ache marks the moment when divine intention presses toward relationship, signaling that God's purpose has not yet found its human correspondence. Calling, therefore, begins not as function but as summons—the disturbance created when God speaks with intent to dwell, to lead, and to form a people under His care.

Sin did not silence this ache. When Adam and Eve hide among the trees, Scripture again reveals the Shepherd's heart. God walks in the garden "in the cool of the day" (Gen 3:8), calling out, "Where art thou?" (3:9). Augustine noted that God's question is not investigative but pastoral— the call of a Shepherd seeking His lost sheep. [4] He does not approach with thunder; He approaches with longing. His voice is gentle, not because sin is light, but because His love is heavy. The Shepherd aches for communion restored.

The call of God originates in the heart of God Himself, born not from reaction but from divine love and purpose. Because God loves what He calls, He guards it; because He guards it, He establishes boundaries around it; and He confronts whatever threatens it.

The rod, therefore, is not arbitrary authority but the Word of God functioning in love—love made firm, love made resolute, love refusing to surrender what it has chosen through the call. This same rod that corrects and protects the called is also wielded against the enemies of the promise, dispersing dark powers and false gods, and lies that seek to devour what God has spoken.

Just as Abraham stood over the covenant sacrifice, driving away the birds of prey until God Himself sealed the promise, so the Word of the Lord stands guard over divine calling, repelling spiritual opposition and preserving covenant purpose. In this way, the rod does not contradict love but expresses it fully: guarding what God loves, guiding those He has called, protecting them from corruption, and forcefully opposing every power that seeks to destroy what His love has ordained.

The rod is the Word of God acting in love—guarding the call, setting holy boundaries, and forcefully opposing every power that threatens the promise - God has spoken. So Genesis continues to unfold this ache and protection through the lives of its shepherds.

**Abel: The First Discernment**

Abel, the first shepherd mentioned in Scripture, appears not preaching but perceiving. He offers "the firstlings of his flock" (Gen 4:4)—not because a command forced his hand, but because his heart discerned the Shepherd's delight. Wenham observes that Abel's sacrifice is an act of spiritual intuition, an offering shaped by attentive longing rather than instruction. [5] Abel becomes the first human who responds to God not with speech but with perception. His ministry is pure pastoral discernment.

**Enoch: The Walk**

Enoch, Abel's spiritual successor, brings pastoral longing to its highest point. "Enoch walked with God" (Gen 5:24), a phrase repeated for no other antediluvian. Jewish tradition in Sirach calls Enoch a man of "perfect devotion," whose intimacy with God distinguished him from his generation. [6] Enoch speaks nothing in Genesis; instead, he walks. His ministry is not proclamation but presence—the daily companionship of the Shepherd and His friend. Enoch embodies the truth that the pastor's first calling is fellowship, not speech.

**Noah: The Remnant Shepherd**

This ache continues through Noah. Genesis repeats the Enoch phrase: "Noah walked with God" (Gen 6:9). Before Noah constructs an ark, he constructs intimacy. Before he shepherds creation into a new world, he shepherds his own heart in companionship with the Shepherd. Walton notes that Noah's obedience flows from relationship; the ability to hear extraordinary instruction grows only in the soil of relational fidelity. [7] Noah becomes the shepherd of a remnant because he first learned to walk the silent paths of faithfulness.

**Abraham: The Father-Shepherd**

Then God calls Abram, not because he was a warrior or philosopher, but because he possessed a shepherd's heart. The divine reasoning is explicit: "For I know him, that he will command his children" (Gen 18:19). The word tsavah (צָוָה) here means more than give orders—it means to guide, to direct, to shepherd a household forward. [8] Abraham longs for a son, longs for a land, longs for the promise. He is the shepherd of holy desire, carrying covenant hope like a staff through barren geography looking for the promise of God.

**Isaac: The Silent Watcher**

Isaac is the contemplative shepherd. He "went out to meditate in the field at eventide" (Gen 24:63), seeking God in open sky and quiet air. Rabbinic commentary calls Isaac the patriarch of stillness, one who perceives God in silence rather than speech. [9] Pastoral ministry begins here—in the quiet field where the shepherd listens for the rustle of divine movement.

**Jacob: The Wrestling Shepherd**

Jacob shepherds Laban's flocks for decades and confesses the price: "In the day the drought consumed me, and the frost by night; and my sleep departed from mine eyes" (Gen 31:40). This is the confession of a tired shepherd—a man who carries the ache of responsibility. Yet Jacob also wrestles with God; he refuses to release the Shepherd without a blessing. His longing becomes struggle, and his struggle becomes transformation. [10]

**Joseph: The Shepherd of Nations**

Finally comes Joseph—shepherd boy turned shepherd of empires. His ministry is anchored not in eloquence but in perception. He sees destiny in dreams, famine in symbols, providence in betrayal. Waltke notes that Joseph's "sight" functions as a pastoral discernment on a grand scale, guiding nations through crisis. [11] Genesis ends as it begins—with a shepherd who sees, discerns, and responds.

These lives, woven together, reveal the shape of pastoral calling: The call to ministry begins not with a message but with a longing. Not with a sermon but with a Shepherd. Not with words but with sight. The ache is the birthplace of all true preaching.

## 2. When the Shepherd Opens the Eyes of the Heart

Longing prepares the soul for revelation. In Genesis, the ache becomes the doorway into sight, sound, and discernment—the three pastoral senses that define the Shepherd's work. The God who sees the formless deep and the God who calls to the hiding pair also awakens human perception. Ministry begins when the Shepherd opens the eyes of the heart.

Genesis teaches that revelation is not merely the transfer of information. It is the unveiling of God's heart to a shepherd's spirit. Before the preacher stands before a congregation, he stands before the Shepherd who calls his name. This revelation unfolds in three movements: seeing, hearing, and discerning—and these three movements shape the pastoral office from the very beginning.

### A.  Seeing — The Shepherd's First Sense

The Scriptures say repeatedly, "And God saw..." (Gen 1:4, 10, 12). Vision is the Shepherd's first work. The Hebrew verb ra'ah (רָאָה) is used not only for physical sight but for spiritual perception—seeing as God sees, recognizing what God recognizes. [12] God sees the barren earth, sees Adam's hiding, sees Abel's offering, sees Hagar's tears, sees Abraham's faith, sees Jacob's fear, sees Joseph's suffering.

Seeing shapes the calling. This is why ministry cannot begin in the pulpit. It must begin in the pasture—where the shepherd watches over what God has entrusted and looks for what God reveals.

Even the patriarchs' callings begin in vision:

- Abraham sees a smoking firepot and flaming torch pass between the pieces (Gen 15).
- Jacob sees angels ascending and descending (Gen 28).
- Joseph sees sheaves bowing and stars shining (Gen 37).

These are not random scenes. They are shepherding visions—revelations of divine activity, guidance, and destiny. In the pastoral stream, seeing is not optional. It is vocational.

### B. Hearing — The Shepherd's Second Sense

Revelation deepens through hearing. Before the preacher speaks, he must recognize the Shepherd's voice.

- Adam hears the sound of God walking (Gen 3:8).

- Noah hears the divine warning (Gen 6:13).

- Abraham hears promises under the stars (Gen 15:5).

- Jacob hears his name spoken in the night (Gen 46:2).

- Joseph hears interpretations whispered by the Spirit (Gen 40–41).

Hearing forms obedience. Childs notes that "hearing in the Old Testament is covenantal; it binds the hearer to the Speaker." [13] In other words, the revelation is relationship. The Shepherd speaks so the sheep may respond. Communication is the sheep hearing His voice. The call of the Shepherd is profound and He calls in love.

## C. Discerning — The Shepherd's Third Sense

The final movement is discernment—the ability to interpret what is seen and heard. The Hebrew bin (בִּין) means "to understand, distinguish, perceive." Von Rad calls this the wisdom dimension of Genesis. [14] Joseph interprets dreams as a shepherd who "discerns what God is revealing for the sake of life."

Discernment is the Shepherd's inner compass:

- Abraham discerns the three visitors as divine messengers.
- Jacob discerns angelic presence.
- Joseph discerns famine's future.
- Judah discerns repentance through a broken heart.

Revelation in Genesis is not doctrinal abstraction—it is God's heart laid bare before His shepherds so they may guide His flock. Revelation forms shepherds. It shapes their soul, sharpens their eye, awakens their ear, and deepens their capacity to carry God's ache for His people. Ministry begins when the Shepherd opens the eyes of the heart.

---

## 3. When the Shepherd Searches Through Silence

Genesis is the seedbed of pastoral longing, but the ache does not end there. It echoes through Israel's history, reverberates in Second Temple Judaism, and is heard again in the early church. Longing becomes the dominant spiritual rhythm—not because God is absent, but because the people's hearts have grown dull. The ache intensifies whenever the Shepherd must search through silence.

### A. The Famine for Hearing

Amos foresees a time when there will be "a famine… of hearing the words of the LORD" (Amos 8:11). Not a famine of Scripture—the scrolls were intact—but a famine of hearing (shemoaʻ). [15] When ritual replaces reverence and instruction loses intimacy; the Shepherd's voice becomes rare. This echoes the days of Eli when "the word of the LORD was precious" (1 Sam 3:1), meaning scarce, infrequent, weighty. Klein notes that the silence was not divine abandonment but a spiritual condition—the ear was closed, not the heavens. [16]

## B. The Shepherd's Search in the Prophets

Isaiah describes Israel's condition this way: "Hear ye indeed, but understand not" (Isa 6:9). Hearing without comprehension is pastoral tragedy. Watts comments that this judgment is "diagnostic, not punitive." [17] The Shepherd laments the dullness of His flock.

## C. Qumran: Longing in the Wilderness

The Dead Sea Scrolls capture the ache with stunning clarity. The Qumran community accused the temple priests of ḥalaqot ("smooth things")—teaching that was polished but powerless, technically correct but spiritually empty.[18] Martínez and Tigchelaar note that the community believed only the humble could receive the "raz nihyeh," the mystery of God's plan.[19] Revelation belonged not to scholars but to shepherds of God's heart.

## D. Rabbinic and Christian Witness

Rabbis emphasized that God chooses shepherds because they "know how to care for every sheep." [21] Early Christians echoed this theme:

- Irenaeus saw Abel as the pattern of the righteous shepherd. [22]
- Chrysostom said, "He who would preach must first walk with God as Enoch did." [23]

- Gregory the Great wrote that the pastor must be "a contemplative first, a laborer second." [24]

Across centuries, the Shepherd's ache is the unbroken thread.

### E. What All of This Means

The historical witness is unmistakable: God always raises shepherds in times of silence. God always awakens longing before restoring hearing. God always forms a watchman before sending a preacher.

The ache prepares the ear. The ear prepares the voice. The voice prepares the people.

### 4. When the Shepherd Awakens the Watchman Within

The ache of Genesis is not merely descriptive; it is formative. God does not unveil His longing simply to stir emotion—He reveals it to awaken vocation. The Shepherd's ache becomes the shepherd's calling. Every preacher, every pastor, every teacher, every spiritual father or mother must learn the Genesis lesson: ministry begins in longing, but it matures in watching.

The prophet Ezekiel later captures this dynamic when God says, "I have set thee a watchman unto the house of Israel" (Ezek 3:17). But long before Ezekiel stood upon the spiritual walls of Israel, the first watchmen walked the fields of Genesis—Abel guarding the flock, Enoch walking with God, Noah preparing for a storm, Abraham interceding for Sodom, Jacob wrestling in the dark, Joseph discerning the dawn of famine.

Every one of them became a watchman because every one of them carried the ache.

### A. The Watchman's Eyes

A shepherd cannot afford blind spots. The pastoral office is the office of sight—watching over souls, noticing subtle shifts in hearts, discerning movement in the unseen places. When God told Abraham, "Lift up now thine eyes" (Gen 13:14), He was not simply giving him geography—He was forming a watchman. Revelation begins when eyes are lifted.

## B. The Watchman's Ear

Watchmen listen differently. They listen not only for words but for whispers—movements, tremors, warnings carried on the wind. Noah heard the thunder of coming judgment before anyone else heard a sound. Samuel heard God call his name in the night. Daniel heard the voice of God in Nebuchadnezzar's cryptic dreams. Hearing is the watchman's vigilance.

## C. The Watchman's Heart

The heart of a watchman must be soft enough to ache but strong enough to endure. Pastoral ministry is tender, and tender things wound easily. Yet Genesis shows us shepherds who feel deeply but stand firmly—Abraham interceding for the wicked, Jacob weeping while blessing Pharaoh, Joseph weeping as he forgives his brothers. The shepherd's heart must be bruised enough to love and healed enough to lead.

## D. The Watchman's Walk

Finally, the watchman must walk with God. Enoch walked. Noah walked. Abraham walked through the land. Jacob walked toward reconciliation. Joseph walked into destiny. Walking steadies the watchman's soul—it is the slow, faithful rhythm of obedience.

Thus, the response demanded by the Shepherd's ache is this:

**"See as He sees. Hear as He hears. Discern as He discerns. Walk where He walks."**

Only then can the preacher speak the Shepherd's Word with accuracy and compassion.

## 5. When the Shepherd Forms a People

Longing does not end with the Shepherd, nor with the patriarchs, nor with the watchmen of Scripture. Longing becomes the furnace where God forms His people. Revival does not begin with miracles or strategies or programs—it begins when the Shepherd awakens longing in the heart of His flock. That longing is the beginning of renewal.

### A. Longing Restores Hearing

Before Israel heard the covenant at Sinai, they groaned under their bondage (Exod 2:23). Their longing rose like incense. Renewal begins when the people ache for God's voice again. Jesus Himself said, "My sheep hear my voice" (John 10:27). Hearing returns when longing is restored.

### B. Longing Restores Walking

Enoch walked with God. Noah walked with God. After the exile, God promised, "I will walk among you" (Lev 26:12). Renewal is not first about activity—it is about proximity. Revival is the restoration of walking with the Shepherd.

### C. Longing Restores Discernment

Genesis ends with Joseph discerning the purposes of God: "Ye thought evil against me; but God meant it unto good" (Gen 50:20). Renewal restores the ability to see beyond circumstance into divine intention. Pastors and congregations alike rediscover how to interpret the movements of God.

### D. Longing Restores Ministry

Every true ministry begins in longing for God. Not longing for results, not longing for success, not longing for reputation—longing for the Shepherd. Abel longed to please Him. Enoch longed to walk with Him. Noah longed to obey Him. Abraham longed to know Him. Jacob longed to be blessed by Him. Joseph longed to fulfill His purpose.

The ministry of preaching does not begin in a classroom, but in a call. Not in articulation, but in ache. And so the chapter concludes where Genesis begins:

**The Shepherd forms His people through longing.**

He leads them into revelation through ache. He restores their hearing through desire. He shapes their calling through discernment. He awakens their voice by awakening their hearts.

Longing is not the end of ministry—it is its beginning.

---

**Conclusion — The Shepherd and the Call**

If you stand quietly in Genesis, you begin to notice the pattern. The Shepherd sees before He speaks. He calls before He commands. He longs before He sends. The ache is His first gift to humanity—the pull that draws us out of hiding, the hunger that opens our ears, the thirst that makes us watchful.

This ache is the birthplace of every shepherd God will ever raise.

It appears in Abel's offering. It pulses in Enoch's walk. It deepens in Noah's obedience. It groans in Abraham's pilgrimage. It wrestles in Jacob's night. It dreams in Joseph's destiny.

The ache becomes the first curriculum of the preacher's soul.

Every pastor who stands to proclaim the Word must first feel the weight of the Shepherd's longing—His longing for His people, His longing for holiness, His longing for fellowship, His longing for sons and daughters who will hear His voice again. This longing prepares the way for what comes next.

For just as Genesis reveals the Shepherd's ache, the next movement of Scripture reveals something deeper—a structure, a rhythm, a divine pattern through which God forms every minister He calls.

It is written into the Torah's very architecture. It is hidden in plain sight. It is the pattern behind the ache. And that pattern reveals to us the foundations of the call.

The pastoral calling therefore has its basis in the heart of God, is guarded by the rod of His Word, and is expressed through the staff as the shepherd echoes the heart and voice of God to the people entrusted to him.

---

**NOTES**

[1] The verb רחף occurs only three times in the Hebrew Bible (Gen 1:2; Deut 32:11; Jer 23:9); the maternal/paternal eagle imagery in Deut 32:11 is the classic exegetical parallel; see Terence E. Fretheim, Genesis, NIB 1 (Nashville: Abingdon, 1994), 342; Nahum M. Sarna, Genesis, JPS Torah Commentary (Philadelphia: Jewish Publication Society, 1989), 6; cf. BDB, 934.

[2] Victor P. Hamilton, The Book of Genesis: Chapters 1–17, NICOT (Grand Rapids: Eerdmans, 1990), 120–21.

[3] Genesis Rabbah 2.4; 8.2; see Jacob Neusner, Genesis Rabbah: The Judaic Commentary to the Book of Genesis, 3 vols., BJS 104–106 (Atlanta: Scholars Press, 1985), 1:21–23, 76.

[4] Augustine, On Genesis against the Manichees 2.23.35–36 (PL 34:215); cf. Sermons on Selected Lessons of the New Testament 77.1 (NPNF[1] 6:247–48).

[5] Gordon J. Wenham, Genesis 1–15, WBC 1 (Waco, TX: Word, 1987), 102.

[6] Sirach 44:16 (LXX and Masada Hebrew fragment); see also 49:14.

[7] John H. Walton, Genesis, NIVAC (Grand Rapids: Zondervan, 2001), 305–6.

[8] Victor P. Hamilton, The Book of Genesis: Chapters 18–50, NICOT (Grand Rapids: Eerdmans, 1995), 30–31.

[9] Rashi on Gen 24:63; cf. Genesis Rabbah 60:14 and 56:11.

[10] On Jacob's wrestling as pastoral struggle and longing, see Gerhard von Rad, Genesis: A Commentary, rev. ed., OTL (Philadelphia: Westminster, 1972), 345–47.

[11] Bruce K. Waltke with Cathi J. Fredricks, Genesis: A Commentary (Grand Rapids: Zondervan, 2001), 525–27.

[12] Francis Brown, S. R. Driver, and Charles A. Briggs, A Hebrew and English Lexicon of the Old Testament (Oxford: Clarendon, 1907), 906–12 (ra'ah).

[13] Brevard S. Childs, Old Testament Theology in a Canonical Context (Philadelphia: Fortress, 1985), 98–100.

[14] Gerhard von Rad, Wisdom in Israel, trans. James D. Martin (Nashville: Abingdon, 1972), 144–57.

[15] Hans Walter Wolff, Joel and Amos, Hermeneia (Philadelphia: Fortress, 1977), 331–33.

[16] Ralph W. Klein, 1 Samuel, WBC 10 (Waco, TX: Word, 1983), 26–28.

[17] John D. W. Watts, Isaiah 1–33, WBC 24 (Waco, TX: Word, 1985), 80–82.

[18] Geza Vermes, The Complete Dead Sea Scrolls in English, rev. ed. (London: Penguin, 2011), 51–52; the phrase is חֲלָקוֹת (ḥalaqot) or "doers of smooth things."

[19] Florentino García Martínez and Eibert J. C. Tigchelaar, The Dead Sea Scrolls Study Edition, 2 vols. (Leiden: Brill; Grand Rapids: Eerdmans, 1997–1998), 1:75–77 (1QS 3–4) and 4QInstruction references.

[20] Midrash Bereshit Rabbah 8:13; 19:9; see H. Freedman and Maurice Simon, trans., Midrash Rabbah: Genesis, 2 vols. (London: Soncino, 1939), 1:62, 158.

[21] Pesiqta deRab Kahana 26:9; Midrash Tanhuma (Buber) Genesis 6.

[22] Irenaeus, Against Heresies 4.20.3 (ANF 1:488).

[23] John Chrysostom, On the Priesthood 6.4 (NPNF[1] 9:76).

[24] Gregory the Great, Pastoral Rule 2.5; trans. George E. Demacopoulos, Popular Patristics Series (Crestwood, NY: St. Vladimir's Seminary Press, 2007), 89–90.

# CHAPTER TWO

**PASTORAL STREAM – THE CRY ECHOES THE CALL**

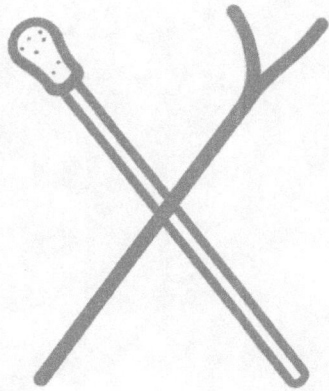

# CHAPTER TWO

## The Call of God and Heart of a Preacher

The ache that began in the heart of God does not remain in heaven. When the Spirit broods over the formless void and the Father walks in the garden calling "Where are you?", something irreversible is set in motion. The divine longing — holy, watchful, discerning — awakens a corresponding cry in the creature formed in His image. What started as the Shepherd's ache becomes the soul's hunger for a living Word.

Every movement of God in history confirms this pattern: before reformation becomes visible, before revival shakes a nation, before preaching rises with clarity, there is a quiet ache in the human spirit — a yearning for a Word that breathes.

---

**Genesis - The Staff that Comforts and the Heart That Responds**
If the rod reveals God's authority issuing and guarding His call, the staff reveals the shepherd's obedient response—echoing God's heart and voice in faithful care for the flock entrusted to him. Human longing in Genesis is not autonomous desire but the echo of having been addressed by the divine voice.

The pastoral calling originates not in human compassion or vocational inclination, but in the heart of God Himself. God calls before the shepherd responds, and He guards what He calls through the rod of His Word—establishing boundaries, confronting enemies, and preserving the promise against corruption and assault. The rod, therefore, belongs first to God, not to the pastor; it is the divine authority by which the call is protected and ordered. The ministry of the staff flows in response to that call, as the shepherd echoes the heart and voice of God to the people entrusted to his care. Where the rod guards the calling, the staff guides the called; where the rod confronts what threatens the flock, the staff comforts and guides those who walk within the safety the rod has established. Together, rod and staff reveal a pastoral ministry that neither originates in human strength nor functions by human will, but faithfully reflects the love, authority, and presence of the Shepherd Himself.

The heart longs because it has been summoned. This response is neither self-generated nor self-interpreting; it is awakened by covenant speech and sustained by pastoral presence. The staff signifies this answering movement: support, correction, and perseverance under care.

Longing is thus vocational before it is emotional—it arises when the human person recognizes, often dimly, that their life is now oriented by the Word that has already spoken. In this way, the heart's response is not the origin of calling but its confirmation of the call. The heart seeks because it has been sought; it awakens because it has been called. Genesis presents this dynamic not as sentiment but as formation—the shaping of a people who learn to walk in response to God's initiating call.

The response of the human heart in Genesis is not self-generated longing, but obedience awakened by the Word of God. The heart responds for the sake of the call. This answer arises not from inward searching but from a heavenly summons; it is the echo of divine speech received and perceived, even though imperfectly understood.

This response is therefore Word-based before it is emotional— scriptural faith taking its earliest form as attentiveness, turning, and movement toward the One who has spoken. The staff signifies this answering life: it shows support for the journey, guidance and correction along the way, and perseverance under pastoral care. Genesis presents response not as autonomous desire but as the beginning of obedience, the shaping of a heart that learns to live in answer to the Word that has called.

## 1. The Ache Before the Word: Longing as the First Revelation

Every story of God's renewal begins in silence. Not the silence of abandonment, but the fertile, hovering silence of Genesis 1:2—the silence before a Word reshapes chaos into cosmos. Scripture repeatedly reveals that God's movements begin not with spectacle but with ache; not with thunder, but with thirst. Before God reforms a nation, He awakens desire. Before He raises a prophet, He stirs hunger. Before He renews preaching, He disrupts the interior life with a yearning nothing else can satisfy.

Genesis gives us the grammar of this longing. After the fall, when shame hides humanity among the trees, God calls, "Where art thou?" (Gen 3:9). The Hebrew verb qārā' does not merely mean "to call" but "to summon into relationship."[1] It is an aching summons—God's pastoral hunger for communion meeting humanity's fractured soul. Even after rebellion, the divine initiative does not recede; it intensifies. The God of Genesis is not aloof. He walks. He calls. He searches. He clothes. He promises. He binds Himself in covenant.

Longing of love is the first movement of grace.

This divine ache appears again in Abraham. God's Word comes to him—not because Abraham sought God, but because God sought Abraham (Gen 12:1). Walter Brueggemann emphasizes that the entire Abraham narrative is "the story of a God who intrudes with promise before performance."[2] Abraham's longing awakens after God's self-disclosure. Grace precedes desire.

Jacob encounters longing in the night, wrestling until he receives a blessing. Joseph embodies longing in exile, holding to dreams God placed in him long before fulfillment. Moses' longing appears in the wilderness, stirred by a bush he "turned aside to see"—a desire that opens the door to revelation (Exod 3:3).[3]

Thus from the beginning, longing for God is not a human invention; it is a divine gift. This is call is God's invitation.

Moses later interprets Israel's entire wilderness experience as the pedagogy of longing: "that He might make thee know that man doth not live by bread only, but by every word that proceedeth out of the mouth of the LORD" (Deut 8:3). The Hebrew phrase kol motsa' pî YHWH—"everything issuing from the mouth of YHWH"—signifies ongoing speech. Revelation is not static; it proceeds. [4]

To hunger for the Word is to hunger for God Himself. This longing becomes the heartbeat of Israel's spiritual life. From the psalmist panting for commandments (Ps 119:131) to the prophets lamenting the drought of hearing (Amos 8:11), Scripture presents this longing not as deficiency but as wisdom. Desire is the doorway through which God reenters the life of a people.

Second Temple literature intensifies this theme. At Qumran, longing becomes a communal identity. The sect describes itself as "the poor in spirit" ('anawim rûaḥ), those whose humility opens them to divine mystery (1QHa).[5] They believe revelation belongs to the brokenhearted listener, the one who waits in yearning. The "Maskil," the righteous leader of the community, is not defined by intellect but by capacity for hearing—the result of God giving him an "ear of knowledge." [6]

Thus, longing is not emotional excess; it is theological necessity. It is the soul's admission that human wisdom is insufficient and divine speech is essential. It calls to repentance by faith, grace before obedience, hunger and transformation. It is the soil and soul where preaching is conceived.

Every preacher God raises He first aligns with longing for Divine relationship and speaks directly to the desire with the heart. As deep calls unto deep. So God calls the heart of the preacher.

---

## 2. The Hunger for Voice: Longing as Wisdom's Beginning

Longing is not only the doorway into revelation—it is the posture by which wisdom is received. The wisdom literature of Israel repeatedly frames longing as the beginning of spiritual intelligence: "I opened my mouth and panted: for I longed for thy commandments" (Ps 119:131). The verb ʾāhâ (panting) describes the physicality of desire—the embodied yearning for divine instruction. [7]

The Psalmist reveals the paradox: desire does not cloud understanding; it unlocks it. "The entrance of thy words giveth light" (Ps 119:130). The Hebrew pēthaḥ ("opening") refers not to a mere doorway but an unfolding, a revelation that breaks open what was closed. [8] Wisdom is not extracted from Scripture by intellectual technique; it is received through spiritual hearing.

This openness—this longing—is illustrated in the quiet crisis of Eli's day: "the word of the LORD was precious"—rare (1 Sam 3:1). Revelation was not absent because God had withdrawn; revelation was absent because hearing had ceased. Ralph Klein notes that the crisis in Eli's priesthood was not moral alone but "a collapse of hearing." [9] Into this silence, God speaks a boy's name—"Samuel." Longing answers that whisper: "Speak, LORD; for thy servant heareth."

Isaiah names this divine-human dynamic with surgical clarity: "He wakeneth mine ear to hear as the learned" (Isa 50:4). The prophet attributes his capacity for revelation not to skill but to divine awakening. The Hebrew yāʿîr ("He awakens") suggests God rouses the ear from spiritual sleep. [10]

This theme explodes in Second Temple texts. In 4QInstruction (4Q417)—one of the most theologically sophisticated wisdom compositions at Qumran—revelation is reserved for those the sect calls "the humble of spirit" (רוח ענוים). The text proclaims: *"When the ears of the meek are opened, then the mysteries (razim) of existence will shine forth." *[11] The razim are not intellectual puzzles; they are the deep structures of God's providence and covenantal purpose.

Humility before Him awakens hearing God Himself; hearing awakens revelation through His Word.

Rabbinic tradition echoes this. In m. Berakhot 5:1, the rabbis teach that "the Shekinah dwells with him who has a broken heart." [12] Midrash Tehillim adds: "The spirit of prophecy rests only on the modest and the humble." [13] In both cases, desire precedes knowledge; longing precedes revelation; humility precedes illumination.

Thus, longing is not weak; it is wise. Longing is not emotional instability; longing is spiritual readiness. Wisdom is not first intellectual—it is relational. The wise person longs for God's voice more than for answers, more than for solutions, more than for escape.

The preacher who does not long for God will never hear from God. The preacher who longs will be taught of God. Longing is God's gift and the preacher's calling. The aloneness of your heart when all is silent – that longing is your heart calling to you through the shadows and speaking to you- giving you God's desire all the while developing the heart of God – the heart of a shepherd.

---

## 3. The Famine for Hearing: When the Scroll Remains but the Voice Withdraws

If longing is the seed of revelation, then famine is the death of hearing. Few judgments in Scripture are as terrifying as Amos's prophetic word: "a famine…of hearing the words of the LORD" (Amos 8:11). The famine is not the absence of Scripture—the scrolls remain—but the absence of Divine encounter. The Hebrew phrase shemoaʿ divrê YHWH means "the capacity to hear the words of YHWH." [14] This famine is relational, not textual.

The tragedy deepens when we see that this famine often begins in religious environments—not in pagan lands, but in sanctuaries. In Eli's day, the lamp of God still burned; sacrifices still occurred; priests still ministered. Yet "the word of the LORD was rare." Ritual continued, revelation did not.

Midrash Shmuel diagnoses the crisis: "The vessels were unclean, so the lamp grew dim." [15] The sanctuary was operational but spiritually hollow. The scroll remained in the priest's hands, but the priest no longer shook when he held it - they lost the fear and reverence for God.

Isaiah intensifies the indictment: "Hear ye indeed, but understand not; and see ye indeed, but perceive not" (Isa 6:9). The Hebrew structure uses doubling—shamoaʿ tishmeʿu... u-reʾoh tireʾu—to show deliberate dullness. [16] Hearing had become habitual but not transformative. Sight had become informational but not revelatory. Revelation ceased not because God stopped speaking but because the people trained themselves not to listen.

This pattern continues in the Second Temple period. The Qumran community viewed the Jerusalem priesthood as spiritually compromised. They accused them of being ʿōsê haḥalaqôt, "doers of smooth things" (CD 1.18), teachers who softened Torah into convenience and removed its prophetic edge. [17] They believed the temple establishment preserved the letter but lost the voice.

Qumran's complaint was not just political. It was spiritual.

They saw a priesthood with access to Scripture but without access to mystery; a ministry with the scroll but without the Spirit. The famine of hearing had set in.

This famine is the great enemy of preaching. A preacher may hold the Bible yet not tremble at its voice. A congregation may gather weekly yet never hear the living God. A nation may preserve religious memory yet forget the God who spoke.

And yet, famine is never the final word. Famine prepares longing. Longing opens the ear. And where the ear opens, revelation returns.

Famine breaks the ground where revival will grow.

## 4. The Reborn Sanctuary — Longing and the Restoration of Hearing

If longing exposes the famine, then humility restores the sanctuary. Scripture presents hearing not as an intellectual act but as a covenant grace—something God gives to the contrite. Isaiah captures this with piercing clarity: "To this man will I look, even to him that is poor and of a contrite spirit, and trembleth at my word" (Isa 66:2 KJV). The Hebrew phrase nēkeh wə-nishbar rûaḥ ("stricken and broken spirit") conveys the image of interior collapse—an openness created by divine pressure. [18]

Hearing God is not a faculty; it is a formation.

### Qumran and the Ear God Opens

Second Temple Judaism deepened this insight. The Qumran community called themselves "the poor in spirit" (ענוים רוח), echoing Isaiah. They believed God "opened their ears" to raz nihyeh— "the mystery of what is happening" (1QHa XI). [19] Simply- they believed that God opened their eyes to interpret the events in their lives, country, and nation through the Word. Revelation was not a right to be demanded; it was a gift given to the humble. Qumran's "Maskil," the enlightened leader, was not chiefly a scholar but a hearer—one whose ear God had formed. [20]

In 4QInstruction, revelation is described as "the light for the humble" (אור לענוים), given when God "uncovers the ear" (יגלה אזן).[21] This phrase does not appear in the Hebrew Bible, but the concept does: "He opened their ears, but none listened" (Job 36:10).[22] Qumran understood revelation as divine initiative awakening human longing.

Longing is not merely desire; it is receptivity.

### The Sanctuary as a Hearing Place

This dynamic appears in the architecture of Israel's worship. Leviticus begins with: "And the LORD called unto Moses" (Lev 1:1). The Hebrew vayyiqra' signals revelation's origin in divine initiative. Moses does not enter the sanctuary to speak; he enters to hear. Preaching begins in listening. [23]

In the Tent of Meeting, God's voice came "from above the mercy seat, from between the two cherubim" (Num 7:89). Rabbinic tradition describes this not as audible thunder but as intimate communication—"a voice that spoke to Moses." [24] Revelation was born in attentiveness.

This is why Israel's great confessional begins with hearing: "Hear, O Israel" (Deut 6:4). Before Israel obeys, before Israel worships, Israel listens.

**Humility Restores the Prophetic Ear**

Throughout Israel's history, revelation is renewed when humility returns:

- Moses removes his sandals (Exod 3:5).
- Samuel says, "Speak, LORD" (1 Sam 3:10).
- David says, "Open thou mine eyes" (Ps 119:18).
- Isaiah cries, "Woe is me!" (Isa 6:5).
- Ezra opens the book, and the people stand in reverence (Neh 8:5–6). [25]

In each instance, God speaks where longing prepares the heart.

Preaching that does not emerge from humility becomes noise. But preaching born in longing becomes flame.

The sanctuary is not first architectural; it is interior. It is the place where longing meets revelation, where humility becomes hearing, where the preacher becomes a vessel.

Longing rebuilds the sanctuary within because it echoes the heart of God.

## 5. The Cry That Moves Heaven — Longing as Prophetic Formation

Longing matures into a cry. Scripture distinguishes between passive desire and covenantal desperation. The Psalms name this cry qārā'—to call, summon, cry out in urgent dependence: "In the day of my trouble I will call upon thee" (Ps 86:7). The cry assumes two things:

1. God is near.
2. God hears.

God answers this cry with qōl—His voice. Psalm 29 describes the "voice of the LORD" (qōl YHWH) as shattering cedars, shaking wildernesses, dividing flames. This is not metaphorical flourish; it is theological claim: **God's voice breaks what binds and builds what belongs.** [26]

### The Pattern of Prophetic Formation: qārā' → qōl

This dynamic—cry → voice—is the root system of prophetic ministry.

- Samuel cries in innocence; God answers with revelation (1 Sam 3). [27]
- Isaiah cries in unclean lips; God answers with commissioning (Isa 6). [28]
- Jeremiah cries in inadequacy; God answers with fire (Jer 1; 20:9). [29]
- Ezekiel collapses; God raises him with the Spirit (Ezek 2:1–2). [30]
- The apostles cry in confusion; Jesus answers with understanding (Luke 24:45).

The call narratives of Scripture reveal a consistent pattern: Longing is the first turning. Cry is the second. Revelation the third. Sending the fourth.

## The Word Made Flesh and the Cry for Hearing

In Christ, longing finds its fulfillment. Jesus is Himself the Word who answers human cry. His ministry begins with a longing people—John's disciples, those hungry for righteousness, the poor in spirit. Jesus does not crush longing; He cultivates it.

He says, "Blessed are they which do hunger and thirst after righteousness" (Matt 5:6). The Greek peinōntes and dipsōntes denote ongoing hunger and thirst—longing as continual posture. [31]

The early Church carried this into its preaching. Their sermons began in the cry of Pentecost: "What shall we do?" (Acts 2:37). Peter's preaching is not technique; it is answer to longing. When the Ethiopian eunuch asks, "How can I understand, except some man should guide me?" (Acts 8:31), Philip steps into longing with revelation.

The preacher is not first a speaker but a listener. Not first an orator but one who has cried. Not first a herald but a hearer of the Voice. Longing forms prophetic ministry of the Word. Cry awakens the call.

---

## 6. Longing and Sending — When Hunger Becomes Apostolic Commission

Longing is not the conclusion; it is the threshold of mission. Every major commissioning scene in Scripture begins not with confidence but with ache.

### Moses: Longing in the Wilderness

Moses' calling begins with longing disguised as curiosity. He turns aside, and God calls. Terence Fretheim notes that Moses' turning is "the hinge of divine encounter"—his longing for something more than Midian's silence opens the way for God's sending. [32]

God's voice answers his longing with a mandate: "Come now therefore, and I will send thee" (Exod 3:10).

### Isaiah: Longing in the Temple

Isaiah's vision begins with upheaval. Uzziah is dead; the throne of Judah is shaken. Isaiah's longing for stability becomes the setting for divine commissioning. Only after he cries, "Woe is me!" does he hear the question: "Whom shall I send?" (Isa 6:8). John Goldingay notes that Isaiah's call "arises organically out of encounter and cleansing, not ambition." [33]

### Jeremiah: Longing for Adequacy

Jeremiah's commissioning is born not out of readiness but inadequacy: "Ah, Lord GOD! behold, I cannot speak: for I am a child" (Jer 1:6). His longing for sufficiency opens him to God's promise: "I have put my words in thy mouth" (Jer 1:9). [34]

### The Apostles: Longing for Understanding

After the resurrection, the disciples long for clarity. Jesus responds by opening their minds to understand Scripture (Luke 24:45). Then He breathes on them and says: "As my Father hath sent me, even so send I you" (John 20:21). Gordon Fee notes this is both empowerment and commissioning—longing answered with sending. [35]

### Pentecost: Longing Becomes Mission

Before Pentecost, the disciples wait in longing; after Pentecost, they preach in power. Craig Keener argues that Pentecost is "the transformation of longing into mission by the Spirit's descent." [36]

Moshe Weinfeld identifies Deuteronomy as "the classical biblical model of commissioning." [37] What we recognize is that the whole Torah is a fivefold movement from longing to sending. Pentecost commissions and sets the rhythm of the church.

Thus, preaching participates in this divine rhythm. The preacher is formed in longing, shaped in revelation, humbled in response, and released in commission.

Longing becomes apostolic urgency.

---

## 7. When Longing Becomes Renewal — The Beginning of All Preaching

This chapter ends where the journey begins: with hunger. Not the hunger that weakens, but the hunger that awakens. Longing is the birthplace of every revival, the seedbed of every renewal, the quiet ache that precedes every outpouring.

Revival history confirms what Scripture teaches:

- Jonathan Edwards said true revival begins when people "pant after the Word." [38]

- John Wesley recorded that the Spirit fell where people "hungered and thirsted after righteousness. [39]

- George Whitefield preached until "hunger for Christ" shook England and the colonies. [40]

- Evan Roberts testified that the Welsh Revival began with a simple cry: "Lord, bend us." [41] Longing is the spark that ignites reformation.

**Here is the Truth – This God-given Longing Precedes Every Movement of God**

- Longing preceded Sinai.

- Longing preceded Isaiah's commission.

- Longing preceded exile's restoration (Neh 8).

- Longing preceded John the Baptist's ministry.

- Longing preceded Pentecost.

- Longing precedes Christ's return (Rev 22:17).

Thus, the ministry of preaching begins not with technique, training, or skill—but with ache.

- Longing opens the ear.
- Longing awakens the heart.
- Longing prepares the sanctuary.
- Longing summons the Voice.
- Longing precedes renewal.

And so the preacher enters the pulpit not as performer but as seeker, not as expert but as listener, not as an analyst but as one who has heard God's cry and answered with longing.

This is the first movement of the Fivefold Rhythm. This is the pastoral stream of Genesis. This is the beginning of the Ministry of Preaching. Before the preacher speaks for God, he must long for God. Before he teaches the covenant, he must hear the Voice. Before he carries the Word, he must hunger for the Word. Longing is the doorway. Longing is the invitation. Longing is the beginning of renewal.

May every preacher in this final hour rediscover the sacred rhythm:

Hear Him—then proclaim Him.

---

**NOTES**

1. Francis Brown, S. R. Driver, and Charles Briggs, A Hebrew and English Lexicon of the Old Testament (Oxford: Clarendon, 1907), 894.

2. Walter Brueggemann, Genesis (IBC; Atlanta: John Knox, 1982), 114–119.

3. Terence E. Fretheim, Exodus (Interpretation; Louisville: John Knox, 1991), 48–55.

4. Jeffrey H. Tigay, Deuteronomy (JPS Torah Commentary; Philadelphia: JPS, 1996), 88–95.

5. Florentino García Martínez and Eibert J. C. Tigchelaar, eds., The Dead Sea Scrolls Study Edition (Leiden: Brill, 1997), 1:169–180 (1QHa).

6. Bilhah Nitzan, Qumran Prayer and Religious Poetry (Leiden: Brill, 1994), 57–63.

7. James L. Mays, Psalms (Interpretation; Louisville: John Knox, 1994), 385–388.

8. James Limburg, Psalms (WBC; Louisville: Westminster John Knox, 2000), 401–402.

9. Ralph W. Klein, 1 Samuel (WBC 10; Waco: Word, 1983), 27–36.

10. Brevard S. Childs, Isaiah (OTL; Louisville: Westminster John Knox, 2001), 396–400.

11. Matthew J. Goff, Discerning Wisdom: The Sapiential Literature of the Dead Sea Scrolls (Leiden: Brill, 2013), 88–92.

12. Mishnah Berakhot 5:1.

13. Cf. Midrash Tehillim on Psalms 29 in William G. Braude, The Midrash of the Psalms, vol. 1 (New Haven: Yale University Press, 1959, 363-370).

14. Hans Walter Wolff, Joel and Amos (Hermeneia; Philadelphia: Fortress, 1977), 253–260.

15. Mordecai Samuel, Midrash Shmuel, trans. Jacob Neusner (Atlanta: Scholars Press, 1988), 17.

16. John D. W. Watts, Isaiah 1–33 (WBC 24; Waco: Word, 1985), 94–98.

17. Geza Vermes, The Complete Dead Sea Scrolls in English, rev. ed. (London: Penguin, 2011), 52–55.

18. Joseph Blenkinsopp, Isaiah 56–66 (AB 19B; New York: Doubleday, 2003), 285–288.

19. García Martínez and Tigchelaar, DSSSE, 1:169–172.

20. Bilhah Nitzan, Prayer and Poetry at Qumran (Leiden: Brill, 1994), 57–63.

21. Matthew J. Goff, "The Place of 4QInstruction," in The Dead Sea Scrolls at Sixty (Leiden: Brill, 2010), 213–229.

22. Marvin H. Pope, Job (AB 15; New York: Doubleday, 1973), 275–277.

23. Jacob Milgrom, Leviticus 1–16 (AB 3; New York: Doubleday, 1991), 131–135.

24. Sifre Numbers 85.

25. Tamara C. Eskenazi and Eleanore P. Judd, The Torah: A Women's Commentary (URJ Press, 2008), 1220–1225.

26. Patrick D. Miller, They Cried to the Lord (Minneapolis: Fortress, 1994), 65–71.

27. Klein, 1 Samuel, 31–36.

28. Childs, Isaiah, 55–59.

29. J. A. Thompson, The Book of Jeremiah (NICOT; Grand Rapids: Eerdmans, 1980), 201–205.

30. Daniel I. Block, The Book of Ezekiel: Chapters 1–24 (NICOT; Grand Rapids: Eerdmans, 1997), 95–102.

31. R. T. France, The Gospel of Matthew (NICNT; Grand Rapids: Eerdmans, 2007), 168–171.

32. Fretheim, Exodus, 54–55.

33. John Goldingay, Isaiah (Understanding the Bible Commentary; Grand Rapids: Baker, 2001), 56–60.

34. Thompson, Jeremiah, 147–152.

35. Gordon D. Fee, God's Empowering Presence (Peabody: Hendrickson, 1994), 803–807.

36. Craig S. Keener, Acts: An Exegetical Commentary, vol. 1 (Grand Rapids: Baker, 2012), 787–821.

37. Moshe Weinfeld, Deuteronomy and the Deuteronomic School (Oxford: Clarendon, 1972), 290–298.

38. Jonathan Edwards, The Works of Jonathan Edwards, vol. 4 (Yale: Yale University Press, 1959), 78–83.

39. John Wesley, Journal, 5 June 1739.

40. George Whitefield, Journals (London: Banner of Truth, 1960), 112–119.
41. Eifion Evans, The Welsh Revival of 1904–1905 (Carlisle: Banner of Truth, 1969), 45–49.

# CHAPTER THREE

## THE FIVE-FOLD VOICE: TORAH AS THE CANONICAL FOUNDATION

# CHAPTER THREE

## THE FIVE-FOLD VOICE: TORAH AS THE CANONICAL FOUNDATION

### The Need for Clarity in a Fragmented Ecclesial Landscape

The contemporary Church finds itself navigating a wide range of interpretations concerning the nature, function, and duration of the resurrection and ascension-gift ministries listed in Ephesians 4:11. Across denominational traditions, questions continue to surface regarding whether these ministries persist today, whether some of them were strictly limited to the first century, and how they operate in relation to one another.[1] These questions are not peripheral. They bear directly on the Church's identity, mission, and maturity.

Behind their questions, lies a deeper and more pervasive longing — a desire for theological clarity and ecclesial coherence. This longing is not rooted in the pursuit of novelty, nor in the impulse of modern pragmatism. Rather, it reflects the enduring conviction that Christ Himself established a particular pattern for the equipping and growth of His people, a pattern the Church must not treat lightly.[2] The desire for clarity arises precisely because the ministries in question belong not to human invention but to the ascended Christ, whose gifts shape the Body into His likeness.

This longing has clear biblical precedent. Israel, standing at Sinai, expressed a similar desire when they pleaded, "Speak thou with us, and we will hear" (Exod 20:19 KJV), seeking a mediated but intelligible articulation of God's covenant will.[3] The young Samuel, ministering in the transitional age between judges and monarchy, embodied the same posture when he answered the divine call: "Speak, LORD; for thy servant heareth" (1 Sam 3:10 KJV).[4] These moments reflect a fundamental spiritual instinct: the people of God long to hear God's Word clearly, to understand His will, and to walk faithfully within the covenant He has established.

The early Church carried this same concern as it navigated its formative decades. The apostolic writings demonstrate an ongoing effort to ensure that teaching, prophecy, pastoral care, evangelistic mission, and apostolic oversight worked together in ordered harmony. [5] Unity and maturity were not expected to arise spontaneously. They were the fruit of Christ's gifts operating rightly within the community.

In the modern context, the longing for clarity is intensified by the divergent interpretations that have emerged around spiritual gifts. Some voices argue that the miraculous or foundational gifts ceased with the apostolic age. [6] Others collapse distinctions between ministries — such as viewing "pastors and teachers" as a single office — or downplay the continuing function of apostles and prophets. [7] Still others affirm the continuation of all gifts but struggle to articulate their interrelation or purpose in the ongoing life of the Church.

These differing perspectives carry real consequences. If the gifts Christ gave are misunderstood, misapplied, or neglected, the Church risks missing the very means Christ intends for its formation. Conversely, when these gifts are recognized within their biblical shape, the Body of Christ is strengthened in doctrine, discernment, mission, and unity. [8] This is why the longing for clarity must lead to careful, covenantal discernment.

This chapter therefore enters the priestly task: to examine the Scriptures with attentiveness, to listen to the broader historical witness of the Church, and to interpret the ascension gifts within the canonical architecture that stretches from Torah to the New Testament. The theological framework developed in Appendix A argues that these gifts do not emerge as isolated ecclesial titles, but as the continuation and fulfillment of a fivefold revelatory pattern embedded in the Pentateuch. [9]

This opening section has attempted to articulate the longing that drives this inquiry — a longing not for novelty, but for fidelity. The next section turns directly to the central biblical text, Ephesians 4:11–16, where the voice of the ascended Christ through the apostle defines the purpose, duration, and function of these gifts. In this revelatory movement, we begin to see how the ministries Christ gave serve as instruments for bringing His people into maturity and unity.

---

**Revelation: Christ Distributing the Five-Fold Voice**

Before the Church can discern how the ascension gifts operate, it must first listen again to the voice of the ascended Christ. Ephesians 4:11–16 is not a peripheral note in Pauline theology; it is the center of Paul's vision for ecclesial maturity. As such, it warrants close, careful, priestly attention.

To anchor the discussion clearly in Scripture, we begin with the text itself.

---

**Ephesians 4:11–16 (KJV)**

> *11 And he gave some, apostles; and some, prophets; and some, evangelists; and some, pastors and teachers;*
> *12 For the perfecting of the saints, for the work of the ministry, for the edifying of the body of Christ:*
> *13 Till we all come in the unity of the faith, and of the knowledge of the Son of God, unto a perfect man, unto the measure of the stature of the fulness of Christ:*
> *14 That we henceforth be no more children, tossed to and fro, and carried about with every wind of doctrine, by the sleight of men, and cunning craftiness, whereby they lie in wait to deceive;*
> *15 But speaking the truth in love, may grow up into him in all things, which is the head, even Christ:*

> *16 From whom the whole body fitly joined together and compacted by that which every joint supplieth, according to the effectual working in the measure of every part, maketh increase of the body unto the edifying of itself in love.*

---

## A. The Ascended Christ as the Source of the Five-Fold Gifts

Paul grounds the entire section not in ecclesial creativity, but in the gift-giving action of the risen and ascended Christ. "And He Himself gave…" *kai autos edoken* (καὶ αὐτὸς ἔδωκεν) signals a direct act of divine agency.[10] The ministries listed are not human offices built out of expedience; they are gifts distributed by Christ Himself as He governs His Body from His enthroned position.

The context of Ephesians 4 makes this explicit. Paul has just cited Psalm 68:18 — "When he ascended up on high, he led captivity captive, and gave gifts unto men" — applying Christological fulfillment to a royal enthronement psalm.[11] As several scholars note, the imagery corresponds to ancient Near Eastern coronation motifs in which a victorious king distributes spoils as signs of his rule.[12] Paul's theological point is unmistakable: the ascension of Christ results in the distribution of ministries essential to the Church's growth.

This immediately places the five ministries within a canonical frame. The Torah blueprint, outlined in Appendix A and the Conceptual Guide, demonstrates that God's voice is revealed in five streams: pastoral (Genesis), priestly (Exodus), prophetic (Leviticus), evangelistic (Numbers), and apostolic (Deuteronomy). These streams converge in Christ, and Christ distributes them to His Church.[13] Thus, the ascension gifts are not ecclesial experiments; they are the continuation of the Torah's revelatory structure through the risen Messiah.

## B. The Gifts Listed: Apostles, Prophets, Evangelists, Pastors, Teachers

### 1. Apostles (ἀποστόλους)

The term *apostolos* describes one who is "sent," carrying both delegated authority and covenantal responsibility.[14] While the Twelve hold a unique foundational role (Rev 21:14), the New Testament also speaks of a broader circle of apostles (e.g., Barnabas, Andronicus, Junia, Epaphroditus).[15] Paul's usage suggests that apostolic ministry continues beyond the foundational witness of the resurrection — functioning as missionary architects who plant, order, and establish communities in the gospel.

### 2. Prophets (προφήτας)

Prophets (prophetas) continue the Levitical pattern of a people shaped by the direct speech of God. New Testament prophecy is not equal to Scripture, but functions as Spirit-inspired exhortation, discernment, and direction for the community. [16] It simply means one who speaks on behlf of God – aligned with the canon of Scripture with focus on edification not novelty. The prophetic voice guards the Church from deception (cf. 1 Thess 5:20–21) and works in tandem with apostolic and teaching ministries to maintain doctrinal integrity.

### 3. Evangelists (εὐαγγελιστάς)

Evangelists embody the wilderness herald of Numbers — summoning people toward repentance, faith, and allegiance to Christ. Philip is the clearest example (Acts 21:8), showing that evangelists not only preach the gospel but catalyze new communities and often operate cross-culturally. [17]

### 4. Pastors (ποιμένας)

The pastoral role corresponds to the Genesis pattern of shepherding — guiding, guarding, and nurturing God's people.[18] Pastoral ministry focuses on relational care, spiritual formation, and the cultivation of communal wholeness.

### 5. Teachers (διδασκάλους)

Teachers are guardians of doctrine, ensuring the community remains grounded in the apostolic message. [19] Though pastors and teachers share a definite article, the nouns are plural, and thus the Granville Sharp rule does not collapse them into one office. [20] Their functions overlap, but they are not identical. This distinction is essential for understanding the architecture of Christ's distribution of gifts.

Together these five expressions constitute the voice of Christ among His people — a fivefold distribution of the ministry He embodied perfectly.

---

### C. The Purpose Clause: "For the Perfecting of the Saints…"

Paul identifies three purpose clauses introduced by the preposition πρός ("toward/for"):

1. For the perfecting *"katartismos"* (καταρτισμὸν) of the saints

2. For the work of ministry

3. For the edifying of the Body of Christ

Each clause builds upon the previous, forming a progressive logic:

Christ gives the fivefold gifts→ the saints are equipped → ministry is released → the Body is built up.

The term *katartismos* denotes restoration, mending, or equipping — often used of setting a broken bone or outfitting a ship for voyage. [21]

In covenantal terms, it describes the process of ordering the people for their vocation. The fivefold ministries therefore serve not as hierarchical offices but as formational gifts, shaping the people of God into a mature and functioning community.

---

## D. The Eschatological Horizon: "Till we all come…"

Ephesians 4:13 is the linchpin of the argument:

"Till we all come…" mechri katantesomen hoi pantes (μέχρι καταντήσωμεν οἱ πάντες). Until we all, together arrive… eis andra teleion – into the one Man…

The temporal clause introduced by mechri ("until") reveals that the gifts continue until the Church reaches four realities:

1. Unity of the faith

2. Knowledge of the Son of God

3. A perfect/mature man (ἄνδρα τέλειον)

4. The measure of the stature of the fullness of Christ

No serious interpreter argues that the global Church has reached this eschatological fullness. [22] Therefore, the continuation of the gifts is not charismatic optimism — it is the direct implication of Paul's grammar.

Here the cessationist model falters: if the gifts were temporary, the maturity they were meant to produce would be unreachable. Christ does not give temporary means for ongoing ends. [23]

The ascension gifts continue because the Church's maturation continues.

## E. The Protective Function: Guarding Against Deception

Verse 14 adds another dimension:

"That we henceforth be no more children, tossed to and fro…"

Paul employs maritime imagery — instability, waves, winds — to describe doctrinal vulnerability. [24] The gifts of Christ function as stabilizing forces:

- Apostles anchor communities in the gospel.
- Prophets expose deception and false motives.
- Evangelists confront syncretism with the news of Christ.
- Pastors protect the flock.
- Teachers clarify truth.

Without all five, the Church becomes susceptible to winds of doctrine.

---

### F. The Growth of the Body: "Fitly Joined Together…"

In verse 16, Paul describes the Body using architectural language found also in Ephesians 2:21: "fitly joined together" (συναρμολογούμενον).[25] The imagery reflects temple-construction language rooted in the Torah pattern — the tabernacle joined by divinely measured frames and couplings (Exod 26–27).[26] The Body is now the living temple, joined by the ministry Christ distributes.

The final outcome of the fivefold voice, therefore, is self-edification in love — the Body participating in its own growth as each member functions properly.

---

### Witness: The Testimony of Scripture and the Historical Church

Having listened to the voice of the ascended Christ in Ephesians 4:11–16, we turn now to the witness of Scripture and the history of the Church. For if these ministries are intended to persist "till we all come" (Eph 4:13), then we should find evidence that the apostles themselves expected their continuation — and that the generations following them recognized these gifts as ongoing.

This historical witness, when taken alongside Scripture, clarifies that the five-fold voice Christ distributes is not an ecclesial anomaly but a consistent feature of Christian life from the apostolic age through the patristic era and beyond.

---

## A. The Scriptural Witness: Continuity Beyond the Apostles

### 1. Prophecy in the New Testament Churches

Prophetic ministry is assumed as ongoing throughout the early Christian communities. Paul commands:

> "Despise not prophesyings. Prove all things; hold fast that which is good." (1 Thess 5:20–21)

These instructions only make sense if prophecy continues beyond the immediate reach of the apostles. Moreover, prophecy appears not as extraordinary but as normative within worship (1 Cor 14:1, 29–33).[27] Paul does not restrict such expressions to the apostolic circle; instead, he expects "all" to potentially participate as the Spirit wills (1 Cor 12:7, 11).[28]

### 2. Apostolic Oversight Beyond the Twelve

The New Testament itself names apostles beyond the Twelve:

- Barnabas (Acts 14:14)

- Andronicus and Junia (Rom 16:7)

- Epaphroditus (Phil 2:25; *apostolos* in a broader sense)

These individuals were not eyewitnesses of the resurrection. Their title reflects functional ministry — pioneering, establishing, fathering, and overseeing communities. [29] This alone challenges the assumption that apostolic ministry ended when the last original apostle died.

### 3. Teachers, Pastors, and Evangelists as Ongoing Functions

Unlike the Twelve, offices such as evangelist, pastor, and teacher are nowhere said to be temporary. Timothy is charged to "do the work of an evangelist" (2 Tim 4:5), and elders are repeatedly commanded to shepherd (ποιμαίνειν) the flock (Acts 20:28; 1 Pet 5:1–4).[30] These commands presume ongoing roles essential for ecclesial life.

### 4. The Function, Not the Canonical Role, Continues

The New Testament distinguishes between:

- Foundational apostles/prophets who bear revelatory authority (Eph 2:20)

- Functional apostles/prophets who edify and guide communities without writing Scripture

This distinction aligns with the Torah pattern: Moses stands uniquely as lawgiver, but prophetic and priestly voices continue. [31] Similarly, the apostolic foundation is unique, yet apostolic ministry continues functionally.

---

## B. The Early Church Witness: Prophecy, Apostleship, and Spiritual Gifts After the First Century

The generations immediately following the apostles offer unmistakable testimony that the gifts continued.

## 1. The Didache (late 1st–early 2nd century)

The Didache reflects organized instructions for apostles and prophets who visit churches, assuming their normal presence. [32] Prophets are to be tested, not dismissed; apostles are honored if their conduct aligns with Christ.

## 2. The Shepherd of Hermas (2nd century)

The Shepherd describes ongoing prophetic revelation, distinguishing between true and false prophets and providing criteria for discernment. [33] This only makes sense in a context where prophecy is active.

## 3. Justin Martyr (mid-2nd century)

Justin writes:

"The prophetic gifts remain with us even to the present time." [34]

His statement explicitly refutes the idea that gifts ceased with the apostles.

## 4. Irenaeus (late 2nd century)

Irenaeus testifies that believers in his day exercised healing, prophecy, tongues, and discernment. [35] His witness is particularly compelling because he was a disciple of Polycarp, who himself was a disciple of the apostle John. This places Irenaeus in direct continuity with the apostolic stream.

## 5. Tertullian (early 3rd century)

Tertullian describes the presence of prophetic visions and supernatural guidance within the church community, viewing them as normal operations of the Spirit. [36] He contrasts this vitality with what he perceived as spiritual decline in heretical groups.

### 6. Origen (mid-3rd century)

While noting some diminishment of gifts in his day, Origen still affirms that miracles and manifestations occurred among believers committed to holiness. [37] His admission that some decline was due not to divine cessation but human coldness parallels later comments by John Chrysostom.

### 7. Chrysostom (4th century)

Chrysostom famously laments the absence of certain gifts in his own era but never attributes this to divine cessation. He attributes loss to spiritual decline, not to a theological ending of gifts. [38]

Across the patristic strata, the testimony is consistent: the gifts continued.

---

## C. The Witness of the Medieval Church

Though often overlooked, the medieval period also retained charismatic expressions:

- Hildegard of Bingen reported prophetic visions and spiritual counsel. [39]

- Bernard of Clairvaux ministered with healing and miracles. [40]

- The mendicant movements emphasized charismatic poverty and Spirit-led mission. [41]

These witnesses demonstrate that spiritual gifts, though sometimes diminished or poorly understood, persisted throughout church history.

## D. The Reformation and Post-Reformation Voices

Reformation leaders, while reacting to abuses, did not deny the possibility of charismatic operation:

- Martin Luther acknowledged divine healing and prophetic insight. [42]

- John Calvin affirmed the reality of miraculous signs, though he viewed them as less frequent. [43]

- The Puritans such as John Owen recognized extraordinary works of the Spirit among believers. [44]

Notably, the cessationist system as articulated today did not exist in the Reformation; it emerged more formally in the 17th–19th centuries.

---

## F. Reformation Witness: Preaching as the Convergence of All Five Ministries

The Reformers recovered not only the primacy of Scripture but also a robust theology of preaching as the living speech of God. Far from restricting preaching to didactic instruction, they understood it as the dynamic event in which God addresses His people with pastoral care, priestly instruction, prophetic confrontation, evangelistic summons, and apostolic ordering.

### 1. Calvin: Preaching Is Prophetic

John Calvin repeatedly affirmed that preaching is prophetic in nature. In his commentary on Ephesians 4, he identifies pastors and teachers not as mere "lecturers" but as those who speak with the prophetic authority of the Word applied to the present moment.[45] He writes:

> "God designs to consecrate the mouths of men to be for Him a herald,
> and in them He would have us hear His own voice."[46]

In Calvin's theology, preaching is not simply teaching. It is a prophetic act, because in preaching, Christ speaks through human ministers to confront, comfort, convict, and restore His people.[47]

Calvin's Institutes further reinforces this point:

> "When the gospel is preached by men, it is as if God Himself did speak."[48]

Thus, for Calvin, preaching participates in the prophetic voice of Christ, not as new revelation, but as the Spirit-empowered exposition of Scripture applied prophetically to the congregation.

## 2. Luther: The Preacher as Prophet

Martin Luther also emphasized the prophetic dimension of preaching. He described preaching as "the living voice of the gospel" (viva vox evangelii) and insisted that when Scripture is proclaimed faithfully, God Himself speaks. [51] Luther frequently compared gospel proclamation to the prophetic ministry of the Old Testament, calling preachers "prophets of the Word" who confront sin and call for repentance.[49]

## 3. Reformed Orthodoxy: The Prophetic, Priestly, and Royal Offices in Preaching

Following Calvin and Luther, the Reformed scholastics (e.g., Turretin, Voetius, Perkins) described preaching as a triple-office ministry that reflects Christ's own offices as Prophet, Priest, and King.[50] The preacher:

- teaches (prophetic office)

- intercedes and mediates pastoral care (priestly office)

- orders the community for obedience (royal/apostolic office)

This aligns naturally with the five-fold pattern of Ephesians 4.

## 4. The Five-Fold Voice Converging in Preaching

While not using the term "five-fold ministry," the Reformers essentially taught its functional reality:

- Preaching is pastoral, feeding and guarding the flock with the Word.

- Preaching is priestly, instructing in covenant truth of the Word.

- Preaching is prophetic, confronting sin and calling to holiness based on the Word.

- Preaching is evangelistic, summoning hearers to faith and a response to the Word.

- Preaching is apostolic, articulating the Word to clarify the Church's foundational truths and shaping its communal direction.

Thus, preaching embodies the whole voice of Christ — the very reality Paul describes when he says that Christ "gave" these ministries for the building up of His Body (Eph 4:11–12).

## 5. Modern Scholarship Recognizes the Same Pattern

Recent homiletic scholarship affirms this insight. Thomas G. Long, for instance, argues that true preaching "is the continuation of the prophetic ministry of Jesus."[51] James P. Torrance describes preaching as a "participation in the continuing ministry of Christ."[52] Even scholars who reject continuationism admit that preaching retains prophetic characteristics.[53]

The implication is clear:

Preaching should never be reduced to a single stream.

It is the convergence of all five.

When the Church preaches with only one voice — only teaching, or only evangelism, or only pastoral comfort — it truncates the full expression of Christ's ministry.

But when preaching embodies the five-fold voice —pastoral, priestly, prophetic, evangelistic, and apostolic —the Church hears Christ in fullness, and the Body grows toward maturity.

---

**E. Modern Cessationism and Its Limitations**

Cessationist thought, especially in its strict form, was crystallized in the writings of B. B. Warfield, who argued that miracles ceased because their purpose was to authenticate the apostles.[54] However:

1. The New Testament never states this purpose exclusively.

2. Miracles and gifts appear in non-apostolic settings and by non-apostolic individuals (e.g., Stephen, Philip, Ananias).[55]

3. The "authenticating purpose" does not account for Ephesians 4:13's eschatological framework.

4. Warfield wrote in polemic against early Pentecostalism, not as a neutral exegete.[56]

When evaluated in the full light of Scripture, the early Church, the medieval and Reformation traditions, and the global witness of the Spirit's work, strict cessationism cannot sustain its historical, theological, or exegetical claims; the five-fold voice is woven into the very fabric of the Church's life from Pentecost onward

## Recovering the Five-Fold Voice for the Contemporary Church

The cumulative witness of Scripture, history, and canonical theology presses upon the contemporary Church with unavoidable clarity: the ministries Christ distributed in His ascension are neither optional nor antiquated. They belong to the essential structure of Christian maturity. The question before the modern Church, therefore, is not whether the five-fold voice exists, but whether we will recognize and cooperate with it.

The Church stands at a moment remarkably parallel to several prior turning points in redemptive history. Like Israel at the threshold of the Promised Land (Num 27:17), the Church requires shepherds who lead in alignment with God's word rather than in reaction to cultural pressures. Like the early Christians navigating post-apostolic transition, we must discern how the Spirit continues to equip the Body in the absence of the original eyewitnesses. And like the Reformation, we find ourselves confronted anew with questions about authority, teaching, and the living voice of God in the gathered assembly.

The response demanded of us is neither reactionary nor ideological. It is deeply theological. It begins with returning to Christ's own design for the formation of His people — a design expressed not in scattered verses, but in a unified canonical pattern.

---

### A. The Ecclesial Consequence of Neglecting the Five-Fold Voice

When the Church restricts or neglects any of the ministries Christ gave, predictable distortions arise. Each gift serves a specific formational role, and the absence of one is not compensated simply by increasing another.

### 1. Without Apostolic Ministry — The Church Loses Order and Mission

Apostolic oversight provides architectural clarity, grounding communities in the gospel and sending them outward. Where apostolic ministry is absent, churches either stagnate inwardly or drift toward novelty without grounding. [57]

### 2. Without Prophetic Ministry — The Church Loses Discernment

Prophets function as guardians of moral and doctrinal clarity. [58] They confront the Church when it drifts into complacency or compromise. Without their voice, the Church becomes susceptible to cultural accommodation.

### 3. Without Evangelistic Ministry — The Church Loses Missional Urgency

Evangelists embody the outward proclamation of Christ's victory. When their voice diminishes, the gospel becomes internalized rather than proclaimed. [59]

### 4. Without Pastoral Ministry — The Church Loses Spiritual Care

Pastors embody the shepherding heart of God — nurturing, healing, and guiding. Without them, communities lack relational cohesion and spiritual formation. [60]

### 5. Without Teaching Ministry — The Church Loses Doctrinal Stability

Teachers ground the Church in sound doctrine and protect it from error.[61] In their absence, unity is impossible and spiritual maturity remains elusive.

Taken together, these ministries represent a single five-fold expression of the voice of Christ. Neglecting one distorts the whole. Amplifying one to the exclusion of the others fractures the Church. The pattern of

Ephesians 4 does not permit selective emphasis; it demands holistic participation.

---

## B. Preaching as the Primary Convergence Point of the Five-Fold Voice

As demonstrated historically, preaching is not a subset of the five-fold ministries but the platform through which all five converge.

### 1. Preaching is Apostolic

It declares Christ's lordship and orders the community around apostolic truth. It commissions the next generation to follow God's Word.

### 2. Preaching is Prophetic

It confronts sin, exposes idols, and calls the Church into covenant faithfulness. Reminding church of God's voice in Scripture and pleading for God's heart. [62]

### 3. Preaching is Evangelistic

It summons hearers to repentance, faith, and new birth - embodiment. [63]

### 4. Preaching is Pastoral

It feeds, guards, comforts, and exhorts the flock.

### 5. Preaching is Teaching

It expounds upon Scripture with clarity and doctrinal precision.

This is why the Reformers insisted that faithful preaching is the living voice of God (*viva vox Dei*) — not in the sense of new revelation, but as the Spirit's application of Scripture to God's people. [64] Preaching, rightly understood, is the place where the five-fold voice becomes audible, tangible, and transformative.

---

## C. The Five-Fold Voice and the Unity of the Church

Ephesians 4 links the five-fold ministries not only to maturity but to unity.

Unity is not achieved by eliminating distinctions but by embracing Christ's distributed voice. [65]

The Church often attempts unity by:

- flattening ministries into one office,
- suppressing certain gifts,
- adopting managerial models,
- emphasizing uniformity over complementarity.

Yet Scripture presents unity as the harmonization of diverse ministries. Where each gift is honored, unity emerges organically. Where one gift is elevated or diminished, unity fractures.

This canonical pattern aligns with the Torah architecture:

- Genesis: Pastoral beginnings
- Exodus: Priestly instruction
- Leviticus: Prophetic holiness
- Numbers: Evangelistic summons
- Deuteronomy: Apostolic sending

Christ embodies all five. The Spirit distributes all five. The Church must reflect all five.

Unity therefore requires not uniformity, but full expression.

---

**D. The Five-Fold Voice and Spiritual Maturity**

Paul's eschatological horizon — "till we all come…" — makes clear that the gifts remain operative until the Church reaches the measure of the stature of the fullness of Christ (Eph 4:13).

This maturity is:

- Christological — measured by the likeness of Christ
- corporate — experienced by the whole Body
- doctrinal — grounded in unity of faith
- experiential — growth in knowledge of the Son
- ethical — reflected in truth-in-love (v. 15)
- structural — the Body joined and supplied by every part (v. 16)

Such maturity is impossible through one voice alone.

- A teacher can explain doctrine but cannot replace the prophetic call to holiness.
- A pastor can tend the flock but cannot substitute for apostolic structure.
- An evangelist can call people into covenant but cannot by himself supply the doctrinal formation or communal structure that the Church requires.

Christ distributes five expressions of His own ministry so that the Body may bear the fullness of His life.

---

### E. The Call to Recover the Five-Fold Voice

The task before the contemporary Church is not to invent a new ministry structure, nor to adopt pragmatic leadership models, but to return to the canonical foundation.

This recovery requires:

1. Theological clarity — recognizing the five-fold voice as Christ-given, Spirit-empowered, and canonically rooted. [66]

2. Ecclesial humility — acknowledging where traditions have overemphasized or underemphasized certain gifts.

3. Pastoral discernment — identifying and cultivating the gifts within the congregation.

4. Doctrinal fidelity — ensuring that the five-fold functions remain grounded in Scripture rather than personality or innovation.

5. Missional focus — allowing the five-fold voice to propel the Church outward in witness and inward in holiness.

The five-fold voice is not a model to adopt but a pattern to receive—an architectural framework grounded in Scripture and given by the ascended Christ for the building up of His Body.

---

### The Five-Fold Voice and the Future of the Church

The recovery of the five-fold voice is an invitation into renewal. Whenever God restores His voice among His people, renewal follows. Scripture records this pattern with remarkable consistency. When the Torah was rediscovered under Josiah, the people renewed the covenant

(2 Kgs 23:1–3). When the prophetic word returned through Haggai and Zechariah, the temple was rebuilt (Ezra 5:1–2). When Ezra taught the Law, the exiles wept and rejoiced as their identity was restored (Neh 8:8–12). When Christ preached in Galilee with authority, lives were reordered around the kingdom (Mark 1:14–15). When the Spirit was poured out at Pentecost, the Church emerged as a people formed by apostolic doctrine, prophetic utterance, evangelistic witness, pastoral care, and the teaching of Scripture (Acts 2:42–47). [67]

Renewal is, in every age, the fruit of hearing God's full voice again.

The five-fold ministries represent the manifold voice of Christ, and whenever that voice becomes clear in the Church, the people of God recover their identity, their unity, their mission, and their joy.

### A. Renewal Begins Where Christ's Voice Is Heard in Full

Renewal does not begin with programs, strategies, or innovations.

It begins when the Church hears Christ again — clearly, covenantally, canonically.

Each of the five ministries — apostolic, prophetic, evangelistic, pastoral, and teaching — carries a distinct resonance of Christ's voice. When these are present and honored, the Church experiences a balanced, holistic articulation of the gospel. [68]

- The apostolic voice restores order, mission, and gospel architecture.
- The prophetic voice restores holiness, repentance, and moral clarity.
- The evangelistic voice restores urgency and outward movement.
- The pastoral voice restores identity, healing, and spiritual formation.

- The teaching voice restores understanding, doctrine, and discernment.

When the Church attempts renewal through one voice alone, it inevitably becomes distorted.

But when the Church receives all five as the ascended Christ distributes them, renewal becomes the natural outcome of obedience.

---

### B. Renewal Flows from the Canonical Architecture of Torah

Appendix A demonstrates that the five-fold voice is not a late ecclesial development but a deeply embedded canonical pattern originating in the Torah. This pattern forms the backbone of biblical revelation:

- Genesis gives the pastoral origin — the God who walks with His people.
- Exodus establishes the priestly instruction — the God who teaches and forms.
- Leviticus reveals the prophetic voice — the God who calls to holiness.
- Numbers embodies the evangelistic summons — the God who sends His people.
- Deuteronomy articulates the apostolic commissioning — the God who forms a covenant people and sends them into inheritance. [69]

This architecture is not abolished in Christ; it is fulfilled in Him (Matt 5:17).

And the ascended Christ distributes this five-fold voice to His Church so that the Torah's formative structure becomes the Church's formative structure.

Renewal occurs wherever the Church returns to this canonical foundation.

---

## C. Renewal Requires Discernment, Not Novelty

The recovery of the five-fold voice is not a license for novelty, charisma without accountability, or ecclesial experimentation. Instead, it calls for:

1. Discernment — ensuring gifts operate in alignment with Scripture.

2. Accountability of the Word — maintaining order, doctrine, and communal health.

3. Integration — recognizing that each gift depends upon the others.

4. Humility — receiving Christ's gifts without elevating personalities or creating hierarchies.

5. Continuity — grounding all ministry in the once-for-all revelation of Christ as witnessed in Scripture.[70]

Renewal is not a reinvention of the Church's structure; it is the Church learning to walk again in Christ's own pattern.

---

## D. Renewal Through Preaching: The Five-Fold Voice Made Audible

Since preaching is the convergence point of the five ministries, renewal often begins where preaching is reformed. When preaching:

- recovers its apostolic clarity,
- restores its prophetic sharpness,
- renews its evangelistic urgency,
- reclaims its pastoral tenderness,
- regains its teaching precision,

the Church hears Christ again. [71]

And when Christ's voice is heard, renewal follows.

This is why the Reformers viewed preaching as central to renewal: the pulpit is where the five-fold voice becomes audible to the gathered saints. As Calvin wrote, "When the gospel is preached, it is as if God Himself were speaking." [72] Such preaching reforms hearts, corrects doctrine, and reorders the entire ecclesial life around Christ.

---

### E. Renewal Leads the Church Toward Eschatological Maturity

Paul's eschatological horizon ("till we all come...," Eph 4:13) reveals that the five-fold voice is not only restorative but teleological. It points the Church toward its consummate identity — a Body reflecting the mature stature of Christ.

Thus, renewal is not an end in itself. It is a journey toward the fullness of Christ:
- unity of faith,
- experiential knowledge of the Son,
- doctrinal stability,

- truth expressed in love,
- a Body joined and supplied by every part,
- growth that arises from Christ, the Head.

This is the eschatological vision of renewal. It is not emotional intensity, organizational momentum, or emotional excitement. It is transformation into the likeness of Christ, shaped by the voice of Christ, mediated through the gifts of Christ.

## F. Renewal and the Eschatological People of God

The recovery of the five-fold voice also aligns the Church with its eschatological destiny — the Bride made ready (Rev 19:7). The ministries Christ distributes prepare the people for the day of His appearing.

- Apostles prepare the Church structurally.
- Prophets prepare the Church morally.
- Evangelists prepare the nations spiritually.
- Pastors prepare believers relationally.
- Teachers prepare the Church doctrinally.[73]

The result is a people "fitly joined together" (Eph 4:16) who bear the fullness of Christ's life and love.

---

## G. Renewal Summarized

Renewal occurs when the Church:

1. Recognizes the ascended Christ as the source of the five-fold voice.

2. Receives the canonical architecture of these ministries.

3. Responds with ecclesial humility and biblical fidelity.

4. Reforms preaching to embody all five dimensions.

5. Restores the balance of ministries within the local and global Body.

6. Returns to the Torah foundation fulfilled in Christ.

7. Reaches toward maturity and unity Paul describes in Ephesians 4.

The result is a Church renewed in identity, grounded in Scripture, empowered by the Spirit, and prepared for the Lord's return.

The five-fold voice is not a model to adopt — it is the canonical shape of Christ's own ministry, given to His people until we reach the fullness of His glory.

What emerges from Scripture is a pattern of ministry, and a recognizable movement of formation. Wherever God speaks, acts, dwells, sends, and renews, people are changed in ordered ways. Longing is awakened, truth is proclaimed, lives are instructed, holiness is embodied, faith is tested in motion, and a people are re-aligned for inheritance. This rhythm does not originate in preaching technique or ecclesial design; it appears wherever God is faithfully at work among His people.

This movement will be traced further in Appendix A, where the same formative logic is shown to arise from the ascension of Christ in Ephesians 4, rooted in Torah's covenantal grammar, and echoed across diverse New Testament witnesses.

---

**NOTES**
1. [Richard B. Gaffin Jr., Perspectives on Pentecost: New Testament Teaching on the Gifts of the Holy Spirit (Phillipsburg, NJ: Presbyterian & Reformed, 1979), 21–34.

2. John Calvin, Institutes of the Christian Religion, trans. Ford Lewis Battles (Philadelphia: Westminster, 1960), 4.3.1–3.

3. Nahum Sarna, Exodus (JPS Torah Commentary; Philadelphia: Jewish Publication Society, 1991), 120–123.

4. David T. Tsumura, The First Book of Samuel (NICOT; Grand Rapids: Eerdmans, 2007), 197–201.

5. Luke Timothy Johnson, The Writings of the New Testament, 3rd ed. (Minneapolis: Fortress Press, 2010), 292–306.

6. B. B. Warfield, Counterfeit Miracles (New York: Charles Scribner's Sons, 1918), 3–32.

7. Harold W. Hoehner, Ephesians: An Exegetical Commentary (Grand Rapids: Baker Academic, 2002), 544–546.

8. Gordon D. Fee, Paul's Letter to the Ephesians (NICNT; Grand Rapids: Eerdmans, 2010), 492–509.

9. See Appendix A, "The Canonical Architecture of the Ascension Gifts,

10. Harold W. Hoehner, Ephesians: An Exegetical Commentary (Grand Rapids: Baker Academic, 2002), 527–530.

11. Andrew T. Lincoln, Ephesians (WBC 42; Dallas: Word, 1990), 243–246.

12. John H. Walton, Ancient Near Eastern Thought and the Old Testament (Grand Rapids: Baker Academic, 2006), 311–315.

13. Cf. Appendix A, "The Fivefold Pattern from Torah to the Fullness of Christ," in The Final TMP Book.pdf .

14. Karl Heinrich Rengstorf, "ἀπόστολος," in TDNT, 1:407–445.

15. F. F. Bruce, The Epistle to the Galatians (NIGTC; Grand Rapids: Eerdmans, 1982), 248–249.

16. Craig Keener, The Spirit in the Gospels and Acts (Peabody, MA: Hendrickson, 1997), 242–249.

17. Eckhard J. Schnabel, Early Christian Mission, vol. 1 (Downers Grove: IVP Academic, 2004), 392–397.

18. Philip J. King, Jeremiah: An Archaeological Companion (Philadelphia: Westminster, 1993), 85–87.

19. Douglas J. Moo, The Letters to the Colossians and to Philemon (PNTC; Grand Rapids: Eerdmans, 2008), 276–278.

20. Daniel B. Wallace, Greek Grammar Beyond the Basics (Grand Rapids: Zondervan, 1996), 270–290.

21. Walter Bauer, Frederick W. Danker, William F. Arndt, and F. Wilbur Gingrich, A Greek-English Lexicon of the New Testament and Other Early Christian Literature, 3rd ed. (BDAG) (Chicago: University of Chicago Press, 2000), 526.

22. Markus Barth, Ephesians 4–6 (AB 34A; Garden City, NY: Doubleday, 1974), 479–487.

23. Thomas R. Schreiner, Spiritual Gifts: What They Are and Why They Matter (Nashville: B&H, 2018), 56–61.
24. Clinton E. Arnold, Ephesians (ZECNT; Grand Rapids: Zondervan, 2010), 259–261.
25. Frank Thielman, Ephesians (BECNT; Grand Rapids: Baker Academic, 2010), 287–289.
26.
27. Carol Meyers, Exodus (NCBC; New York: Cambridge University Press, 2005), 211–218.
28. Gordon D. Fee, God's Empowering Presence: The Holy Spirit in the Letters of Paul (Peabody, MA: Hendrickson, 1994), 56–61.
29. Anthony C. Thiselton, The First Epistle to the Corinthians, NIGTC (Grand Rapids: Eerdmans, 2000), 944–50.
30. F. F. Bruce, Paul: Apostle of the Heart Set Free (Grand Rapids: Eerdmans, 1977), 289–95.
31. Thomas R. Schreiner, Paul, Apostle of God's Glory in Christ (Downers Grove, IL: InterVarsity Press, 2001), 384–87.
32. Moshe Weinfeld, Deuteronomy 1–11, AB 5 (New York: Doubleday, 1991), 19–23.
33. The Didache, in The Apostolic Fathers, ed. Michael W. Holmes, 3rd ed. (Grand Rapids: Baker Academic, 2007), 3–35.
34. The Shepherd of Hermas, in The Apostolic Fathers, ed. Michael W. Holmes, 3rd ed. (Grand Rapids: Baker Academic, 2007), 358–410.
35. Justin Martyr, Dialogue with Trypho, in The Ante-Nicene Fathers, ed. Alexander Roberts and James Donaldson, vol. 1 (Peabody, MA: Hendrickson, 1994), 169.
36. Irenaeus, Against Heresies, 5.6.1, in The Ante-Nicene Fathers, ed. Alexander Roberts and James Donaldson, vol. 1 (Peabody, MA: Hendrickson, 1994), 531–32.
37. Tertullian, Against Marcion, 5.8, in The Ante-Nicene Fathers, ed. Alexander Roberts and James Donaldson, vol. 3 (Peabody, MA: Hendrickson, 1994), 446–47.
38. Origen, Against Celsus, 1.46, in The Ante-Nicene Fathers, ed. Alexander Roberts and James Donaldson, vol. 4 (Peabody, MA: Hendrickson, 1994), 415–18.
39. John Chrysostom, Homilies on First Corinthians, Hom. 29.1, in Nicene and Post-Nicene Fathers, Series 1, vol. 12, ed. Philip Schaff (Peabody, MA: Hendrickson, 1994), 168–70.
40. Hildegard of Bingen, Scivias, trans. Columba Hart and Jane Bishop, CWS (New York: Paulist, 1990), 59–65.
41. Bernard of Clairvaux, Sermons on the Song of Songs, trans. Kilian Walsh, 4 vols. (Kalamazoo, MI: Cistercian Publications, 1971–80), 1:23–29.
42. Lawrence S. Cunningham, Saint Francis of Assisi (Collegeville, MN: Liturgical Press, 2004), 33–41.
43. Martin Luther, Table Talk, trans. William Hazlitt (London: Reeves and Turner, 1872), 375–79.
44. John Calvin, Institutes of the Christian Religion, 3.2.4, ed. John T. McNeill, trans. Ford Lewis Battles (Philadelphia: Westminster, 1960), 1:536–37.
45. John Owen, The Holy Spirit, ed. William H. Goold, 3 vols., Works of John Owen 3 (Edinburgh: Banner of Truth, 1967), 3:267–74.
46. B. B. Warfield, Counterfeit Miracles (New York: Charles Scribner's Sons, 1918), 3–32.
47. Stanley M. Burgess, The Holy Spirit: Medieval Roman Catholic and Reformation Traditions (Peabody, MA: Hendrickson, 1997), 22–29.
48. John Calvin, Commentary on the Epistle to the Ephesians, trans. William Pringle (Edinburgh: Calvin Translation Society, 1854), 277–279.

49. Calvin, Institutes, 4.1.5.

50. T. H. L. Parker, Calvin's Preaching (Louisville: Westminster John Knox, 1992), 25–32.

51. Calvin, Institutes, 4.1.9.

52. Martin Luther, Sermons of Martin Luther, ed. John Nicholas Lenker (Grand Rapids: Baker, 1983), 1:12–15.

53. Timothy J. Wengert, Reading the Bible with Martin Luther (Grand Rapids: Baker Academic, 2013), 121–128.

54. Francis Turretin, Institutes of Elenctic Theology, trans. George Musgrave Giger (Phillipsburg, NJ: Presbyterian & Reformed, 1992), 2:497–503.

55. Thomas G. Long, The Witness of Preaching, 3rd ed. (Louisville: Westminster John Knox, 2016), 33–35.

56. James B. Torrance, Worship, Community, and the Triune God of Grace (Downers Grove: IVP Academic, 1997), 67–72.

57. John Stott, Between Two Worlds: The Challenge of Preaching Today (Grand Rapids: Eerdmans, 1982), 87–92.

58. Darrell L. Bock, A Theology of Luke and Acts (Grand Rapids: Zondervan, 2012), 365–372.

59. Amos Yong, The Spirit Poured Out on All Flesh: Pentecostalism and the Possibility of Global Theology (Grand Rapids: Baker Academic, 2005), 104–109.

60. Michael Green, Evangelism in the Early Church (Grand Rapids: Eerdmans, 2004), 46–63.

61. Eugene H. Peterson, The Pastor: A Memoir (New York: HarperOne, 2011), 103–118.

62. Kevin J. Vanhoozer, Hearers and Doers: A Pastor's Guide to Making Disciples Through Scripture and Doctrine (Bellingham, WA: Lexham, 2019), 57–68.

63. T. H. L. Parker, Calvin's Preaching (Louisville: Westminster John Knox, 1992), 25–32.

64. John Stott, The Gospel: A Life-Changing Message (Grand Rapids: Zondervan, 2008), 112–120.

65. Timothy George, The Theology of the Reformers, rev. ed. (Nashville: B&H Academic, 2013), 92–97.

66. Gordon D. Fee, Pauline Christology (Peabody, MA: Hendrickson, 2007), 361–365.

67. Craig S. Keener, Gift & Giver: The Holy Spirit for Today (Grand Rapids: Baker Academic, 2001), 154–162.

68. G. K. Beale and Benjamin L. Gladd, The Story Retold: A Biblical-Theological Introduction to the New Testament (Downers Grove: IVP Academic, 2020), 212–220.

69. Christopher J. H. Wright, The Mission of God: Unlocking the Bible's Grand Narrative (Downers Grove: IVP Academic, 2006), 412–418.

70. See Appendix A, "The Canonical Architecture of the Ascension Gifts," in The Final TMP Book.pdf .

71. Michael Horton, People and Place: A Covenant Ecclesiology (Louisville: Westminster John Knox, 2008), 165–172.

72. Hughes Oliphant Old, The Reading and Preaching of the Scriptures in the Worship of the Christian Church, Vol. 4 (Grand Rapids: Eerdmans, 2002), 38–49.

73. Calvin, Institutes, 4.1.9.

74. John Webster, The Domain of the Word: Scripture and Theological Reason (London: T&T Clark, 2012), 99–105

# Exodus:

## Priestly Stream

## Teaching the Truth in Covenant

# CHAPTER FOUR

## THE MINISTRY OF THE PRIEST

**Introduction to the Ministry of Access**

The priestly stream is the steady backbone of the covenant community. If the prophetic voice confronts, the evangelistic voice summons, and the apostolic voice sends, the priestly voice structures, orders, and guards the covenant life of God's people. The priest does not simply stand beside the altar — he stands between God and the people as an active agent of access of redemption and healing.

Scripture consistently locates national and communal failure not first in prophetic silence, but in priestly neglect. When the priests cease to guard the Word, false worship proliferates. When holy things are mishandled, judgment falls—not because God is capricious, but because access has been corrupted. Nadab and Abihu are not punished for false prophecy but for unauthorized approach. Eli's failure is not ignorance of revelation but refusal to restrain what defiles worship. Malachi's indictment is not that the people lack zeal, but that the priests have despised the table of the LORD.

This danger is not rooted in personality or power, but in custodianship. The priest does not invent the covenant; he preserves it. He does not originate the Word; he guards it. He does not create access; he stewards it. His authority is quiet, enduring, and therefore decisive. When exercised faithfully, it stabilizes the people of God across generations. When compromised, it prepares the ground for every other failure.

**Priestly Covenant Teaching: Word Lived and Word Read**

The defining task of the priest as covenant teacher is twofold: to live out the Word in proximity to the altar and tabernacle, and to read and teach that same Word publicly to the people. Priestly authority does not arise from abstract instruction, but from embodied obedience. The priest first orders his own life around the holy place—handling sacrifice, guarding access, and dwelling near the presence of God—so that the Word he teaches is not just spoken, but lived. Instruction flows from proximity.

This pattern reaches its clearest expression in the example of Ezra. Ezra does not function primarily as prophet or reformer, but as priestly scribe. He stands among the people, opens the Book of the Law, reads it aloud, and gives the sense so that the people understand. The power of this moment lies not in novelty or confrontation, but in restoration through clarity. The Word is recovered, made audible, and interpreted within covenant bounds. Worship is renewed because the Word is rightly handled.

Ezra embodies the priestly danger and responsibility. He does not apply judgment as a prophet nor establish new ground as an apostle. He reorders the life of the people by restoring the Word to its rightful place. His life and ministry demonstrates that when the Word is guarded, lived, and taught faithfully, covenant renewal follows naturally. When the Word is neglected, even sincere worship collapses into confusion.

The priest, therefore, is dangerous not because he speaks loudly, but because he teaches steadily. By living under the Word at the altar and reading the Word to the people, he shapes what a community believes and becomes, faithful and holy people. Over time, this authority determines whether the people drift from the covenant or remain anchored within it.

**Priestly Judgment, Eternal Meaning, and Covenant Accountability**

Scripture presents priestly judgment not only as punishment for ritual error, but as consequence for acting out the covenant law without understanding—or teaching—the eternal weight of what was being enacted. Priests were entrusted not only with performing the statutes of worship, but with discerning and transmitting their meaning within God's redemptive purpose. When the law was reduced to performance without comprehension, and worship continued without instruction, the priesthood failed in its highest responsibility. This failure is repeatedly indicted in Scripture—not because sacrifices ceased, but because their significance was obscured. The priest was charged to "teach Jacob thy judgments" and to "put difference between holy and unholy," a task that presupposes understanding, not mechanical obedience. Judgment, therefore, falls when priests enact holy rites while remaining blind to their covenant purpose and neglect to instruct the people accordingly.

In this light, the priesthood bore responsibility to recognize that the law pointed beyond itself – to redemption—to discern its telos—and to prepare the people for the fulfillment God Himself would bring.

This does not mean that every priest possessed absolute messianic clarity, but it does mean covenant faithfulness: to see acceptable sacrifice demanded obedience, that atonement required righteousness, and that access to God anticipated a greater mediation and fulfillment.

**Preserving the Form without Understanding the Meaning**
Where the priests failed to perceive and teach these realities, they preserved form while forfeiting meaning. Such blindness rendered them unable to recognize the Messiah when He came—not because revelation was absent, but because the law they enacted daily had never been rightly understood or taught as pointing toward its fulfillment.

The priests had ministered the covenant without apprehending God Himself in relationship. Thus, priestly judgment in Scripture is consistently tied to misunderstanding eternity while handling holy things in time, and to neglecting the sacred duty of instruction that would have prepared the people—and the priests themselves—for the coming of Christ. Below shows the revelation and flow of the teaching requirement God reveals.

- Torah: Priests are commanded to teach, discern, and guard meaning (Lev 10:10–11; Deut 33:10).
- Prophets: Judgment falls for corrupted teaching, not absent ritual (Mal 2; Ezek 44).
- Ezra: Restoration comes through understanding, doing, and teaching the law (Ezra 7:10; Neh 8).
- Gospels: Jesus indicts leaders for knowing the Scriptures yet missing their witness to Him (John 5:39).
- Second Temple / DSS: Priestly interpretation is tied to covenant destiny and eschatological alignment.

Based on these passages - teaching priest is now responsible for asking:

- What does this act reveal about God's redemptive purpose?
- What does this law prepare the people to recognize?
- What blindness results if this is not taught?

**The Ministry of Access is the Guardianship of the Word**

The ministry of access is the priestly guardianship of the Word by which nearness to God remains possible. From the beginning, access to the presence of God has always been ordered by what God has spoken and preserved through those entrusted with its care.

The priest therefore serves as the steward of access precisely because he is first the custodian of the Word. Where the Word is faithfully guarded, the way to God remains clear and the life of the covenant remains stable; where the Word is neglected, distorted, or surrendered, access collapses—not because God withdraws, but because the path has been obscured. Thus the priest both guards the Word and guides the people, yet guardianship must always govern guidance, for only what is preserved can be rightly entered.

He brings God's Word to the people, and he brings the people's worship to God. This dual movement defines the priestly stream. The priest is the living bridge between revelation and response — the one who receives the covenant on behalf of the people and ensures that the people walk in it faithfully. Without the priestly stream, the covenant remains distant. With it, the covenant becomes livable and accessible.

In Scripture, the priest is never a ceremonial accessory. He is the steward of access, the keeper of the door. The people do not approach God casually; they approach through priestly ministry of the Word. They do not invent worship; they are instructed in worship.

They do not guess at holiness; they are taught holiness through the Word. The priest embodies covenant clarity. Where the prophet cries, "Return to the covenant." The priest explains, "This is the covenant." Where the evangelist calls, "Enter the kingdom," the priest teaches, "This is how kingdom people live." Where the apostle commissions, "Go," the priest anchors, "Remember the Word."

The priest is God's authorized interpreter of His ways. The priest is the guardian of sacred memory. The teacher of the sacred Word. The priest is the teacher of holiness, the keeper of order, the instructor of the soul.

And in every generation, the priestly stream remains essential because the covenant is not self-executing. It must be taught, guarded, and handed down. The priest keeps the people aligned with what God has spoken, ensuring that worship is not creativity but covenant fidelity.

The teaching priest makes access to God possible. He nurtures access to the Word, this means continual access to His presence. Access to the covenant is preserving life under God's rule.

The priestly stream therefore shapes preaching with clarity, structure, and holy precision. It is the stream that keeps the Church rooted, steady, grounded, and faithful — the voice that holds us to what God has said so we may walk in what God has promised. Without a faithful priest teaching the Word – there is no stability to a body of believers.

**The Heart That Guards the Living Word**

Whenever God awakens His people, He therefore raises a priesthood—a people entrusted with the holy task of guarding, unfolding, and transmitting the meaning of His Word.

This conviction stands at the center of Israel's Scriptures. The priest is not first a ritual officiant, nor first a custodian of sacrifice. He is the steward of divine knowledge. Malachi speaks with unflinching clarity: "For the priest's lips should keep knowledge, and they should seek the law at his mouth: for he is the messenger of the LORD of hosts" (Mal 2:7 KJV). The Hebrew phrase "the priest's lips should keep knowledge" is שִׂפְתֵי־כֹהֵן יִשְׁמְרוּ־דַעַת (siftei-kohen yishmeru-da'at). The verb yishmeru ("should keep/guard") comes from the root שָׁמַר / shāmar, meaning "to guard, watch, keep, preserve," a term used of Adam's calling to "keep" the garden (Gen 2:15),[2] of watchmen guarding a city (Ps 127:1), and of Levites guarding holy space (Num 1:53).[3] Thus the priest is a guardian of knowledge—daʿat—a rich Hebrew term denoting not abstract data but covenantal understanding, relational wisdom, and the internalization of God's ways.[4]

Malachi's second claim intensifies the weight of the office: the priest is a mal'āk YHWH ṣĕbā'ôt—"a messenger of the LORD of hosts." In the ancient Near Eastern world, a royal messenger carried the authority of the throne; to misrepresent the message was an act of treason.[5] Malachi applies this political imagery to the priesthood: to distort the Word of God is treason against the covenant itself. Teaching is not a matter of opinion but of fidelity. The priestly stream is thus born from divine trust: God entrusts His Word to human lips and expects those lips to guard it.

The Torah reinforces this vocation at every turn. The word Torah itself, often reduced in English to "law," derives from the Hebrew root יָרָה / yārāh, meaning "to teach, instruct, direct," and even "to shoot an arrow."[6] Torah is God's instruction—His arrow of guidance shot into the human heart. The priest, therefore, is God's archer: he draws back the bow of revelation and releases truth with accuracy. This is why Deuteronomy blesses Levi with the words: "They shall teach Jacob thy judgments, and Israel thy law" (Deut 33:10 KJV). Teaching is not secondary to priesthood; it is its essence.[7]

The Psalms describe Torah not as static statute but as voice (Ps 29; Ps 119). The Qumran community later described their calling as those who "hear His glorious voice" (1QS 8:14).[8] Torah was heard before it was read. It lived before it was studied. Even its written form carried the expectation of being interpreted by consecrated hearts.

Israel's history reveals what happens when this priestly calling is ignored. Hosea laments, "My people are destroyed for lack of knowledge" (Hos 4:6 KJV). The crisis is not intellectual but covenantal—the priests "forgot the law of [their] God," and the people perished with them. Here daʿat again means covenantal awareness; it is the loss of orientation, the collapse of memory, the erosion of their identity.[9] When priests fail to guard knowledge, the people lose the path, they lose sight and spiritual vision.

This tragedy became acute in the centuries leading to Christ. The Second Temple period was marked by priestly fragmentation. Political entanglements, compromises with foreign powers, and internal corruption hollowed the priesthood's authority. Many Israelites lamented that those entrusted to teach the Torah had instead obscured it.

The Qumran sect, withdrawing from Jerusalem, articulated this lament with sharp force. In their Community Rule, the priests are described as the true spiritual leaders of Israel, "the sons of Zadok," chosen "to teach His righteous judgments" and to maintain the purity of interpretation.[10] They contrasted themselves with the Jerusalem establishment, accusing the temple priests of becoming 'ōsê haḥalaqôt—"doers of smooth things."[11] This idiom refers to those who soften the demands of Scripture, turning difficult commands into convenient ones and dulling the sharpness of divine revelation. To Qumran, such teachers were not merely misguided—they were dangerous. Smooth teaching produced crooked hearts and blinded the people.

Their Habakkuk Pesher goes further, accusing the priests of "lying about the teaching" because "they have not sought the Lord."[12] For them, doctrinal corruption flowed from spiritual neglect. The interpretive crisis was not rooted in insufficient learning but in insufficient holiness. The heart that failed to seek God produced teachings that failed to represent Him. Thus, for Qumran, the first task of the priest was purity; the second was interpretation; the two could never be separated.

Later rabbinic reflection echoed this ancient concern. Midrash Tanhuma warned: "If the priest distorts the Torah, he destroys the foundation of the world." [13] Teaching, then, is not neutral. It either upholds creation or destabilizes it. It either forms a holy people or fractures them.

This is the world into which Ezra steps—a moment where teaching had become urgent, where understanding had grown thin, and where the covenant people needed clarity more than comfort. Ezra is called "a ready scribe in the law of Moses" (Ezra 7:6 KJV), but the Hebrew description implies more: a man skilled in interpretation, devoted to the text, shaped by obedience. Scripture says, "Ezra had prepared his heart to seek the law of the LORD, and to do it, and to teach in Israel" (Ezra 7:10 KJV). The pattern is divine: seek → do → teach. Interpretation must flow from obedience, and obedience must flow from intimacy with God's Word.

His ministry reaches its zenith in Nehemiah 8. There, the people gather "as one man" to hear Scripture. Ezra opens the scroll, and immediately the people stand—a physical reflex to the rediscovered weight of revelation. As he reads, the Levites move among the people, "giving the sense" and "causing them to understand the reading." The Hebrew term מְפֹרָשׁ / meforāsh means "to explain, to interpret, to make clear," [14] a word later connected to the developing tradition of perush (commentary). This is exposition in its earliest biblical form. And as understanding dawns, repentance erupts. The people weep, not from emotional manipulation, but because clarity has pierced them. Revelation has become interpretation, and interpretation has become transformation.

Ezra's ministry reveals the priestly stream in full: the Word opened with holiness, explained with accuracy, and applied with power. It is this stream that will shape the New Testament church, the apostolic community, and the entire history of Christian preaching.

---

### The Witness of the Deas Sea Scrolls

The priestly stream widens as Israel enters the tumultuous centuries before the coming of Christ. The Babylonian exile had humbled the nation; the return had rebuilt its walls; but the heart of the people still needed shaping. Teaching was no longer simply a responsibility—it had become how the covenant itself survived. And yet the priesthood entrusted with this sacred work often faltered. Politics had crept into the temple courts, foreign influence diluted the sanctity of worship, and internal rivalries eroded the clarity of doctrine. In this atmosphere of tension and longing, the priestly vocation did not disappear; it became contested, fragmented, and fiercely debated.

The Second Temple period makes this especially clear. The Sadducean priesthood, aligned with political power and controlling the sacrificial system, laid claim to authority but lacked the reverence for Scripture that earlier generations had held. The Pharisees, committed to oral tradition and rigorous halakhic interpretation, offered a counter-vision of faithfulness. The Qumran community, withdrew altogether, convinced that the Jerusalem establishment had forsaken the covenant.

In their writings preserved among the Dead Sea Scrolls, we discover a community wrestling for the soul of Israel's teaching ministry. Their Community Rule (1QS) identifies priests as the center of communal life: those appointed "to teach His righteous judgments" and to "preserve all the mysteries of His wisdom."[15] This priestly task was not merely intellectual; it was rooted in consecration. Only those purified in spirit and life could interpret Torah rightly. In their view, interpretation divorced from holiness was inherently corrupt.

Their critique of the Jerusalem priesthood was unsparing. In the Habakkuk Pesher—a commentary applying Habakkuk's oracle to their own generation—the Interpreter accuses the temple priests of having "lied about the teaching," explaining that they erred because "they have not sought the Lord."[16] Here lies a profound theological insight: the Qumran community believed that false teaching begins in the heart, not the mind. Failure of devotion precedes failure of doctrine. To mishandle Scripture is ultimately to misrepresent the God who gave it, and this is why the priestly vocation demanded holiness.

Later Jewish tradition affirms this burden. Midrash Tanhuma, reflecting on the priest's role in preserving Torah, declares that "if the priest distorts the Torah, he destroys the foundation of the world."[17] The idea is unmistakable: teaching is not marginal. It is cosmic. It either upholds or undermines the very order God established. For Israel, the loss of faithful teaching did not just result in ignorance; it brought collapse. When priests failed to guard knowledge, the people lost the path.

## The Witness of the New Testament

This tension sets the stage for the Gospels. Into a world of fractured priesthoods, theological factionalism, and longing for authoritative interpretation stepped Jesus of Nazareth—not just as a teacher but as the Word made flesh. His teaching astonished because He spoke "as one having authority, and not as the scribes" (Matt 7:29 KJV). His voice did not echo tradition; it revealed the heartbeat of the Lawgiver. When He preached the Sermon on the Mount, He did not relax the Torah but exposed its deepest intent (Matt 5:17–48). His teaching possessed the dual qualities of priestly ministry: clarity and consecration. He clarified God's will and embodied it perfectly.

The most priestly of all His teaching moments occurred on the Emmaus road, where "He expounded unto them in all the scriptures the things concerning Himself" (Luke 24:27 KJV). The Greek diermēneuō ("to interpret fully") signifies a priestly act: opening the Scriptures, unfolding meaning, guiding disciples from confusion into recognition. Their hearts burned, not from emotion, but from illumination (Luke 24:32). Jesus did what every priest had failed to do perfectly—He interpreted Scripture in purity and revealed its fulfillment in Himself.

The early church inherited this priestly ministry and treated it as sacred trust. Acts 2:42 tells us that the believers "continued steadfastly in the apostles' doctrine," a phrase denoting disciplined devotion. Teaching formed the backbone of community life. The apostles were not only preachers of experience but interpreters of revelation. Their sermons in Acts reveal a deep engagement with Scripture—reading, explaining, applying, and proclaiming Christ from the Law, Prophets, and Psalms.

## The Church Fathers

The earliest Christian writings beyond the New Testament confirm this centrality of teaching. Clement of Rome insisted that ministers were appointed "to proclaim the message... not from themselves, but from what Christ entrusted."[18] Ignatius of Antioch admonished believers to honor those who expound the Word "with accuracy," for the church's unity depended on doctrinal fidelity.[19] The Didache, likely the earliest Christian handbook, offered strict criteria for discerning true teachers, insisting their doctrine align with the "way of life" given by Jesus.[20] For the early church, teaching was not a ministry; it was the ministry that shaped all others.

This priestly stream deepened in the great centers of Christian learning. In Alexandria, Origen developed a method of Scriptural interpretation that combined rigorous study with spiritual insight. He believed the preacher must "open the Scriptures as Christ did on the road to Emmaus,"[21] enabling believers to encounter Christ in the text. His commentary work set a precedent for Christian exposition: Scripture must be handled with reverence, precision, and prayer.

The Eastern fathers carried the priestly stream further. John Chrysostom, the "golden-mouthed" preacher of Antioch, taught that the preacher's life must "be the interpretation of the sermon,"[22] binding holiness of life to faithfulness of teaching. His homilies reveal that exposition was not just intellectual analysis but pastoral formation. He did not simply explain Scripture; he shepherded souls through it.

The Reformation recaptured this priestly vision with prophetic power. While Martin Luther restored Scripture to the people by shattering the medieval mediatorship of hierarchy, it was John Calvin who fully embodied the ancient teaching priesthood. His relentless exposition of Scripture—interrupted only by exile or sickness—revealed a man convinced that the people of God must be anchored in the Word. He insisted that pastors "handle Scripture as a priest handles holy things,"[23] a statement that echoes Malachi's ancient warning.

The Puritans extended this vision in profound pastoral depth. Their preaching, saturated with Scripture, aimed at shaping the conscience, not merely informing the mind. They viewed the pulpit as the priestly table where the Word was broken like bread and distributed to the people. Later, John Wesley united priestly teaching with evangelistic urgency, requiring Methodist preachers to engage in rigorous biblical study and accountability. Revival did not bypass teaching; it demanded it.

## The Priestly Witness —Faithfulness to God's Word

If the priestly stream is the ministry of access, then the priestly witness is the ministry of fidelity. The priest stands before the people not as a creative innovator but as a faithful steward of what God has already spoken. His authority is not originality but accuracy. His power is not novelty but canonical fidelity — a life rooted in, aligned with, and obedient to the revealed Word of God.

In Scripture, the priest is the guardian of the sacred deposit. He does not amend the covenant to the culture. He does not adjust the revelation of the Word. He does not soften the holiness of God to match the mood of the moment.

His witness is simple and uncompromised: "Thus is the covenant. Walk in it." The priestly witness stands against drift — stands with precision and scriptural exposition and exegesis preserving the meansing. Against covenant confusion — not with opinion, but with Scripture. Against spiritual erosion — not with sentimentality and human tradition, but with the unbending clarity of God's Word that is the ultimate tradition.

The priest embodies Scripture before he teaches it. He lives the covenant before he explains it. His presence itself becomes a stabilizing reminder that the Word does not change. The covenant does not shift. The boundaries do not move. This is why the priestly witness is essential for the life of the Church.

When culture fluctuates, the priest stands with the Word. When trends rise and fall, the priest stands with the canon. When the people forget, distort, or neglect the truth, the priest returns them to the canon.

Canonical fidelity is not rigidity — it is protection. It is the covenant guarded. It is doctrine kept pure. It is worship preserved according to the ways of God rather than the desires of men.

In every generation, God raises up priests — pastors, teachers, shepherds — whose primary witness is faithfulness to the Scriptures, rightly divided and rightly lived. Their priestly task is to ensure that the people of God are formed not by trends, preferences, or personalities, but by the enduring revelation of the canonical Word.

Fidelity to the Word keeps the Church from drifting into sentimentality, syncretism, or self-made religion. It preserves the holiness of the people. It protects the purity of worship. It sustains revival by anchoring zeal in truth. Where the priestly witness is strong, the Church is steady. Where canonical fidelity is upheld, the covenant remains clear. Where the priest stands firm, the people walk in truth. This is the witness of the priestly stream: The Word preserved. The covenant guarded. The people kept in the truth that makes them free.

The witness of history converges on a single truth: whenever God restores His people, He restores teaching. Whenever He prepares a generation, He raises teachers. Whenever He reforms the church, He reforms the pulpit. The priestly stream is the anchor of renewal, the safeguard of holiness, the foundation of discernment. Without it, revival collapses. With it, revival matures.

---

**Renewal Through Priestly Teaching**

The priestly stream is not only an ancient pattern; it is the living artery through which renewal flows in every generation. Revival often begins with the cry of hunger, but it is sustained by the restoration of scriptural teaching. The Spirit may ignite a moment, but only the Word can establish and sustain a movement. The fire that falls must find a place to rest, a structure strong enough to hold the weight of glory. And throughout Scripture, that structure is always built by priests.

This is why every great turn in Israel's history begins with a rediscovery of the Word. The story of King Josiah is paradigmatic. When Hilkiah the high priest found the forgotten scroll of Torah in the temple ruins, he placed it into the hands of the scribe Shaphan, who read it before the king. As the words reached Josiah's ears, the Scripture says he tore his garments (2 Kgs 22:11), a gesture of covenant grief and sudden awakening. Scholars note that the Hebrew verb qara' (to tear) signals not mere sorrow but recognition—Josiah saw in the mirror of Torah the distance between God's covenant and the nation's condition. [28] Revival was born not from emotion but from revelation. The Word pierced the king, and the king led the nation back to God.

A similar pattern shapes the reforms of Hezekiah. Before songs could rise in the temple courts, the priests had to cleanse the holy place (2 Chron 29:5–15). Chroniclers emphasize the rhythms of sanctification more than the spectacle of celebration. [29] The Levites carried out the filth, restored the vessels, and reestablished priestly order—only then did worship ascend. The prophetic songs returned not because the singers were inspired, but because the priests had been faithful. Fire always comes where order has been restored.

Even Ezra's renewal, though filled with public weeping and repentance, is fundamentally a revival of teaching. The people "wept when they heard the words of the law" (Neh 8:9 KJV), not just because conviction fell, but because understanding dawned. The Hebrew binah ("understanding") implies insight that penetrates the soul. [30] It was understanding, not sentiment, that shook the nation awake. The priestly stream revealed the path, and the people walked it.

These biblical moments reveal an often-overlooked truth: revival collapses without teaching. Zeal without knowledge is unstable; passion without Scripture is volatile. The prophetic cry awakens, but only the priestly word establishes. The fire must be tended with clarity lest it burn uncontrolled.

Jesus Himself modeled this union of fire and form. The crowds marveled at His teaching because His authority cut through the haze of competing interpretations (Mark 1:22). And though His ministry was filled with signs and wonders, the Gospels give extraordinary attention to His exposition of Scripture. His longest recorded conversations are not miracles but teachings—the Sermon on the Mount, the kingdom parables, the temple debates, and the Emmaus exposition. Renewal flowed from His words because He upheld and fulfilled the priestly calling. When He declared, "Man shall not live by bread alone, but by every word that proceedeth out of the mouth of God" (Matt 4:4 KJV), He restored Torah to its rightful place in the soul.

The apostles carried this same conviction. Paul cautioned Timothy that teaching must be guarded "as a good deposit" (2 Tim 1:14), using the Greek parathēkē, a term from banking and legal custody. [31] The Word entrusted to them was not to be altered or neglected. Everywhere Paul went, he established churches by evangelizing and by teaching "the whole counsel of God" (Acts 20:27). His letters to Corinth and Galatia demonstrate a fierce commitment to doctrinal integrity, confronting distortions with priestly gravity. Renewal demanded accuracy.

This priestly burden becomes acute in the final days. Paul's warning to Timothy is chillingly prophetic: "The time will come when they will not endure sound doctrine" (2 Tim 4:3 KJV). The phrase "sound doctrine," *hugiainousa didaskalia*, literally means "healthy teaching."[32] When the priestly stream dries up, the church becomes sick. When teaching becomes distorted, the body weakens. In such times, God raises teaching priests—who refuse the lure of "smooth words," who resist the seduction of novelty, and who guard the flock with truth rather than trends.

Our time resembles the spiritual climate our Lord Jesus and Apostle Paul described. Information floods the modern world, yet understanding remains scarce. Sermons abound, yet scriptural clarity often diminishes. The ease of access to Scripture has not guaranteed depth of comprehension. Indeed, the abundance of voices has sometimes produced confusion rather than conviction. We live in a moment where the famine Amos foresaw—a famine "not of bread… but of hearing the words of the LORD" (Amos 8:11)—returns not because Scripture is unavailable, but because priestly teaching is rare. [33]

The rise of "smooth things" (Isa 30:10) is a perennial danger. Qumran accused the Jerusalem priests of being 'ōsê haḥalaqôt—teachers of smooth words. [34] Light preaching produced light people. Jeremiah described such leaders saying, "Peace, peace; when there is no peace" (Jer 6:14), healing the wound of the people lightly—the Hebrew qalal meaning "to make trivial, insignificant." [35] Teaching without weight breeds disciples without stamina. Shallow doctrine produces shallow devotion.

This is why the priestly stream must rise again in our time. The last-days church cannot be carried by emotional fervor or cultural relevance. She must become a people shaped deeply by Scripture—a people taught, formed, and strengthened by the priestly ministry of the Word. Apostles may govern, prophets may ignite, evangelists may gather, pastors may shepherd, but teachers ground the His Church in the truth without which all other ministries falter.

Yet the priestly stream does not operate in isolation. It intertwines with the fivefold gifts as the bloodstream of their effectiveness. Apostles establish doctrine because they interpret the foundation laid by Christ and the prophets. [36] Prophets call the people back to Torah-shaped holiness. Evangelists proclaim the gospel with precision because they know the Scriptures that testify of Christ. Shepherds feed the flock with wisdom that flows from the Word. Teachers, of course, stand at the core of this work, but all five vocations rely on the priestly dimension of truth.

John Calvin captured this unity when he wrote that pastors "handle Scripture as a priest handles holy things." [37] The Word is not a tool for ministry; it is the content of ministry. The preacher is not a performer but a steward. Holiness of life and accuracy of teaching converge. The more deeply the church stands in this priestly stream, the more clearly she will discern the voice of her Shepherd.

This priestly restoration will mark the last-days church. Revelation depicts a people who "follow the Lamb whithersoever he goeth" (Rev 14:4 KJV). Such following demands discernment. And discernment demands teaching. It is the priestly stream that grants the church eyes to see, ears to hear, and hearts to remain faithful in times of deception. Where the Word is opened faithfully, the Bride is formed beautifully.

Thus revival demands not only fire but form, not only longing but learning, not only awakening but anchoring. The Spirit kindles the flame, but priests tend the lamp. When the priestly stream flows pure, the light of revelation burns bright.

## The Renewal That Forms Faithful People

The priestly stream ultimately flows toward a single purpose: to form a people capable of carrying the glory of God in the final hour. Teaching is not an academic exercise, nor merely a skill; it is the shaping force by which God fashions a covenant people into His likeness. Revelation without formation produces instability; zeal without grounding produces imbalance. But when the Word is opened faithfully—when the priestly stream flows pure—the people of God become a living sanctuary prepared for His presence.

This has always been God's intent. From the moment He called Israel out of Egypt, He declared that they would be to Him "a kingdom of priests, and an holy nation" (Exod 19:6 KJV). The Hebrew phrase mamlekhet kohanim ("kingdom of priests") is astonishing. Israel was not to have priests only in the tribe of Levi; she was to become a priestly nation.[38] Priesthood was always meant to be communal. The Levites were a model, not a monopoly. Through faithful teaching, the entire people were to be shaped into a priestly identity—a people whose very lives interpreted the covenant before the nations.

The prophets foresaw this priestly renewal coming. Isaiah announced a coming day when God's people would be "called the priests of the LORD… ministers of our God" (Isa 61:6 KJV). The Hebrew kohanei YHWH ("priests of the LORD") is used there not of clergy but of the restored people of God.[39] Ezekiel envisioned a renewed temple from which the river of life would flow (Ezek. 47), but that river flows only after the priestly order is restored and the Word of the Lord is obeyed (Ezek 44). Teaching is the gate through which the river moves.

When Jesus formed His disciples, He did so through teaching. Even after the resurrection, before ascending into heaven, He "opened their understanding, that they might understand the scriptures" (Luke 24:45 KJV). The Greek dianoigō ("to open, to unlock, to cause to see") is the language of priestly insight.⁴⁰ The risen Christ's final act before enthronement was not a miracle but an exposition. He restored the priestly stream in the hearts of His followers because only a taught people can be a faithful people.

The book of Acts reveals this renewal in motion. The church grows because "the word of God increased" (Acts 6:7 KJV). Luke's phrasing, *ho logos tou Theou ēuxanen,* implies organic expansion—the Word itself spreads like seed.⁴¹ Whenever the apostles taught, communities flourished; whenever false teaching threatened, the apostles confronted it with priestly authority. Teaching was the means by which the church maintained fidelity amid pressure, persecution, and cultural upheaval.

Paul's vision of the church in Ephesians embodies this priestly renewal. Christ ascends to give gifts—apostles, prophets, evangelists, pastors, and teachers—to equip the saints for the work of ministry (Eph 4:11–12). But the ultimate aim is maturity: "that we henceforth be no more children… tossed to and fro… by the sleight of men" (Eph 4:14 KJV). Teaching guards the church from deception, stabilizes her against false winds, and forms her into the fullness of Christ. The fivefold gifts function in harmony, but the priestly stream running beneath them ensures that their ministry aligns with the Word. ⁴²

This priestly formation becomes even more vital in the eschatological horizon. Jesus warned of a time when many false prophets would arise and deceive many (Matt 24:11). Deception inevitably thrives where teaching falters. The final contest of the age is between belief and unbelief and true interpretation and false interpretation—between the voice of the Shepherd and the seduction of imposters. John's First Epistle makes clear that fidelity to the apostolic teaching becomes the dividing line between truth and deception (1 John 4:1–6).⁴³ In the last days, the priestly stream becomes the lifeline of the church.

Revelation reaches the same conclusion. The glorified Christ addresses the churches not primarily with visions but with words—rebukes, exhortations, corrections, and promises. "He that hath an ear, let him hear what the Spirit saith unto the churches" (Rev 2–3). Hearing requires teaching; teaching requires priestly discernment. When the Word is compromised, candlesticks are removed.

Yet the climax of Revelation offers a radiant picture of the priestly renewal God intends. John sees a people who "follow the Lamb whithersoever he goeth" (Rev 14:4 KJV). Such following demands understanding. Later he beholds the redeemed standing before God's throne, singing a new song, and described as "kings and priests unto God" (Rev 1:6; 5:10). This is the fulfillment of Exodus 19:6: the entire people of God become priests. The Bride is priestly because she reflects the image of her Bridegroom, who is both Priest and King. [44]

This is the renewal toward which the priestly stream flows: a people instructed by the Word, purified in truth, strengthened by doctrine, and prepared for the presence of God.

Only such a people can stand faithful in the final hour. The last-days church will be marked not by novelty but by depth, not by restlessness but by rootedness, not by mere inspiration but by illumination. She will be a people who know the Scriptures, discern the voice of the Shepherd, and reject the seductions of false teaching. She will carry the fire of revival, yes—but also the clarity of interpretation. She will be lit by the prophetic flame but grounded by the priestly Word.

**Renewal: Guarding the Boundaries of Holiness**

Renewal does not happen in a vacuum. Revival fire can fall suddenly, but it is sustained only when the people of God learn how to walk within the holy boundaries of the covenant. This is where the priestly stream becomes essential — because renewal without priestly clarity will always collapse into confusion, mixture, and emotional drift.

The priestly stream does not only convey truth; it establishes the safe boundaries within which renewed life flourishes.

In Scripture, the priest does more than read the law — he discerns, distinguishes, and defines. He separates clean from unclean, holy from common, true from counterfeit. His ministry creates the space where God can dwell among His people without that presence becoming destructive. The priest is the custodian of distinction.

When renewal comes, the renewed community must rediscover these covenant distinctions — not as legalism, but as the environment of life. A revived heart must learn how to live revived. A renewed people must learn where the covenant lines are drawn. The priestly voice guards those lines. Renewal fails when boundaries are lost. Renewal thrives when boundaries are recovered.

The priestly stream reminds the people that holiness is not improvisation. Revival is not spiritual anarchy but a restoration of God's Divne order. Renewal is not enthusiasm without order. The fear of the Lord requires definition — what God accepts and what He rejects, what He blesses and what He forbids.

The priest is the custodian of distinction. When renewal comes, the renewed community must rediscover covenant distinctions. A renewed people must learn where the covenant lines are drawn. The priestly voice guards those lines and does this through teaching the Word.

In seasons of renewal, the priestly voice becomes indispensable because it answers the question every awakened heart eventually asks: *"Now that God has changed me — how do I walk in His ways?"*

The priest answers with clarity: *Here is the covenant Word. Here is holiness. Here is the way of life. Here are the boundaries that protect the fire God has given you.*

Renewed congregations without priestly guidance will burn brightly for a moment and then wander into confusion. But a renewed people with priestly clarity will burn with sustained, accelerating fire — because they know where God walks, where God speaks, and where God draws the line. This is why the priestly stream is essential for renewal: It keeps the fire pure. It keeps the community safe. It keeps the covenant intact. It keeps the people walking in the fear, joy, and order of the Lord.

Renewal needs revelation, but it also needs boundaries. The priestly stream gives the renewed people both.

This is the renewal God desires: A church taught by God. A church shaped by Scripture. A church formed by the priestly stream. A church ready for the Bridegroom. The longing for the Word has become understanding. Revelation becomes formation. Witness becomes conviction. Conviction provides the soil for revival.

Renewal prepares a people for glory — and for the living Word that will now confront them in the prophetic stream.

---

**NOTES**

1. Ludwig Koehler and Walter Baumgartner, The Hebrew and Aramaic Lexicon of the Old Testament (Leiden: Brill, 1994), 1461–1463.

2. HALOT, 1586–1588.

3. Jacob Milgrom, Numbers (JPS Torah Commentary; Philadelphia: JPS, 1990), 14–16.

4. William L. Holladay, A Concise Hebrew and Aramaic Lexicon of the Old Testament (Grand Rapids: Eerdmans, 1988), 77.

5. K. Lawson Younger, "The Messenger in the Ancient Near East," Journal of Biblical Literature 110 (1991): 281–290.

6. Koehler and Baumgartner, HALOT, 432–434.

7. Moshe Weinfeld, Deuteronomy and the Deuteronomic School (Oxford: Clarendon, 1972), 175–178.

8. Florentino García Martínez and Eibert Tigchelaar, The Dead Sea Scrolls Study Edition (2 vols.; Leiden: Brill, 1997–1998), 1:79.

9. Francis I. Andersen and David Noel Freedman, Hosea: A New Translation with Introduction and Commentary (AB 24; New York: Doubleday, 1980), 356.

10. García Martínez and Tigchelaar, DSSSE, 1:107–112.

11. Ibid., 1:13–19.

12. Ibid., 1:15.

13. John T. Townsend, trans., Midrash Tanhuma (Hoboken: Ktav, 1989), 1:45–47.
14. David M. Levy, "Ezra the Scribe," Israel My Glory 45, no. 2 (1991): 12–14.
15. Florentino García Martínez and Eibert J. C. Tigchelaar, The Dead Sea Scrolls Study Edition (2 vols.; Leiden: Brill, 1997–1998), 1:107–112.
15. Martínez and Tigchelaar, DSSSE, 1:13–19.
16. John T. Townsend, trans., Midrash Tanhuma: Translated into English with Commentary (Hoboken: Ktav, 1989), 1:45–47.
17. Clement of Rome, 1 Clement 42–44, in Bart D. Ehrman, The Apostolic Fathers, vol. 1 (Loeb Classical Library; Cambridge: Harvard University Press, 2003), 65–71.
18. Ignatius, Philadelphians 2–3, in Ehrman, Apostolic Fathers, 2:245–247.
19. Didache 11–13, in Michael W. Holmes, The Apostolic Fathers (3rd ed.; Grand Rapids: Baker Academic, 2007), 347–351.
20. Origen, On First Principles 4.1–3, trans. G. W. Butterworth (New York: Harper & Row, 1966).
21. John Chrysostom, Homilies on Matthew 4.2, in Nicene and Post-Nicene Fathers, Series 1, vol. 10 (Edinburgh: T&T Clark, 1888).
22. John Calvin, Institutes of the Christian Religion 4.3.1, trans. Ford Lewis Battles (Philadelphia: Westminster, 1960
23. Marvin A. Sweeney, I & II Kings: A Commentary (Louisville: Westminster John Knox, 2007), 433–435.
24. H. G. M. Williamson, 1 and 2 Chronicles (New Century Bible Commentary; Grand Rapids: Eerdmans, 1982), 354–359.
25. Ludwig Koehler and Walter Baumgartner, HALOT, 133–134.
26. Philip H. Towner, The Letters to Timothy and Titus (NICNT; Grand Rapids: Eerdmans, 2006), 505–507.
27. Ibid., 568.
28. Elizabeth Achtemeier, "Amos 8:11–12," Interpretation 35 (1981): 279–282.
29. Florentino García Martínez and Eibert J. C. Tigchelaar, DSSSE, 1:13–19.
30. J. Andrew Dearman, Jeremiah and Lamentations (NIVAC; Grand Rapids: Zondervan, 2002), 81–83.
31. G. K. Beale, The Temple and the Church's Mission (NSBT 17; Downers Grove: IVP Academic, 2004), 314–330.
32. John Calvin, Institutes 4.3.1
33. Brevard S. Childs, The Book of Exodus: A Critical, Theological Commentary (OTL; Philadelphia: Westminster, 1974), 348–350.
34. John D. W. Watts, Isaiah 34–66 (WBC 25; Waco: Word, 1987), 318–320.
35. N. T. Wright, Luke for Everyone (Louisville: Westminster John Knox, 2004), 306.
36. Darrell L. Bock, Acts (BECNT; Grand Rapids: Baker Academic, 2007), 272–274.
37. Gregory K. Beale, The Book of Revelation (NIGTC; Grand Rapids: Eerdmans, 1999), 404–412.
38. Richard Bauckham, The Theology of the Book of Revelation (Cambridge: Cambridge University Press, 1993), 94–102.

39. G. K. Beale, The Temple and the Church's Mission (Downers Grove: IVP Academic, 2004), 330–348.
40. Richard B. Hays, The Moral Vision of the New Testament (San Francisco: HarperCollins, 1996), 459–464.
41. J. Ramsey Michaels, Revelation (IVPNTC; Downers Grove: InterVarsity, 1997), 121–128.
42. David E. Aune, Revelation 1–5 (WBC 52A; Dallas: Word, 1997), 61–67.
43. G. R. Osborne, Revelation (BECNT; Grand Rapids: Baker Academic, 2002), 89–94.
44. Larry Hurtado, Lord Jesus Christ: Devotion to Jesus in Earliest Christianity (Grand Rapids: Eerdmans, 2003), 590–595.

# LEVITICUS:

# THE PROPHETIC STREAM- THE LIVING WORD

# CHAPTER FIVE

## PROPHETIC PREACHING: DECLARATION OF THE LIVING WORD

### The Cry That Burns and The Voice That Calls

The prophetic stream, once revealed at the heart of Leviticus, does not lie dormant within the sanctuary walls. It moves across Israel's history with a living pulse, taking place in men and women, whose lives become vessels of that same divine voice. Scripture does not present these prophets as isolated figures but as participants in an unfolding drama in which God continues to reveal Himself through those willing to listen. Their stories, far from being scattered episodes, form a coherent witness: the Word is always entrusted to those who stand near the presence, and revelation always carries both the sweetness and the weight of divine fire.

### The Prophet as Ambassador of the Throne

In the books of Kings, the prophet is not a religious accessory to power; he is its interruption. He does not arise from the court, nor does he speak on behalf of popular will. He enters history bearing a message already determined in heaven. The prophet stands as an ambassador of the throne—one sent, not consulted; commissioned, not elected.

This is why the prophet was feared. Kings did not fear prophets because they were unpredictable, but because they were unmanageable. The prophet could not be bribed, scheduled, or silenced without consequence, because he did not speak from himself. He carried the dābār of the LORD—the Word as living reality—and applied it directly to decisions, policies, altars, and lives. When a prophet spoke, heaven's verdict confronted earth's arrangements.

The prophetic office, therefore, is not the establishment of new revelation, nor the expansion of canon. Scripture is not added to by the prophet. Rather, the prophet stands beneath the already-given Word and applies it with immediacy and authority. This is the work of pesher—not invention, but enforcement. Where the priest declares what God has spoken, the prophet declares how that Word now stands against the present moment. He says, "This is the way. Walk in it."

This is why prophetic preaching is dangerous. It is dangerous not because it is sensational, but because it is precise. It collapses the distance between hearing and obedience. It refuses to allow Scripture to remain abstract, general, or postponed. It confronts kings who have normalized compromise, systems that have learned to coexist with disobedience, and religious structures that have mistaken continuity for faithfulness. Prophetic preaching brings the unchanging Word of God into direct collision with changing human arrangements.

In Kings, this danger is embodied. Prophets are imprisoned, hunted, wounded, or killed—not because they are reckless, but because they are faithful. In one of the most sobering prophetic moments, a prophet must himself be wounded in order to deliver the Word. His injury is not incidental; it is interpretive. The prophet bears pain so that the truth may be seen. He bleeds first because the Word he carries cuts deception at its root. The wound authenticates the message: prophetic authority is never exemption from cost, but submission to it.

This reveals the nature of prophetic ambassadorship. An ambassador does not create policy; he announces it. He does not negotiate terms; he delivers them. He does not soften the message for acceptance; he preserves it for fidelity. To alter the Word is to betray the commission. To withhold it is to abandon the post. The prophet stands publicly identified with the authority he represents, and therefore bears the backlash directed at the throne itself.

Prophetic preaching, then, is not commentary, exhortation, or spiritual insight detached from Scripture. It is throne-speech addressed to a generation. The canon is closed, but the summons is not. The prophet speaks as one sent, declaring that God has already spoken and that His Word now demands alignment. Acceptance is not the measure of faithfulness; accuracy is.

For this reason, the prophet is always under judgment before he speaks to others. He does not stand above the Word, but beneath it. He cannot tame its edge without forfeiting authority, and he cannot escape its weight without disqualifying himself. When prophetic preaching is genuine, it wounds the messenger before it wounds the hearer. It carries both steel and sorrow—truth spoken with fear of the LORD.

To recover the prophetic stream in preaching is not to recover a style or a gifting emphasis. It is to recover heavenly ambassadorship in the pulpit: Scripture applied without apology, truth enforced without cruelty, and obedience summoned without delay. Such preaching will never be safe, because it dismantles false peace in order to restore true peace. It threatens idols so that people may live.

Where prophetic ambassadorship is present, neutrality becomes impossible. Where it is absent, faith quietly decays into preference. The pattern of the prophet reminds every generation that the throne still speaks, the Word still judges, and the way of the LORD still demands to be walked.

**The Pattern of the Old Testament Prophet**

This pattern emerges with striking clarity in the boy Samuel. Israel in his day lived beneath a famine of revelation: "the word of the LORD was precious… there was no open vision" (1 Sam 3:1). Into that silence, a quiet voice speaks in the night—not with spectacle, not with thunder, but with the gentle repetition of a child's name. The simplicity of Samuel's calling reveals the essence of prophetic ministry: the word comes first to those who dwell, without pretense, near the lamp of God. The rabbis note that God's double calling of names— "Samuel, Samuel"—is reserved for moments of deep affection and divine purpose. [1]

Elijah's story reveals another dimension of prophetic revelation. Though associated with fire from heaven, his true commissioning comes not through wind, earthquake, or flame, but through what Scripture calls the qōl demāmāh daqqāh— "the thin whispering voice" (1 Kgs 19:12). Here the prophetic ministry is shown not as the mastery of dramatic signs but as the discernment of God's quietest breath. Elijah learns that prophetic power is not measured by outward force but by inward clarity. The one who hears the whisper can overturn nations. This truth only deepens the prophetic stream: revelation requires not only proximity but stillness, the surrendered ear inclined toward God's heart rather than the tumult of circumstances.

Isaiah steps into the stream from yet another angle—the angle of encounter. His vision in the temple is formative: the holiness of God overwhelms him, exposes him, and then purifies him. Only after confession and cleansing does the voice of the Lord ask, "Whom shall I send?" (Isa 6:8). Isaiah's response— "Here am I; send me"—is not the enthusiasm of ambition but the surrender of a man undone. Prophetic preaching, Isaiah teaches us, is born from a transformed interior. Where holiness is revealed, revelation becomes commission. His ministry becomes a lifelong expression of what he saw in that moment: the exalted Lord, the trembling thresholds, the burning coal, the call that binds the prophet to the God he encountered.

Ezekiel's witness carries the pattern forward with yet more nuance. His encounters do not unfold in a single moment of overpowering vision but across a sequence of Spirit-led acts. First, the Spirit enters him and lifts him to his feet (Ezek 2:1–2), enabling him to receive the divine word. Then he is commanded to eat the scroll, to take the message into himself so that the word becomes inseparable from his own inner life (Ezek 3:1–3). Later, the Spirit lifts him again and carries him to the exiles by the river Chebar (Ezek 3:12–15), setting him in the very place where the word must be spoken. Still later, the hand of the LORD comes upon him and positions him for the next revelation (Ezek 3:22–24). [2]

Ezekiel's ministry is a reminder that prophetic preaching is not static but Spirit-driven. The prophet is shaped by the places the Spirit brings him, the experiences the Spirit guides him through, and the inner dialogue between the Word absorbed and the Word proclaimed. His story holds together the two essential dimensions of prophetic ministry: the word that enters the prophet and the Spirit that carries the prophet.

Not all prophetic activity flows from temple priests or visionary ecstatics. Amos stands as a corrective reminder that prophetic authority is not conferred by lineage. "I was no prophet, nor the son of a prophet," he insists (Amos 7:14), yet God takes him from tending sheep and sends him directly into Israel's religious center to confront counterfeit worship.

His boldness arises not from a pedigree but from a divine interruption. His life demonstrates that prophetic preaching is not a vocational choice but a divine summons—one that God extends even to those working in the humblest corners of society.

In Amos, the prophetic stream reveals its disruptive power, confronting injustice and exposing the superficiality of ritual without righteousness.

As these stories flow together, a unified picture emerges: prophetic preaching is never an abstract office or an inherited role. It is a lived experience of divine relationship. Samuel teaches us the necessity of a hearing heart; Elijah shows the sensitivity required to discern God's quietest whisper; Isaiah reveals the transforming holiness that qualifies a messenger; Ezekiel embodies the Spirit-led movement that shapes a prophet across time; Amos reminds us that God's word can erupt in the life of anyone He chooses.

Together these witnesses form a single, canonical testimony: the prophetic word is always entrusted to those whom God draws close, purifies deeply, and sends boldly. It is revelation that disrupts, restores, and demands response. It is never just speech; it is God's presence expressed through a consecrated vessel.

This is the prophetic stream that flows directly into the ministry of John the Baptist, whose voice in the wilderness becomes the hinge between Torah and Messiah.

---

**Prophetic Expectation in Qumran and Jewish Tradition**

By the time John the Baptist appeared in the wilderness, Israel had already been living for centuries beneath a growing canopy of prophetic expectation. The long silence between Malachi and the Gospels was not empty. It was a season in which the longing for revelation deepened and communities formed around the hope that God would once again speak with clarity. The prophetic stream did not disappear after the exile; it quietly intensified beneath the surface of Jewish life.

Nowhere is this more evident than in the world of the Dead Sea Scrolls. The Qumran community, often identified with the Essenes, understood themselves as "the Way" a people called to prepare the way for the age of visitation. They withdrew from Jerusalem not because they despised the temple but because they believed it had become corrupt and that God's presence had withdrawn from its rituals. In their self-understanding, they were the sanctuary—a "house of holiness" where God continued to reveal His will.[3] The Community Rule (1QS) describes them as those upon whom God has poured "a spirit of holiness," enabling them to discern His mysteries and walk in His covenant.[4] Here, revelation is not a rare experience but a communal vocation. Prophetic insight is expected, cultivated, and guarded. The community confesses that God grants knowledge "through His holy spirit" and that He reveals hidden things "to the humble of spirit."[5] This anticipates precisely what will erupt at Pentecost: a people filled with the Spirit who discern God's heart through revelation and prophetic proclamation.

Even more striking is the prophetic hermeneutic preserved in the Pesharim, particularly Pesher Habakkuk (1QpHab). The Qumran interpreters read Scripture not only as historical record but as a living word addressed to their present moment. The formula pishro ("its interpretation is…") reveals a prophetic style of interpretation in which ancient prophecy unfolds its meaning in contemporary events.[6] They believed that the Teacher of Righteousness—a central figure in their community—was given direct insight into the mysteries of the prophets and that he could unveil God's will for their generation.[7] This was prophetic preaching in its purest Second Temple form: Scripture, Spirit, interpretation, confrontation, and eschatological urgency.

The Damascus Document (CD) reinforces this pattern. It speaks of God raising up a leader "to make known to later generations what He will do in the final age," a prophetic figure who teaches righteousness and renews covenant fidelity.[8] The document envisions the community itself as a remnant called to prepare the way of the Lord, echoing the very language Isaiah uses—a language that will soon be applied to John the Baptist. The parallels are unmistakable. The community saw itself as standing at the brink of fulfillment, interpreting the times in light of Scripture and calling Israel to repentance and purity.

Even the War Scroll (1QM) reveals that the community viewed the coming age as a time when God would again speak through revelation, dreams, visions, and signs. [9] The eschatological war is not fought merely with weapons but with prophetic insight, angelic revelation, and the "voice of God" leading His people. Revelation is not ornamental; it is strategic.

This is the world into which John the Baptist steps—a world longing for a prophetic voice, shaped by centuries of interpretation, expectation, and preparation.

This prophetic atmosphere extended far beyond Qumran. Jewish tradition in the wider Second Temple period was rich with reflection on how God speaks. The rabbis preserved the tradition of the "bat qōl", the "daughter of the voice," the heavenly echo that revealed God's will in the absence of classical prophecy. [10] Though not equivalent to prophetic speech, the bat qōl reflected a conviction that God had not ceased to communicate. The Voice remained, even if softly.

Midrashic traditions deepened this sense of divine communication. Exodus Rabbah teaches that at Sinai the voice of God went out "in seventy languages," revealing that divine speech is universal and seeks every people.[11] Midrash Tehillim on Psalm 29 imagines the "voice of the LORD" as a flame that divides, multiplies, and reaches all creation.[12] The rabbis envisioned a Word that trembles across the world, shaking cedars, splitting flames, and resounding over the waters. This imagery prepares the imagination for Pentecost's fiery tongue and the thunderous sound that accompanies the Holy Spirit's descent upon a prepared people.

The Targums also highlight the prophetic dimension of divine speech. Targum Jonathan on Isaiah 6 expands Isaiah's encounter with vivid detail: angels proclaim the holiness of God with thunderous voice, and the call of the prophet becomes an echo of the heavenly liturgy.[13] Revelation here is not simply information but participation in the heavenly council—a reality that the New Testament echoes when it describes the church as "seated in heavenly places in Christ Jesus" (Eph 2:6). The prophetic call, in Jewish imagination, is always a summons upward and inward toward the holy.

Even apocalyptic texts of the period reflect this prophetic expectation. In 1 Enoch, the prophets of old are shown secrets concerning the future of Israel and the nations, a reminder that prophetic history is ultimately God's history.[14] The Animal Apocalypse (1 Enoch 85–90) interprets Israel's past and future in visionary form, showing that God reveals the meaning of history through prophetic sight. Likewise, Jubilees reimagines Israel's story through angelic revelation, presenting covenant fidelity as the pathway to eschatological blessing.[15] In Sirach (Ben Sira), Wisdom descends from heaven to dwell among God's people, speaking through the Scriptures and guiding the wise—an image that resonates deeply with the prophetic work of the Spirit in the early Church.[16]

All these currents—Qumran, Midrash, Targum, Apocalyptic literature—create a vibrant prophetic landscape. Israel was not prophetically barren in the centuries before the Messiah; she was prophetically pregnant. The longing for a fresh word, the expectation of God's visitation, the careful reading of Scripture as present address, and the conviction that God reveals His mysteries to the humble—these shaped the spiritual world of first-century Judaism.

Only now can we appreciate the full force of John the Baptist's appearance. When he lifts his voice in the wilderness and cries, "Prepare ye the way of the Lord," Israel recognizes the sound—not because it is new, but because it is ancient. It is the Voice from Sinai echoing again. It is Leviticus' call from the tent now thundering in the desert. It is the same prophetic fire that shaped Qumran's community, the same longing preserved in Midrash, the same expectation burning in apocalyptic visions.

John does not emerge in a vacuum. He stands at the convergence of centuries of prophetic yearning. His ministry is the fulfillment of Israel's longing for a messenger who would prepare the way for divine visitation. And his proclamation sets the stage for the One whose voice will shake not only the earth but also the heavens.

This is the prophetic climate Jesus enters. This is the prophetic world that births Pentecost. This is the environment that makes Acts 2 not a surprise but a culmination.

---

**John the Baptizer: The Greatest Prophet**

Prophetic preaching does not end with Israel's prophets. It comes to its height in the figure who stands at the meeting point of ages—the one whom Jesus Himself called the greatest "born of women" (Matt 11:11). John the Baptist embodies the prophetic stream with a clarity that binds the Old Covenant to the New, the sanctuary to the wilderness, and the voice from Leviticus to the revelation of the Lamb of God.

John's message is not novel. It is continuing the true prophetic ministry of Scripture: the Word of the Lord calling His people back to Himself. Everything about John's ministry—his location, his clothing, his diet, his proclamations—testifies that the prophetic stream has not diminished but has intensified. His cry, "Prepare ye the way of the Lord" (Isa 40:3; Matt 3:3), is a call to moral regeneration and a summons to divine visitation.

The wilderness, in biblical imagination, is the classroom of the prophetic vocation. It is where God reveals Himself apart from the distortions of civilization, where idols lose their charm, and where revelation cuts through the illusions of religious security. John preaches from the wilderness because prophetic preaching always originates from a place outside the systems it is sent to confront. His message is uncompromising because he is not shaped by the palace or the temple but by the presence of God hidden in desolate places.

In John, the prophetic stream becomes a sharp and burning instrument, clearing a path for the One who will baptize with the Holy Ghost and fire. His voice is not his own; it is a divine echo, beginning in Leviticus, sounding through Isaiah, and culminating in the cry that awakens Israel to the appearing of her Messiah. The prophetic stream prepares the way for Christ because prophetic preaching always prepares the way for Christ.

---

**Christ the Prophet — The Voice at the Center of the Fire**

In John, the prophetic stream becomes a sharp and burning instrument, clearing a path for the One who will baptize with the Holy Ghost and fire. His voice is not his own; it is a divine echo, beginning in Leviticus, sounding through Isaiah, and culminating in the cry that awakens Israel to the appearing of her Messiah. The prophetic stream prepares the way for Christ because prophetic preaching always prepares the way for Christ.

Yet the stream does not end with John. It disappears into Someone greater.

From the first promise in Deuteronomy, Israel had been waiting for a Prophet like unto Moses—one who would stand in God's presence as Moses did, hear God's voice as Moses did, and make God's will known with a clarity that left no room for confusion:

"The LORD thy God will raise up unto thee a Prophet from the midst of thee, of thy brethren, like unto me; unto him ye shall hearken" (Deut 18:15).

Moses was more than a lawgiver. He was the mediator who went up into the cloud, entered the thunder and the fire, and carried the Word of God down to the people. To promise another Prophet "like unto me" is to promise Someone whose intimacy with God surpasses anything Israel had ever known. The early Church did not hesitate to name this One. Peter stands in Jerusalem and declares that Jesus is that promised Prophet, explicitly joining Deuteronomy 18 to the risen Christ (Acts 3:22–26), and Stephen repeats the same confession before the council

(Acts 7:37).¹⁷ Christ is not simply one prophet among many; He is the promised Prophet, the fulfillment of the prophetic line.

But the New Testament goes further. Hebrews opens with a sentence that shifts the entire understanding of prophecy:

*"God, who at sundry times and in divers manners spake in time past unto the fathers by the prophets, Hath in these last days spoken unto us by his Son"* (Hebrews 1:1–2).

The Greek is even more striking: literally, God has spoken "in a Son " (en huiō) reflective also of "the Son of Man". The prophets were instruments through whom God spoke; the Son is the environment in which God's speech now occurs. The Word no longer stands beside the prophet; the Word has become flesh. ¹⁸

This is why John calls Him the Word (ho logos). "In the beginning was the Word… and the Word was made flesh, and dwelt among us" (John 1:1, 14). The prophets carried witness; Christ carries God's own identity. ¹⁹ He is not only the revealer of God—He is the revelation of God. Everything the prophets glimpsed in fragments; Christ holds in fullness.

You could say it this way:

- As the eternal Son, Christ is the Alphabet of God—the Alpha and Omega from whom every syllable of revelation is formed.
- As the Word, Christ is the complete Speech of God—the content, tone, and intent of God's heart embodied in a Person.
- As the Prophet, Christ is the Voice of God.

The prophets heard phrases from heaven; Christ is the language of heaven. The prophets saw visions; Christ is the image of the invisible God. The prophets echo; Christ originates.

And yet, this exalted Christ does not leave the Church as a silent audience to His prophetic majesty. He draws her into His own prophetic life.

The ecclesia is not only a community that remembers what Christ once said; she is a people in whom Christ continues to speak. The same letter to the Hebrews that exalts the Son as final revelation also warns the Church, "See that ye refuse not him that speaketh" (Heb 12:25). Christ is still speaking. He is the Prophet of the Church—not just in history but in this moment.

This is where prophetic preaching becomes more than gifted communication. Christ is the Prophet, true preaching is participation in His ongoing prophetic ministry. The preacher does not stand in the pulpit as a solitary voice trying to represent Christ from afar. He stands there as a member of Christ's Body, indwelt by the Spirit of the Son, called to let the living Prophet speak again through mortal lips.

The Church, then, is not simply a gathering of hearers but a prophetic people. She is the assembly that listens to the voice of the Son and answers with obedience. In a very real sense, the ecclesia is the community formed by the Word, shaped by the Word, and sent with the Word. Her very existence is prophetic, because she embodies the reality that God has spoken decisively in Christ and is still speaking through Him.

For the preacher, this changes everything.

What this means is because Christ is the Prophet, then the preacher is not an independent religious professional manufacturing weekly content. He is a servant who stands under the Word, in the Word, and before a people who belong to the Word. His authority does not come from his creativity, his personality, or his rhetorical skill. It comes from union with the living Prophet and faithfulness to the written Word that bears witness to Him.

Prophetic preaching, in this light, is not primarily about predicting future events or reporting spectacular impressions. It is about bearing the testimony of Jesus—and Scripture tells us that "the testimony of Jesus is the spirit of prophecy" (Rev 19:10).[20] Whenever Christ is truly proclaimed, His cross is lifted up, His resurrection is announced, His kingship is confessed, and His return is set before the people with urgency and hope, the prophetic stream is flowing again. The voice from the Tent in Leviticus, the voice from the mountain in Deuteronomy, the voice in Isaiah's temple, the whisper to Elijah, the thunder over Ezekiel's river, the cry in John's wilderness—all of it converges into the preaching of Jesus Christ in the power of the Spirit.

This is not abstract theology; it is a charge to every preacher who steps into a pulpit in these last days. You are not called to be clever; you are called to be clear. You are called to inform, reform, and to compel. You are not called to echo the culture; you are called to echo the Christ who is Himself the Echo of the Father's heart.

To preach Christ as the Prophet is to let the voice of God be heard again in the congregation. To preach Christ as the Alphabet is to let the Spirit arrange the letters of Scripture into living words that pierce and heal. To preach Christ as the Word is to become, for a brief sacred moment, a living conduit through whom heaven addresses earth.

When this happens—when Christ the Prophet stands at the center of the sermon—the ecclesia remembers who she is. She is not an audience; she is an army. She is not a social club; she is a covenant people. She is not a consumer group; she is a company of those who have heard the voice of the Son and now carry that voice into the streets, the nations, and the last days.

The prophetic stream does not stop at Christ; it flows through Christ into His Body. And every time a preacher yields the pulpit to the living Word, that stream runs fresh again.

---

**Prophetic Preaching in the Early Church: The Spirit's Fire Made Audible**

Pentecost does not mute the prophetic voice; it magnifies it. When the Spirit descends upon the disciples, the first sign was the ability to speak in other tongues and bold proclamation of the Word of God. Peter's sermon in Acts 2 is not a carefully crafted apologetic but an eruption of Spirit-born revelation. He interprets Scripture through the lens of

Christ's resurrection, confronts Israel's sin, and calls for repentance—all marks of prophetic preaching. [21]

---

**The Prophetic Function vs. the Priestly Function in Preaching**

The priestly voice and the prophetic voice stand side by side in Scripture like two sentinels on opposite sides of the same covenant. They are not rivals. They are not interchangeable. And they are not optional. One guards the covenant. The other confronts the people when they fail the covenant.

The priestly function is steady hands, careful borders, and covenant maintenance. The priest teaches what God has said. He preserves the pattern. He holds Israel to the holiness God has already revealed (Exodus–Leviticus). He keeps the house clean, the knowledge clear, and the worship ordered. The priestly stream is all about clarity, continuity, and covenant fidelity.

But the prophetic function is different. It is not maintenance — it is interruption. It is not calm explanation — it is holy confrontation. The prophet enters when the system cracks, when the breach is opened, when the rituals grow hollow, when the sermons lose their sting, when the people drift but pretend they have not. If the priest guards the covenant, the prophet guards the heart of the covenant by declaring exactly how the people have broken it.

The priest says: "This is the way of the Lord."

The prophet says: "You have left the way of the Lord — return."

The priest trains the people in what God has spoken, but the prophet exposes where the people have stopped listening.

The priest builds the walls. The prophet tests the walls — and trumpets the warning when they begin to fracture. The priest maintains holiness teaching. The prophet confronts unholy living.

Prophetic voice is necessary because covenant communities drift. They drift slowly, politely, religiously. They drift while singing. They drift while offering sacrifices. They drift while quoting the right verses. And because drift never feels like rebellion, God raises a prophet to make the drift undeniable. The prophetic stream exists for conviction, confrontation, and the call to return. It prevents the covenant from becoming a museum exhibit maintained by priests but deserted by the people.

The prophetic ministry is the mercy of God refusing to let His people die in quiet compromise

The early Church never treated prophecy as a fringe phenomenon. It was woven into the normal life of the community. Agabus prophesies a coming famine (Acts 11:28), and later he reveals the suffering that awaits Paul (Acts 21:10–11). The church in Antioch receives prophetic direction that initiates the first missionary movement (Acts 13:1–3). Paul's instruction to the Corinthians assumes a congregation in which prophecy is frequent, Spirit-led, and ordered for the edification of all (1 Cor 14:1–5, 24–33).

This is one of the great misconceptions of the modern Church—the belief that prophetic ministry existed only for a short period in early Christian history. But the early Church fathers confirm that prophetic preaching continued as an essential dimension of the Church's pastoral and missional life. The Didache gives instructions for discerning true and false prophets, insisting that a genuine prophet must live the message he preaches, embodying the holiness of God rather than exploiting His people. [22]

Origen, in his homilies, speaks of preaching as the unfolding of Scripture through a mind illuminated by the Spirit.[23] Chrysostom describes the preaching moment as a time when "grace flows from heaven" into the gathered assembly.[24] Calvin echoes this when he writes that preaching is prophetic because "God uses the mouths of His ministers as instruments of His Spirit, so that He Himself may speak to us by their lips."[25] Luther adds that preaching is the "living voice of the Gospel," where Christ Himself draws near to His people.[26]

The Reformation does not diminish prophetic preaching; it restores it. Calvin argues that the pastors who faithfully expound Scripture are truly prophets—not because they predict future events but because they interpret the will of God for their generation. [27] Prophetic preaching, in Calvin's understanding, is not ecstatic speech but the Spirit-illumined proclamation that makes the timeless Word timely. The preacher becomes, in Calvin's language, the "mouth of God," not by personal authority but by faithful submission to Scripture and the Spirit's illuminating power. [28]

This is a vital truth: prophetic preaching is not primarily foretelling but forth-telling, the Spirit-borne unveiling of God's Word for the present moment. The preacher does not manufacture revelation; he discerns and declares it. The same Spirit who descended at Sinai and filled the prophets of old now fills the Church, causing the Word of Christ to dwell richly within her (Col 3:16).

Wherever the Spirit is present, prophetic preaching is possible. Wherever the Word is preached faithfully, prophetic preaching is happening. Here is the principle – He is always present so prophetic preaching should not be an exception to the Word. If flows naturally from the Word and a relationship with God.

---

**Witness of Revival History: Fire in the Pulpit**

The prophetic stream that begins in Leviticus, flows through the prophets, and erupts in the early Church continues its course through every major revival in Christian history. Without exception, revival has always been carried on the shoulders of men and women who preached with prophetic conviction.

In the eighteenth century, George Whitefield's preaching shook the trans-Atlantic world because his words bore the weight of a divine burden. He did not merely expound Scripture; he declared it with a voice burning from the presence of God. His contemporaries said he spoke "as one who had come from the judgment seat." [29]

John Wesley's preaching was equally prophetic. His sermons cut through the formal religion of his day, calling the Church to holiness, repentance, and love burning with the flame of Christ. Wesley believed the preacher must speak with "plainness, power, and urgency," qualities that characterize every prophetic messenger. [30]

In later generations, the Spirit raised up voices like Charles Finney, whose bold calls for repentance sparked awakening across America. Smith Wigglesworth's preaching carried the raw fire of faith that confronted unbelief and ignited spiritual hunger. John G. Lake's sermons carried the conviction that the Word is a living force, and that the Spirit-filled preacher is a vessel of God's healing power. Leonard Ravenhill embodied the prophetic cry for holiness in a generation drifting toward spiritual apathy.

David Wilkerson brought the prophetic Word into the heart of New York City, speaking with unflinching honesty about sin, righteousness, and the coming judgment of God. His preaching was not popular, but it was prophetic—born out of prayer, brokenness, and a burning heart for revival.

Every one of these figures stands in the prophetic stream. They did not just teach; they burned. They did not simply explain the Word; they declared it under divine compulsion. The prophetic voice is recognizable because it carries both the weight of truth and the warmth of God's heart. It confronts but also comforts. It wounds but also heals. It reveals sin but also reveals Christ.

Revival preaching is prophetic preaching—and prophetic preaching is revival preaching. It always brings people to a choice to say yes or no to the Word.

## Renewal Through Prophetic Fire: A Church Reawakened to the Voice of God

If the Church is to experience renewal in the last days, she must rediscover the prophetic stream. We are living in an age saturated with information yet starved for revelation. Sermons abound, but prophetic preaching is rare. We have teachers but few messengers, homilies but little fire, explanations but little encounter.

Prophetic preaching is God's remedy for a Church drifting toward lukewarmness. It is the Word spoken in the flame of divine presence. It awakens slumbering hearts, exposes hidden idols, confronts cultural compromise, and calls God's people back to holiness. It is preaching that carries the sound of eternity—preaching that prepares the Bride for the return of her King.

This is why the prophetic stream stands at the center of Torah. Leviticus reveals that God desires to speak from a consecrated people, and the Church becomes that people through the blood of Christ and the indwelling of His Spirit. The Voice that called Moses now speaks through the Body of Christ. Ephesians 4:11 serves as our waypoint here—not the foundation, but the signpost—showing that Christ Himself continues the fivefold pattern of the divine voice established in Torah, now given to His Church for her maturity and mission.

In the prophetic stream, preaching becomes more than instruction; it becomes encounter. More than exhortation; it becomes unveiling. More than exhortation; it becomes flame.

The Spirit who filled the sanctuary in Leviticus, who spoke through the prophets, who descended at Pentecost, who empowered the Reformers, and who ignited the great awakenings is the same Spirit who longs to restore prophetic fire to the pulpits of our day. So let's look at the renewal and how prophetic preaching happens today.

## The Two-Fold Prophetic Authority

Prophetic ministry in the Church operates on two rails. If either rail is removed, the train derails. If both rails stay aligned, the Church moves forward with clarity, holiness, and authority.

## 1. Authority Resides in the Canonical Word (Prophetic Sermon)

This is the first and immovable rail. The true authority of the prophetic stream is the written, canonical, Spirit-breathed Word of God. Every prophetic sermon, every prophetic burden, every prophetic warning is tethered to this unbreakable anchor. The Word interprets the times. The Word diagnoses the drift. The Word provides the plumb line for correction, conviction, warning, and call.

A prophetic sermon is simply the Word preached as fire — God's holiness pressing upon the conscience, God's grief exposing sin, God's mercy calling for immediate repentance. This is the unchanging, unshakable, "Thus saith the Lord" that stands above every gift, impression, or moment of spiritual sensitivity.

Authority is never personal. Authority is textual – always based on the Word.

## 2. The Spirit of God and Prophetic Sensitivity

If the Word carries the authority, the Holy Spirit gives the sensitivity. The gift does not create new revelation — it awakens the heart to the revelation already given and how it applies now. The gift sharpens discernment, heightens conscience, exposes hidden decay, and opens the pastor's eyes to how the Canonical Word must confront the present moment.

The prophetic gift is how the fire is felt, not what the fire says.

It is the Spirit pricking the heart.

It is the Spirit exposing the rot beneath religious routine.

It is the Spirit revealing where the sermon must strike.

Where the Word provides the sword, the gift provides the aim.

Prophetic gifting does not elevate a person; it intensifies the Word.

Prophetic gifting does not add to the canon; it adds urgency.

Prophetic gifting does not rival or replace Scripture; it drives the hearer back to Scripture and back to the Word. Without that it has no basis.

---

**Conviction, Confrontation, and the Call to Renewal**

The heart of the prophetic preaching stream is not prediction. It is not forecasting geopolitical headlines. It is not speculation dressed up in religious language. Prophecy at its core — in Torah, in the Prophets, in the New Testament — is confrontation with the Word unto repentance.

The prophet's message is not, "Look what is coming." but "Look what you have become — return before it is too late."

If prediction appears, it appears only to intensify repentance. It is never the point. The point is the heart-strike.

Prophets appear when priests alone are not enough. Prophets appear when sermons no longer sting. Prophets appear when the covenant is being maintained but not obeyed.

The prophetic stream is God refusing to let His people drift gently into judgment. He loves His people too much to let them go.

It is His mercy disguised as confrontation. It is His love wrapped in thunder. It is lightning of His holiness breaking into apathy.

The prophet does not comfort the comfortable; he calls the comfortable to the altar. Priests define holiness; the prophet as the voice of God demands it.

The priest keeps the camp clean; the prophet prevents the camp from dying in its own silence. Together they preserve the covenant: One through order. One through fire of the Word applied to the people today.

It is clear that the Church does not need new methods. She needs old fire. She does not need novel strategies. She needs renewed surrender. She does not need louder voices. She needs the Voice. When the prophetic stream flows again, the Church hears God. When the Church hears God, she rises in holiness. And when she rises in holiness, revival is inevitable.

This is the prophetic stream. This is the voice from the Tent. This is prophetic preaching. And this is the fire Christ desires to restore to His Body.

---

**Notes**

1 Louis Ginzberg, The Legends of the Jews, 7 vols. (Philadelphia: Jewish Publication Society, 1909–1938), 4:123–124; Jacob Neusner, The Components of the Rabbinic Documents (Atlanta: Scholars Press, 1997), 112–115.

2 Daniel I. Block, The Book of Ezekiel: Chapters 1–24, NICOT (Grand Rapids: Eerdmans, 1997), 108–121.

3 Lawrence H. Schiffman, Reclaiming the Dead Sea Scrolls (Philadelphia: Jewish Publication Society, 1994), 105–110.

4 1QS 3:7–9 in Florentino García Martínez and Eibert J. C. Tigchelaar, The Dead Sea Scrolls Study Edition, vol. 1 (Leiden: Brill, 1997), 75–77.

5 1QS 4:3–6 in García Martínez and Tigchelaar, DSS Study Edition, 1:75–77.

6 John J. Collins, The Apocalyptic Imagination: An Introduction to Jewish Apocalyptic Literature, 2nd ed. (Grand Rapids: Eerdmans, 1998), 113–118.

7 Schiffman, Reclaiming the Dead Sea Scrolls, 127–131.

8 CD 6:11–19 in García Martínez and Tigchelaar, DSS Study Edition, vol. 1 (Leiden: Brill, 1997), 552–555.

9 1QM 12:1–6 in García Martínez and Tigchelaar, DSS Study Edition, 1:119–123.

10 Jacob Neusner, Midrash as Literature: The Primacy of Form (Philadelphia: Fortress Press, 1987), 34–41.

11 Exodus Rabbah 5:9 in H. Freedman and Maurice Simon, trans., Midrash Rabbah, vol. 3 (London: Soncino, 1939), 65–66.

12 Midrash Tehillim on Psalm 29 in William G. Braude, The Midrash on Psalms, vol. 1 (New Haven: Yale University Press, 1959), 363–370.

13 Targum Jonathan on Isaiah 6 in Bruce D. Chilton, The Isaiah Targum (Wilmington, DE: Glazier, 1987), 12–15.

14 Michael A. Knibb, The Ethiopic Book of Enoch: A New Edition in Light of the Aramaic Dead Sea Fragments, vol. 2 (Oxford: Clarendon, 1978), 150–205.

15 James C. VanderKam, The Book of Jubilees (Sheffield: Sheffield Academic Press, 2001), 18–21.

16 Benjamin G. Wright, Sirach, Hermeneia (Minneapolis: Fortress Press, 2011), 189–205.

17 F. F. Bruce, The Book of the Acts, NICNT (Grand Rapids: Eerdmans, 1988), 58–61.

18 Brevard S. Childs, Introduction to the Old Testament as Scripture (Philadelphia: Fortress, 1979), 318–330; Christopher R. Seitz, Prophecy and Hermeneutics: Toward a New Introduction to the Prophets (Grand Rapids: Baker Academic, 2007), 41–47.

19 Abraham Joshua Heschel, The Prophets, 2 vols. (New York: Harper & Row, 1962), 1:193–197.

20 Michael W. Holmes, ed., The Apostolic Fathers: Greek Texts and English Translations, 3rd ed. (Grand Rapids: Baker Academic, 2007), 365–370.

21 Origen, Homilies on Genesis and Exodus, trans. Ronald E. Heine, Fathers of the Church 71 (Washington, D.C.: Catholic University of America Press, 1982), 45–47.

22 John Chrysostom, "Homilies on the Gospel of John," in Nicene and Post-Nicene Fathers, First Series, vol. 14, ed. Philip Schaff (Peabody, MA: Hendrickson, 1994), 3–6.

23 John Calvin, Institutes of the Christian Religion, ed. John T. McNeill, trans. Ford Lewis Battles, 2 vols. (Louisville: Westminster John Knox, 1960), 4.1.5.

24 Martin Luther, The Babylonian Captivity of the Church, trans. A. T. W. Steinhaeuser (Philadelphia: Westminster Press, 1972), 110–112.

25 Calvin, Institutes, 4.3.4–5.

26 Ibid., 4.1.6.

27 Arnold Dallimore, George Whitefield, vol. 1 (Edinburgh: Banner of Truth, 1970), 89–92.

28 John Wesley, A Plain Account of Christian Perfection (Kansas City: Beacon Hill Press, 1966), 23–25.

29 Robert P. Gordon, 1 & 2 Samuel (Sheffield: JSOT Press, 1984), 84–88; Victor P. Hamilton, Handbook on the Historical Books (Grand Rapids: Baker Academic, 2001), 187–189.

30 Francis Brown, S. R. Driver, and Charles Briggs, A Hebrew and English Lexicon of the Old Testament (Oxford: Clarendon, 1907), 198; Marvin A. Sweeney, I & II Kings: A Commentary (Louisville: Westminster John Knox, 2007), 232–235.

# NUMBERS:

## EVANGELISTIC STREAM - HERALDS OF THE GOOD NEWS

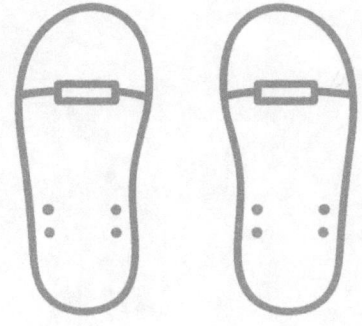

# CHAPTER SIX

## Evangelistic Preaching: Proclaiming the Kingdom

**Introduction**

The evangelistic stream is the engine of response in the rhythm of God. It is the moment when the Word stops being theory and becomes crisis. When truth ceases to be admired and demands an answer. When the wilderness trumpet of God sounds and a person can no longer pretend neutrality. Evangelism is where royal revelation proclamation meets the human will and the unseen realm.

From the wilderness ordering of Israel in Numbers, through the sending ministry of Jesus in the Gospels, and into the apostolic witness of the Epistles, Scripture presents one unified Gospel: the LORD alone reigns, and His reign is revealed by the Holy Spirit through love rather than domination - therefore humanity has a choice.

In the wilderness, God ordered a people around His presence, sounding the summons that called them to Himself. Separating them away from false powers and bringing into covenant allegiance to worship.

In the Gospels, that summons reaches its fullness as Jesus proclaims the Kingdom of God, not as one authority among many, but as the decisive announcement that God Himself has come to reclaim what He loves. God so loved the world that He sent His Son—to defeat the darkness and false powers and then liberate enslaved humanity, by giving Himself for humanity's redemption.

The cross exposes every false god, every rival claim to sovereignty, and every oppressive power as totally and finally defeated- nullified through the sacrifice of Christ. What is true in Him actually is potentially available to us. No evil and unclean power can overcome God's love. The Epistles then proclaim this victory publicly and unapologetically, declaring that Jesus Christ alone is Lord, that all other gods are false and passing, that humanity is summoned to repentance and obedience under His reign.

Evangelistic proclamation, therefore, is neither revivalist spectacle nor abstract doctrine, but the loving and public announcement that the one true God reigns, that the powers have been judged, and that the world is invited—urgently and exclusively—into life, freedom, and restored sonship through Jesus Christ alone.

**Evangelism as the Herald's Cry: "Your God Reigns"**

Biblical evangelism begins with a proclamation, not an invitation. The evangelist comes to those in the wilderness with one announcement: "Your God reigns." This is the essence of the gospel. Before forgiveness is offered, before restoration is promised, before obedience is summoned, the reign of God is declared.

This pattern is established in the wilderness. In Bəmidbar—the book of Numbers—God speaks His Word (dābār) to a people formed outside settled power, security, and systems. The wilderness becomes the place where authority is clarified and allegiance is tested. There, Israel learns that life does not proceed by human ordering but by obedience to the Word of the LORD. Evangelism flows from this wilderness reality: the Word received in the midbar is proclaimed so that all may hear who truly reigns.

The prophets give this proclamation its clearest voice. *"How beautiful upon the mountains are the feet of him that bringeth good tidings... that saith unto Zion, Thy God reigneth."* The good news is not first that circumstances will change, but that God has acted and now rules. The evangelist stands in this prophetic stream as a herald—one who announces publicly and indiscriminately that the reign of God has drawn near.

This announcement carries forward into the New Testament without alteration. John the Baptist cries in the wilderness, preparing the way of the Lord. Jesus begins His ministry with the same declaration: "The kingdom of God that is at hand."

In the Epistles the apostles proclaim Christ crucified and risen as Lord, calling all people everywhere to repent and believe. At every stage, evangelism announces reign before it explains rescue. The kingdom then the cross.

The evangelist, therefore, is not sent primarily to confront kings or structures—that is the work of the prophet. He is sent to the wilderness places of humanity, to crowds and consciences, to announce openly that God reigns and that a way of return has been opened. His message is public, authoritative, and universal. He heralds news that demands response from every hearer.

This proclamation is never neutral. To announce that God reigns is to expose false gods, false rulers, false securities, and false freedoms. Yet it is also profoundly merciful. The same reign that judges rebellion offers grace to the repentant. The wilderness Word that disciplines the multitude also feeds them. The evangelist declares that the King has come not only to rule, but to rescue and redeem. God's love has conquered them all.

To recover the evangelistic stream is to recover the herald's cry. Evangelism is the public announcement that God reigns, the Kingdom has drawn near, and all who hear are summoned to turn and live. Rooted in the wilderness Word and faithful to the throne, the evangelist prepares the way by making the reign of God unmistakably known.

Decision without direction is spiritual stillbirth. Direction without decision is religious moralism. But when both come together through the Word by the Spirit, the kingdom breaks in like fire.

The evangelistic stream refuses to let people nod politely at grace. It demands movement. It demands posture. It demands repentance that shows up in steps, not sentiments. Evangelistic preaching says: Choose. Turn. Follow. Move. Start. Now.

Because the gospel never calls for admiration — it calls for allegiance.

In Scripture, God never separates conversion from commission. Israel leaves Egypt and moves immediately toward covenant. Disciples drop nets and follow Jesus. Paul falls to the ground and rises with a mission. The Spirit descends at Pentecost and sends the Church into the streets. Decision always births direction. Direction always validates decision.

The evangelistic stream is the wilderness cry of God echoing through every generation:

*"How long will you halt between two opinions? Choose this day."*

Not tomorrow. Not eventually. Not when life settles down. Now. Today.

This stream is the holy urgency of God calling the wandering to return, the complacent to awaken, the sinner to repent, and the Church to move from confession to commission.

Evangelistic preaching is not only about getting someone to pray — it's about getting someone to walk. Not only about getting someone saved — but getting them sent. Not just getting them to an altar — but getting them into the harvest.

Decision is the spark. Direction is the flame. Together, they ignite a life of discipleship, mission, and obedience — the very heartbeat of the evangelistic stream.

**The Wilderness Longing: God's Cry for a Wandering People**

The evangelistic stream begins not with human urgency but with divine longing. Before Israel wanders, God yearns; before Moses pleads, God aches; before sermons thunder through prophets and apostles, the Father Himself calls His children home. The Book of Numbers opens upon this tension — a redeemed people between Egypt and promise, between deliverance and destiny, between covenant identity and rebellious desire.

The wilderness becomes the landscape of divine longing, the sacred space in which God reveals His heart for a straying people.

The Hebrew title of the book, Bemidbar ("In the Wilderness"), situates Israel in the place of testing, forming, calling, and responding. [1] In the wilderness, God presses His people, not to destroy them, but to reveal Himself as faithful. The wilderness is the crucible in which God awakens the hunger that no bondage or sin can satisfy. The evangelistic cry is therefore born in the desert — the place where God meets humanity in its frailty and summons it back to Himself.

The opening chapters of Numbers carry the unmistakable cadence of divine order. Tribes are counted, camps arranged, roles assigned. [2] The wilderness is not chaos but formation; God is preparing a people who will bear His name among the nations. Yet this divine ordering sets the stage for the tension that explodes in the book — a holy God leading a restless people. The evangelistic stream emerges at the intersection of divine faithfulness and human resistance.

Even the geography of the wilderness is prophetic. The word midbar (מִדְבָּר) carries within it the root d-b-r, the same consonantal core for "word" (dabar, דָּבָר) and "to speak" (diber, דִּבֶּר).[3] In Hebraic imagination, the wilderness is the place where God speaks. Revelation is not found in the comfort of cities but in the barren spaces where distractions fall silent and the soul stands exposed before its Maker. This is why the prophets constantly return to the wilderness imagery when calling Israel to repent (Hos 2:14–15; Isa 40:3). The wilderness becomes the sanctuary of the evangelist — a place where the Word confronts the wandering heart.

The longing of God is visible even in Israel's journeying structure. When the tribes set out, they do so under the sound of trumpets — silver instruments designed not merely for military alert but for sacred summoning (Num 10:1–10). Trumpets call, warn, and gather. They announce seasons and signify movements. They are the wilderness gospel before there was a New Testament: a divine voice carried through the desert, urging Israel to follow the cloud and obey the call. Jacob

Milgrom notes that these blasts served as "public proclamations of divine guidance," binding the community's movement to the command of God. [4] Evangelistic preaching carries this same resonance — a sound that gathers, warns, awakens, and directs.

The wilderness exposes not only the voice of God but the volatility of the human heart. Israel grumbles, questions, rebels, and resists. The evangelistic stream flows precisely because the human soul is prone to stray. The preeminent theme of Numbers is not geography but response — will Israel trust the God who redeemed them, or will they return to the patterns of Egypt? Gordon Wenham summarizes the crisis well: "Numbers shows Israel hovering between promise and rebellion," they hear God's voice yet struggling to believe and obey." [5] This tension is the birthplace of evangelistic preaching — the confrontation of unbelief with the call to return.

This divine longing appears poignantly in God's lament over Israel's refusal to enter the land after the spies return with their report (Num 14). God's grief is not merely judicial; it is relational. "How long will this people provoke me?" He asks (Num 14:11). Jewish tradition interprets this moment with deep pathos. Sifre Numbers teaches that God wept over Israel's unbelief, comparing their refusal to trust Him to a child rejecting a father's embrace.[6] The evangelistic stream is thus revealed as divine love calling— a Father calling His children back from the edge of destruction.

And yet, in this wilderness struggle, the longing of God is mirrored in the longing of His servant. Moses emerges as the first sustained evangelistic preacher in Scripture — a man bearing the burden of a wandering people and pleading for their return. Moses intercedes, argues, laments, and urges. His words are not mere instructions; they are appeals born from the heart of God. When God threatens judgment, Moses cries out for mercy (Num 14:13–19), standing "between the living and the dead" (Num 16:48), embodying the evangelist's burden to rescue those teetering on the edge of judgment.

Rabbinic tradition regards Moses' intercession as the model of prophetic pleading. Exodus Rabbah observes that Moses "stood in the breach" not as a negotiator but as one who shared God's anguish over Israel in prayer. [7] He spoke in prayer to intercede so that Israel would conform with the mercy God desired to give. Evangelistic preaching continues this pattern — calling people not only to avoid consequences but to return to the love that has pursued them from the beginning.

Even the cloud that guides Israel carries evangelistic symbolism. It moves, stops, and waits — always urging Israel forward, but never forcing them. The cloud is patient, persistent, gentle, and insistent. It symbolizes the God who leads but does not drag, who calls but does not coerce. James Kugel notes that the cloud in Jewish interpretation functions as a "visible sermon," a manifestation of divine presence teaching Israel the rhythm of obedience. [8] The evangelistic word follows the same pattern: calling, pleading, guiding, urging — but never violating the freedom to respond.

In this way, the wilderness becomes the place where God's longing and human longing converge. Israel longs for water, bread, rest, and home. God longs for trust, obedience, faith, and relationship. Evangelistic preaching stands in this tension — announcing that God is near, that His Word is clear, and that His promises remain if His people will turn and follow Him.

Thus the evangelistic stream begins not with rhetorical technique but with longing — God's longing for His people and His people's unfulfilled longing for Him. The wilderness is the womb of evangelistic proclamation. It is where God teaches His people to listen, to trust, to respond, and to return. Every evangelist, every preacher of repentance, every prophetic herald stands in the desert with Moses — sensing both the grief and the hope of God, calling a wandering people back to the One who still speaks.

## The Wilderness as God's Evangelistic Classroom: Revelation That Forms the Voice of the Preacher

The wilderness became a backdrop of hardship; it is the pulpit of God, the first great preaching ground in the biblical story. Here the evangelistic stream becomes unmistakable. God does not simply reveal His will — He summons His people to respond. Revelation in the desert is always proclamation, and proclamation always reaches for the heart. If the wilderness exposes the frailty of Israel, it simultaneously reveals the persistent longing of God, who will not cease calling His people to faith and fidelity.

The Hebrew imagination perceives this with remarkable clarity. The word midbar (מִדְבָּר, "wilderness") shares its root with the word dabar (דָּבָר, "word" or "speech").[8] The desert is the place where God speaks, where His word breaks into the silence of human wandering. Midrash Rabbah marvels that God chose the wilderness for His Torah, "a place belonging to none," so all the world might hear Him without barrier or claim.[9] Revelation, therefore, begins not in privilege but in openness; it is the evangelistic heart of God declaring Himself in a space wide enough for every wandering soul.

Yet this divine speech does not remain abstract. In Numbers, revelation arrives as urgency, as divine insistence that Israel must hear, believe, and respond. Everything God reveals becomes a summons, and the wilderness becomes the arena where revelation forms preachers — human voices raised in echoes of God's own call.

The cloud that rises and settles day by day becomes the first evangelistic gesture. It moves not randomly but "at the command of the LORD" (Num 9:18), pressing Israel to respond with obedience. Too often we imagine this cloud as gentle guidance, but ancient interpreters understood it as divine proclamation, a visible sermon calling the people to align their steps with the will of God. James Kugel notes that early readers saw Israel's journey not only as wandering but as "acted teaching," in which God's presence instructs the nation through rhythm, repetition, and holy insistence.[11] In every lift and rest, the Lord was preaching.

The silver trumpets in Numbers 10 sharpen this truth. Their blast summons, warns, gathers, and sends. Jacob Milgrom calls them "audible proclamations of divine intent," [4] a phrase almost indistinguishable from the work of a herald or evangelist. In their piercing sound, God again is the Preacher, calling His people to assemble, to move, to repent, to prepare. Before any human voice cries out in the New Testament, the trumpets already bear the evangelistic burden of God.

But the evangelistic stream does not end with God's voice from cloud and trumpet. In the wilderness, God raises evangelists — human voices bearing His word, pleading with His people, echoing His longing.

Moses rises first. He has no pulpit. He preaches from the dust, from the edge of rebellion, from the thresholds of mercy and judgment. When Israel murmurs, Moses cries out for them. When they refuse the land, he intercedes with tears and trembling (Num 14:13–19). Rabbinic teachers saw him as the archetypal preacher, a man who "stood in the breach" not to change God but to draw Israel back to the God who longed for them.[12] Moses becomes Israel's evangelist, urging them to believe the promise and follow the One who redeemed them.

But Moses is not alone. From the crisis of the spies emerge Joshua and Caleb, voices burning with the urgency of faith. Their cry — "The LORD is with us… let us go up at once" (Num 14:8–9) — is the gospel distilled to its essence: believe the Word, trust the promise, do not fear. Their proclamation carries an evangelistic ring so clear that later Jewish teachers compared their words to the faith-cry of Abraham. These two men embody the evangelistic calling: urging God's people to respond to what He has revealed.

Aaron, too, becomes an evangelist in the wilderness, though through the ministry of intercession. When plague sweeps the camp, Aaron runs "into the midst of the congregation" with a censer of atonement (Num 16:47). Timothy Ashley observes that Aaron's act is "preaching through sacrifice,"[13] a proclamation of mercy enacted through priestly courage.

Standing "between the living and the dead," he becomes a living sermon: salvation is still possible if Israel will respond.

Even Balaam enters the evangelistic stream, though unwittingly. His oracles ring with divine sovereignty and the rising hope of a star from Jacob (Num 24:17). Early Jewish writings, including portions of the Testament of the Twelve Patriarchs, read Balaam's final word as a messianic announcement,[14] making Balaam's reluctant prophecy one of the earliest evangelistic proclamations to the nations. In the wilderness narrative, the Word of God refuses to be confined; even pagan lips must declare His purpose.

Taken together, these voices reveal a profound truth: the wilderness is the birthplace of evangelistic preaching. God reveals Himself not to satisfy curiosity but to summon response. And when He speaks, He shapes human heralds to carry His call.

This is why Hebrews can say, with startling clarity, "unto them was the gospel preached, as well as unto us" (Heb 4:2). The wilderness is the first gospel arena — a place of proclamation, confrontation, and invitation. Here God preaches. Here evangelists rise. Here revelation becomes response, instruction becomes summons, and God's longing becomes the burden of human voices.

The wilderness teaches Israel to hear the Word. The wilderness shapes Israel to preach the Word.

The wilderness reveals God as the Evangelist who raises evangelists.

In this desert classroom, the evangelistic stream emerges not as a late development but as a foundational movement of God's redemptive work. Revelation becomes proclamation; proclamation seeks response; response opens the way into promise. Evangelistic preaching is not an invention of the New Testament — it is the heartbeat of Numbers, the sound of God calling His wandering people home.

## What the Wilderness Teaches Us About Preaching

The wilderness stories of Numbers are more than ancient history; they are sermons God preached into the life of His people and preserved for every generation of proclaimers.

The evangelistic witness of these narratives reveals the nature of preaching itself—its burden, its tone, its urgency, its hope. In each episode we discover not only what God did, but what God teaches us about the task of calling a wandering people back to Himself. The wilderness becomes the preacher's classroom because the events themselves are evangelistic proclamations shaped by God for the sake of response.

### 1. The Priestly Blessing — Preaching Begins in the Heart of God (Numbers 6:24–26)

One of the first lessons the wilderness teaches about evangelistic preaching is that proclamation begins with God's desire to bless. The priestly blessing—"The LORD bless thee, and keep thee…"—is not a liturgical flourish or a decorative conclusion. It is God's own announcement of His goodwill toward His people. Baruch Levine describes it as a "public proclamation of divine favor,[15] a declaration that God's posture toward Israel is mercy before judgment and peace before confrontation.

What we learn about preaching here is this: authentic evangelistic proclamation always begins with the heart of God for blessing. The preacher does not warn because God is reluctant, but because God yearns to save. Before a single warning is sounded, God places blessing upon Israel's head, teaching every future herald that the evangelistic word must flow from divine kindness before it ever confronts sin.

## 2. The Rebellion Narratives — Preaching Must Name the Truth About the Human Heart (Numbers 11–14)

The wilderness also teaches that evangelistic preaching cannot avoid the truth about human rebellion. Israel's complaints and fear are not side-notes; they are revelations of the unbelief that preaching must confront. Hebrews makes this explicit when it turns back to Numbers and says, "Harden not your hearts" (Heb 3:8). These stories become warnings meant to awaken. Gordon Wenham notes that Numbers records rebellion "not to shame Israel but to instruct future generations in the danger of unbelief."[16]

What we learn about preaching here is: evangelistic proclamation requires courage to name unbelief, idolatry, and fear. It is not condemnation for condemnation's sake—it is mercy articulated through warning. Every sermon calling people to return must reckon with the wilderness truth that the heart resists God unless confronted by His Word.

## 3. The Bronze Serpent — Preaching Lifts Up God's Provision (Numbers 21:4–9)

The bronze serpent becomes the clearest evangelistic witness in the wilderness. Israel sins, judgment falls, and salvation is offered not through human effort but by looking upon God's provision. Jesus Himself interprets this moment as the gospel in miniature: "As Moses lifted up the serpent… so must the Son of man be lifted up" (John 3:14). Rabbinic tradition observed that the serpent had no healing power—its role was to lift Israel's eyes toward God in faith.[17]

What we learn about preaching here is: evangelistic proclamation is essentially the lifting up of God's provision. Preaching points away from human striving and toward the saving act of God. Evangelistic preaching is never self-help—it is beholding. It is not "try harder"; it is "look and live." The wilderness teaches the preacher that the gospel is fundamentally visual: we lift Christ up so that all who look with faith shall live.

## 4. Aaron Running With Incense — Preaching Moves Between the Living and the Dead (Numbers 16:47–48)

In the midst of rebellion, when judgment breaks out as plague, Aaron takes incense and runs into the heart of the assembly. Scripture says he "stood between the living and the dead; and the plague was stayed." This is more than a priestly duty; Jacob Milgrom calls it "atonement in motion,"[18] the kind of action that reveals the urgency of mediation.

What we learn about preaching here is: evangelistic proclamation stands in the middle place, bearing the message of life where death has begun its work. Preaching is not passive instruction; it is an urgent mediatorial act. The wilderness teaches that evangelistic preaching always stands in the gap—between judgment and mercy, rebellion and repentance, death and deliverance—pleading that the plague might be halted.

## 5. Balaam's Oracles — Preaching Cannot Be Contained or Restricted (Numbers 22–24)

The Balaam narratives teach a surprising truth about preaching: God's evangelistic proclamation refuses to be domesticated. Balaam, unwilling and compromised though he is, cannot escape the sovereignty of God's word. The Spirit compels him to speak blessing over Israel and to declare the rising "star out of Jacob," widely understood in Second Temple tradition as a messianic prophecy.[19] James VanderKam notes that these oracles demonstrate God's universal claim, extending beyond Israel into the surrounding nations.[20]

What we learn about preaching here is: the evangelistic word of God is not confined to "acceptable vessels." God speaks through willing servants, reluctant messengers, and even adversarial voices. This teaches every preacher that the gospel belongs to God, not to us. When God desires His word to be heard, He will see that it is proclaimed—even through unexpected mouths. This humbles the preacher and enlarges the evangelistic horizon: the Word must go out.

## 6. Zelophehad's Daughters — Preaching Invites Bold, Faith-Filled Response (Numbers 27)

Not all wilderness witness condemns; some reveals the beauty of faithful response. The daughters of Zelophehad approach Moses with boldness, seeking their inheritance. Their action becomes a witness that faith steps forward even when circumstances discourage it. Dennis Olson observes that their story "embodies courageous engagement with God's revealed will."[21]

What we learn about preaching here is: evangelistic proclamation must not only warn; it must invite. It must call people into bold faith, into forward movement, into the inheritance God desires for them. Evangelistic preaching opens a door and says, "Come—this promise is for you."

## 7. The Wilderness as the Evangelist's Canon

These wilderness narratives—blessing, rebellion, serpent, incense, oracle, inheritance—were written to be preached for examples. Paul turns them into a sermon in 1 Corinthians 10. The author of Hebrews turns them into a warning and a promise in Hebrews 3–4. Jesus Himself preaches the brazen serpent symbolism as the pattern of His own work.

What we learn about preaching here is: the wilderness scenes of Numbers are the first evangelistic texts of Scripture. They define the contours of preaching that calls for response: preaching that blesses, warns, lifts up Christ, mediates mercy, proclaims sovereign truth, and invites faith. The wilderness becomes the canon for evangelistic proclamation.

The preacher who stands in the Evangelistic Stream stands not beside these stories but inside them—proclaiming the same witness, urging the same response, lifting up the same salvation, and trusting the same God who preached first in the desert.

## The Evangelistic Appeal: Preaching as the Call to Return

If the wilderness provides the witness, it also supplies the appeal. Evangelistic preaching is never content to describe truth; it presses for response. It is never satisfied to recount God's acts; it summons hearers into those acts. It unveils the character of God; it calls people to surrender, trust, and obey. The wilderness stories of Numbers demonstrate this with striking clarity: every revelation is crafted toward a decision, and every preacher raised in the desert carries this same urgency.

Israel does not simply observe the cloud; it must rise when it rises and rest when it rests. Israel does not only hear the trumpets; it must assemble, march, or prepare for battle. Israel does not simply witness the bronze serpent being raised; it must look. The wilderness does not teach passive theology — it teaches responsive faith. And because the wilderness is the birthplace of evangelistic preaching, it teaches that true preaching always presses toward a moment of decision.

## The Appeal Rooted in Ache (Numbers 14)

The wilderness reveals that God Himself makes evangelistic appeals. In Numbers 14, when Israel refuses the land, the text captures the ache of God: "How long will this people provoke me?" The divine question is not annoyance but grief. Rabbinic tradition describes God here as "a father whose child will not come when called,"[22] a portrait of divine heartbreak driving the appeal.

What we learn about preaching here is this:

Evangelistic preaching carries the grief of God. It does not threaten from a distance; it pleads from love. It is not angry rhetoric but wounded compassion. The cry of the preacher is the echo of the Father's ache for His wandering children.

### The Appeal and the Word (Numbers 14:7–9)

Joshua and Caleb's cry to Israel is one of the earliest recorded evangelistic appeals: "Rebel not... fear not... the LORD is with us." Their words are not doctrinal clarifications but calls for immediate response. They do not analyze; they urge. They do not debate; they summon. They clearly remind the people of God's Word – His unfailing promise.

Hebrew scholars note that the verbs in their speech are imperatives of persuasion — forms designed to move the hearer toward decisive action.[23] The wilderness teaches that evangelistic proclamation is summons, not suggestion. It carries weight, urgency, and expectation.

Evangelistic preaching is not content to inform; it calls hearers to act upon what has been revealed.

### The Appeal Embodied in Mediation (Numbers 16)

Aaron's act of running with incense reveals another dimension of the evangelistic appeal. He does not shout from afar; he steps into the very heart of the crisis. His intercession becomes invitation — the plague is stopped wherever he stands.

Early Jewish interpreters saw in Aaron's run the model of one who "rescues by standing near,"[24] revealing a truth essential for evangelistic preaching: the word of appeal is most powerful when joined to compassionate presence.

The evangelistic appeal is not just spoken — it is embodied. True evangelistic preaching does not stay safe; it enters the places where death is working and speaks life.

### The Appeal Expanded to the Nations (Numbers 23–24)

Balaam's oracles extend the evangelistic appeal beyond Israel. His reluctant prophecy becomes a call to the nations to recognize the sovereignty of Israel's God. His words declare blessing for those who align with God and trouble for those who resist.[25] The wilderness thus shows that evangelistic preaching is inherently missional. It cannot remain tribal; it must stretch outward.

The evangelistic appeal is global in scope. God uses the wilderness to teach that preaching must reach beyond familiar circles and call all peoples to recognize the authority of the Lord.

**The Appeal Through Experience (Numbers 33)**

When God directs Moses to recount the stages of Israel's journey — every camp, every failure, every mercy — the list becomes a covenantal appeal. This is not nostalgia; it is summons. By remembering where they have come from, Israel is urged toward faithfulness in the present.

James Kugel notes that this catalogue of encampments served as a "liturgical memory,"[26] forming Israel to respond in the future by recalling God's past mercies. The wilderness teaches that evangelistic preaching draws heavily from memory — it retells the story so that hearers might return to God with understanding and conviction.

The evangelistic appeal is strengthened by testimony — the retelling of God's faithfulness becomes the foundation for calling people back to Him.

**The Appeal Grounded in Promise (Numbers 27; 36)**

The closing chapters of Numbers reveal appeals rooted not in warning but in promise. The daughters of Zelophehad step forward with bold faith, and God affirms their inheritance. The tribes are instructed to marry within their clans to preserve the land God intends for them. Promise becomes persuasion.

The evangelistic appeal, therefore, is not only "turn from sin" but also "turn to promise." Evangelistic preaching must hold out the goodness of God's future as clearly as it warns of the danger of rebellion.

The evangelistic appeal is both warning and invitation — a call to turn from destruction and embrace promise. The wilderness holds these together without contradiction, teaching the preacher to do the same.

**The Wilderness Appeal and Apostolic Preaching**

The New Testament writers understood the wilderness appeal as normative for evangelistic proclamation. Hebrews builds its entire exhortation on the patterns of Numbers: "Today, if ye will hear his voice, harden not your hearts" (Heb 3:15). Paul recounts the same wilderness stories in 1 Corinthians 10 to warn and persuade the church, using the appeal logic embedded in Numbers as a template for gospel exhortation.[27]

The evangelistic appeal is not a modern invention. It is the ancient rhythm of God's voice in the wilderness, carried forward by apostles who understood that preaching is the Spirit's means of drawing people into decisive response.

The wilderness teaches us that the evangelistic appeal rises not from human persuasion but from divine revelation, divine grief, divine mercy, and divine promise. It is the call of God Himself echoing through human voices, summoning every wandering heart to return.

---

**The Evangelistic Renewal — From Wilderness Calling to Fivefold Sending**

The wilderness is where God strips us of every voice but His own, and there, in the silence of holy reduction, He provides His Word and forms His herald. The evangelist does not emerge from abundance but from exposure; not from crowds but from solitude; not from triumph but from testing. In the wilderness, God confronts the preacher with Himself—and once a soul has heard the unmediated voice of the Lord in the desolate place, he becomes one who can speak that voice into the desolation of others.

But the wilderness does not merely shape the preacher; it commissions him. Numbers ends not with a settled people but with a summoned people—ready to cross, ready to proclaim, ready to follow the One who spoke them into readiness. This is where the Evangelistic Stream meets the apostolic logic of Ephesians 4:11, for the evangelist is not a late ecclesial development; he is the New Covenant continuation of the wilderness herald.

## The Wilderness as the Cradle of the Evangelist (Numbers → Ephesians 4:11)

Paul's declaration that Christ "gave some... evangelists" (Eph 4:11) is often treated as a New Testament innovation, but the wilderness reveals it as a continuity. The evangelist belongs to the canonical architecture from the beginning. What Paul names, Numbers forms. What Paul commissions, the Torah births. What Paul assigns to the risen Christ, the wilderness shows as the enduring will of God: that His Word be carried by human voices into the places of wandering.

Scholar Andrew Lincoln notes that the evangelist in Ephesians 4 is "a bearer of the gospel whose ministry stands between proclamation and foundation,"[28] precisely what Moses, Joshua, Caleb, Aaron, and even Balaam become in the desert—a mediating voice between divine revelation and human response. The wilderness becomes the pastoral ecology in which the evangelistic office is first shaped.

Thus the renewal of evangelistic ministry in the Church does not begin with innovation but with return—return to the wilderness where God strips, speaks, forms, and sends.

## John the Baptist: The Wilderness Evangelist Who Bridges the Testaments

No figure embodies the wilderness paradigm more fully than John the Baptist. He arises not from the temple nor academy but from the Judean desert, fulfilling the Qumranic expectation that God's revelation would again be heard "in the wilderness" (1QS 8:12–14).[29] John becomes the living hinge between the Testaments, echoing the trumpet of Numbers as he cries, "Prepare ye the way of the Lord" (Isa 40:3; Matt 3:3). His message is pure wilderness proclamation: repent, behold, believe.

What we learn about preaching here is that the evangelist must call from the margin, not the center. John's wilderness is not accidental—it is essential. His voice is clear because his surroundings are bare. He is the embodiment of the wilderness preacher who has been stripped of every distraction so that his clarion message rings without obstruction.

## Jesus in the Wilderness: The Evangelistic Word Tested and Commissioned

Jesus Himself is driven "by the Spirit into the wilderness" (Mark 1:12). He is the Living Word placed in the landscape where the written Word was first proclaimed. His temptations reenact Israel's wilderness failures—hunger, presumption, idolatry—and His victory redefines the evangelistic ministry that will proceed from Him.

What we learn about preaching here is that evangelistic ministry must be tested before it is proclaimed. The evangelist must discover in the wilderness that the Word of God is enough. Jesus' response—"It is written…"—is the model of every wilderness evangelist who refuses to preach from flesh but from revelation. Raymond Brown notes that Jesus' wilderness victory "prefigures the triumph of the gospel over every wilderness of the human heart."[30] The Evangelistic Stream finds its perfect fulfillment in Christ, and from Him it flows into the apostles.

## Philip in Samaria: The Wilderness Voice in the Urban Wild

Philip, one of the first explicitly named "evangelists" in Scripture (Acts 21:8), emerges from a church scattered by persecution—a different kind of wilderness. His ministry in Samaria reflects the wilderness pattern: a place of spiritual confusion, syncretism, and hunger becomes the ground of divine visitation. When Philip preaches Christ, "the people with one accord gave heed," and "there was great joy in that city" (Acts 8:6–8).

What we learn about preaching here is that the wilderness is not always geographical; it is often cultural. Evangelists are sent into the wilderness of fractured cities, overlooked peoples, and spiritually barren places where distraction and idolatry reign. Philip stands in the line of Numbers: one stripped by persecution, carrying the wilderness Word into a wilderness people.

**Paul: The Evangelist to the Gentiles Formed in Arabia**

Paul's evangelistic commission is explicitly tied to a wilderness encounter. "I went into Arabia," he writes (Gal 1:17). The early Church consistently interpreted this as a desert formation paralleling Moses and Elijah.[31] F. F. Bruce notes that Paul's Arabian withdrawal functioned as "a prophetic consecration,"[32] linking him to wilderness tradition and preparing him for the apostolic-evangelistic ministry that would reshape the world.

What we learn about preaching here is that evangelistic authority flows from wilderness encounter. Paul's gospel proclamation to the Gentiles is not the product of expertise but of revelation received in the silent places, where the risen Christ confronted and commissioned him. His entire ministry embodies the wilderness pattern: stripped, confronted, instructed, and sent.

**The Desert Fathers: Wilderness as the Furnace of the Evangelistic Soul**

The wilderness formation of the evangelist does not end with the apostles; it continues in the early Church's most radical witnesses—the Desert Fathers. In the third and fourth centuries, men and women fled the noise of Empire for the silence of Egypt's interior, believing that the desert remained the place where God strips a soul, speaks His Word, and forms a herald. Their movement was not escapism but evangelistic preparation. The desert became their Numbers.

Athanasius, writing of St. Antony, describes the desert as "the school of the soul,"[33] where the heart learns to discern God's voice without the interference of worldly distraction. Antony himself declared, "A man who dwells in the desert is free from a thousand distractions,"[34] capturing in one sentence the very thesis of this chapter: God strips so He may speak.

For the Desert Fathers, the wilderness was not isolation but refinement. The desert was the place where the Word became audible, where temptations stripped illusions, and where prayer became proclamation. Abba Moses the Black taught that a man "must enter his cell and his cell will teach him everything,"[35] echoing Numbers: revelation comes when distraction is removed. Abba Poemen added, "Do not give your heart to that which does not satisfy the heart,"[36] a desert paraphrase of God's wilderness stripping.

What we learn about preaching here is that the evangelist must be shaped where the soul is quiet enough to hear the Word of God without distortion. The Desert Fathers understood that evangelistic power flows not from public ministry but from interior wilderness — a place where one is confronted by God, cleansed by truth, and called again to proclaim His Word.

Their lives become a historical witness that the wilderness remains the ordination ground of the evangelist. Like Moses, Joshua, Caleb, Aaron, John the Baptist, Paul, and Christ Himself, the Desert Fathers remind the Church that the evangelistic voice grows clear only in the place where every competing voice dies.

The evangelistic stream is where the voice of God stops sounding like background music and becomes a summons. It is the blast of the trumpet in the wilderness. It is the moment where revelation demands response. It is God Himself pressing upon human will with a holy urgency that refuses delay.

And this stream has a center: the proclamation of the kerygma — the irreducible gospel message. Not philosophy. Not therapy. Not moral uplift – but the gospel of the Kingdom.

**The kerygma: Christ died. Christ was buried. Christ rose. Christ reigns. Christ is returning.**

This is the burning core of evangelistic preaching. The evangelist does not entertain; he declares. He does not negotiate; he announces.

He does not offer another spiritual option; he proclaims a kingdom that demands surrender. The kerygma creates crisis. Crisis creates a decision. Decision launches direction. This is the work of an evangelist.

---

**Modern Evangelistic Witnesses Under the Wilderness Paradigm**

The wilderness pattern did not cease in the early Church. Every great evangelistic movement in history bears the imprint of the desert:

- John Wesley, who preached outdoors because churches would not receive him, found his voice among miners and common people in windswept fields—a wilderness of social rejection.

- George Whitefield, whose most powerful sermons were delivered in the open air to tens of thousands, carried a voice trained by solitude and suffering.

- Charles Finney kneeling in the woods on the day of his conversion reflects the wilderness place where God strips the soul and gives His Word.

- Billy Graham, after his retreat to the mountains of California in 1949 to settle the authority of Scripture, emerged with the clarity that would define his evangelistic voice for the next sixty years.[37]

What we learn about preaching here is that wilderness is the ordination ground of the evangelist in every age. Whether literal wilderness, cultural wilderness, emotional wilderness, or spiritual wilderness, the pattern holds: God strips, God speaks, God forms, God sends.

**The Renewal of the Evangelistic Office (Ephesians 4:11)**

Ephesians 4:11 is not only an ecclesial list; it is the New Covenant continuation of the wilderness Word. Christ gives evangelists to His Church as a gift because lost humanity remains in the wilderness—wandering, hungry, restless, and in need of the Word that was first spoken in the desert. Paul tells Timothy in the last letter we possess that he wrote do the work of an evangelist. Timothy was the pastor of the largest church in the New Testament at the time – but "do the work of an evangelist and make full proof of thy ministry" (2 Timothy 4:5). The word here is *plerophoreo* – accomplish the work God has given you to do. Evangelistic proclamation therefore is based upon the risen Christ and His work and fully proves the ministry and calling of the preacher by kingdom proclamation.

We understand based on that fact that Kingdom proclamation is then ordered and sustained through the gifts Christ Himself gives to the Church. As Ephesians 4:11–13 makes clear, apostles, prophets, evangelists, pastors, and teachers are not separate agendas but coordinated ministries through which the reign of God is made visible in a people. Apostles establish what Christ has accomplished, prophets guard the truth of that revelation, evangelists announce it publicly so allegiance to the one true God is brought into the open, humanity may respond to the call of His love. Pastors and teachers then nurture those who respond into maturity and faithfulness. The goal of these gifts is not institutional success or personal fulfillment, but the formation of a unified people who grow into the full measure of Christ Himself.

In this way, evangelistic proclamation initiates what pastoral care and teaching sustains, ensuring that the Gospel remains both exclusive in truth and expansive in love, until the Church stands mature, unified, and visibly subject under the Lordship of Jesus Christ.

So the function of the evangelist – to stand in the wilderness of the humanity and announces the kerygma as a royal herald:

> **"The King has come. The cross has spoken. The tomb is empty. The kingdom is at hand. Repent and believe the gospel."**

And in that moment, all neutrality dies. No one encounters the kerygma and stays unchanged. The gospel forces a posture. It forces a "yes" or a "no," a surrender or a resistance, a turning or a tightening.

This is why the evangelistic stream is essential to the fivefold rhythm of preaching: It is the stream that moves the people from revelation to response, from hearing to obeying, from believing to becoming.

The evangelistic voice is God saying: "Choose. Turn. Follow. Step. Live. Now." Because the kingdom does not advance on sentiment — it advances on decisions that birth direction, and direction that births disciples who carry the kerygma to the ends of the earth.

Here is the renewal: the evangelist is not an optional ministry gift but the apostolic continuation of God's wilderness preaching. The Church loses her mission when she loses her evangelists, for evangelists carry the voice that first shook Sinai and later shook Jerusalem at Pentecost.

**The Wilderness And The Evangelist**

Numbers ends with a people prepared to cross into promise, but they carry the wilderness within them—the memory of the God who called them, spoke to them, fed them, corrected them, forgave them, and sent them forward.

Every evangelist carries the same memory. His power does not lie in eloquence but in the Word. His authority does not lie in technique but in the Word. His fire does not lie in emotional force but in revelation received in silence- holy communion with God. His urgency does not lie in strategy but in the God who met him when all else had been removed from his life. Remember Moses. Remember Paul. Remember John the Baptist. You carry that same fire. Do the work of an evangelist.

**Notes**

1. Jacob Milgrom, Numbers (JPS Torah Commentary; Philadelphia: Jewish Publication Society, 1990), xiii–xv.
2. Philip J. Budd, Numbers (WBC 5; Waco: Word Books, 1984), 17–23.
3. Francis Brown, S. R. Driver, and Charles Briggs, A Hebrew and English Lexicon of the Old Testament (Oxford: Clarendon, 1907), 180–182.
4. Milgrom, Numbers, 78–82.
5. Gordon J. Wenham, Numbers (Tyndale Old Testament Commentaries; Downers Grove: IVP Academic, 1981), 25.
6. Sifre Numbers §80, in Jacob Neusner, Sifre to Numbers (Atlanta: Scholars Press, 1986), 227–229.
7. H. Freedman and Maurice Simon, eds., Midrash Rabbah, Vol. 3 (London: Soncino, 1939), 314.
8. James L. Kugel, The Bible As It Was (Cambridge, MA: Harvard University Press, 1997), 368–370.
9. Brown, Francis, S. R. Driver, and Charles Briggs. A Hebrew and English Lexicon of the Old Testament. Oxford: Clarendon, 1907, 180–182.
10. Freedman, H., and Maurice Simon, eds. Midrash Rabbah. Vol. 3. London: Soncino, 1939, 175.
11. Kugel, James L. The Bible As It Was. Cambridge, MA: Harvard University Press, 1997, 355–360.
12. Milgrom, Jacob. Numbers. JPS Torah Commentary. Philadelphia: Jewish Publication Society, 1990, 78–82.
13. Freedman and Simon, Midrash Rabbah, Vol. 3, 314.
14. Ashley, Timothy R. The Book of Numbers. NICOT. Grand Rapids: Eerdmans, 1993, 321–325.
15. Charlesworth, James H., ed. The Old Testament Pseudepigrapha. Vol. 1. New York: Doubleday, 1983, 775–780.
16. Baruch A. Levine, Numbers 1–20 (AB 4; New York: Doubleday, 1993), 210–213.
17. Gordon J. Wenham, Numbers (TOTC; Downers Grove: IVP, 1981), 127.
18. Freedman, H., and Maurice Simon, eds., Midrash Rabbah, Vol. 3 (London: Soncino, 1939), 390–392.
19. Jacob Milgrom, Numbers (JPS Torah Commentary; Philadelphia: JPS, 1990), 136–139.
20. James H. Charlesworth, ed., The Old Testament Pseudepigrapha, Vol. 1 (New York: Doubleday, 1983), 780.
21. James C. VanderKam, An Introduction to Early Judaism (Grand Rapids: Eerdmans, 2001), 78–79.
22. Dennis T. Olson, Numbers (Interpretation; Louisville: Westminster John Knox, 1996), 179–183

23. Freedman, H., and Maurice Simon, eds. Midrash Rabbah, Vol. 3 (London: Soncino, 1939), 313–315.
24. Timothy R. Ashley, The Book of Numbers (NICOT; Grand Rapids: Eerdmans, 1993), 281–283.
25. Jacob Milgrom, Numbers (JPS Torah Commentary; Philadelphia: JPS, 1990), 139–142.
26. James H. Charlesworth, ed., The Old Testament Pseudepigrapha, Vol. 1 (New York: Doubleday, 1983), 780
27. James L. Kugel, The Bible As It Was (Cambridge, MA: Harvard University Press, 1997), 376–379.
28. Gordon D. Fee, The First Epistle to the Corinthians (NICNT; Grand Rapids: Eerdmans, 1987), 442–450.
29. Athanasius, The Life of Antony and the Letter to Marcellinus, trans. Robert C. Gregg (New York: Paulist Press, 1980), 30–32.
30. Athanasius, Life of Antony, 12.
31. Benedicta Ward, The Sayings of the Desert Fathers: The Alphabetical Collection (Kalamazoo: Cistercian Publications, 1975), 138.
32. Ward, Sayings of the Desert Fathers, 170.
33. Andrew T. Lincoln, Ephesians (WBC 42; Dallas: Word, 1990), 253–255.
34. Florentino García Martínez and Eibert J. C. Tigchelaar, The Dead Sea Scrolls Study Edition (2 vols.; Leiden: Brill, 1997–1998), 1:97–102 (1QS).
35. Raymond E. Brown, The Birth of the Messiah (New York: Doubleday, 1993), 272–276.
36. N. T. Wright, Paul and the Faithfulness of God (Minneapolis: Fortress, 2013), 383–385.
37. F. F. Bruce, The Epistle to the Galatians (NIGTC; Grand Rapids: Eerdmans, 1982), 96–100.
38. William Martin, A Prophet with Honor: The Billy Graham Story (New York: Morrow, 1991), 119–123

# Deuteronomy:

# Apostolic Stream - Divine Commissioning

# CHAPTER SEVEN

## APOSTOLIC PREACHING: GOD'S DIVINE CONTINUUM

### The Ache for Continuity: Moses Longs for the Greater Prophet and the Coming Apostolic Age

Moses stands at the edge of the land he will never enter with a longing Scripture refuses to soften. He has spoken the covenant, lifted his hands over Israel, pleaded for their faithfulness, and borne the burden of a nation wandering between promise and rebellion. Yet he knows the truth that every preacher eventually confronts: his voice will fall silent. The Tabernacle will remain, the people will continue, the covenant will endure—but Moses will not. And so Deuteronomy's closing movement becomes a portrait of ache: a leader longing not for succession but for continuity, for a voice that will carry the Word of God beyond his death.

This longing crystallizes in the words of Deuteronomy 18:15–19, where Moses declares, "The LORD thy God will raise up unto thee a Prophet from the midst of thee, of thy brethren, like unto me; unto Him ye shall hearken." It is a promise wrapped in exegesis, a revelation that reveals need. The Hebrew phrase navi' kamoni (נָבִיא כָּמֹנִי)— "a prophet like me"—is not just similarity but succession. Moshe Weinfeld notes that the expression signifies "a continuation of the Mosaic office," not a replacement. [1] Moses is longing for someone who will bear what he bore, speak as he spoke, carry the weight of covenant revelation, and call Israel to obedience in the same divine authority that marked Sinai.

The verbs in the passage deepen this longing. The command "unto Him ye shall hearken" uses the Hebrew shama (שָׁמַע)—to hear, heed, and obey. [2] Moses knows that Israel's future hinges not on institutional structures but on a voice—one they will hear, fear, and follow. The covenant depends on continuity of proclamation and preservation of text. Israel must not only have Torah; they must have a preacher of Torah, one who mediates the divine qōl (קוֹל), the voice that thundered at Sinai and shaped the nation.

Deuteronomy 18 therefore creates the first canonical expectation of apostolic ministry—a divinely sent representative who will speak God's Word with covenant authority. The people will not approach Sinai again; instead, God will send someone who will speak as Moses spoke. The longing for the apostolic office begins here, not in the New Testament.

This expectation intensifies as Deuteronomy unfolds. Moses turns to Joshua in Deuteronomy 31, laying hands upon him and imparting the Spirit of wisdom (Deut 34:9). Joshua becomes the first "sent one"—one who goes before the people in God's name (Deut 31:7–8). The Hebrew concept of commissioning (tsavah, צוה; shalach, שלח) forms the covenantal backbone of apostolic identity: to be sent is to represent, to speak on behalf of, to carry the Word from God to the people and from the people back to God.[3] Joshua is a general; he is the first covenant emissary, a proto-apostolic figure whose leadership embodies the Mosaic pattern.

Yet Joshua, in his faithfulness and bravery, does not satisfy the ache Moses feels. He is valiant, but he is not Moses. He leads, but he does not speak with Sinai's thunder. He enters the land, but he cannot renew the covenant in the way Moses could. He foreshadows another that is coming. The ache remains—Israel needs a voice of the same weight Moses carried, a prophet who will not simply interpret Torah but embody its revelation.

**Apostolic Ministry as Covenant Rule**

In Scripture, God does not send His people into new territory without first establishing His rule within it. Apostolic ministry functions in this way: as a covenant beachhead. The apostle is sent to establish the standard of God's reign where false gods, false worship, and disordered allegiance have long stood unchallenged.

This logic is rooted in Deuteronomy. As Israel stands on the edge of inheritance, the land before them is not religiously neutral. It is filled with rival altars, rival loyalties, and rival claims upon human devotion. Israel is sent to occupy space, and to confront false worship. The central concern of Deuteronomy is both covenant geography, and spiritual allegiance. Will you serve the Lord God in the land? Expansion without covenant faithfulness is impossible.

This is the apostolic pattern. The apostle is sent to establish a foothold of obedience under the Word of God. He carries the standard of covenant faithfulness into places ordered by other gods and other narratives. His task is not first to grow numbers, but to confront false worship with the Word—It is the Word that must be trusted, feared, and obeyed. Apostolic ministry clears ground so that true worship may be restored and sustained.

This confrontation of truth is destructive to all that is false, but propels and provides purpose and hope to those who are bound. Wherever God confronts false gods, He provides hope to the people and the possibility of a new beginning. Deuteronomy consistently joins warning with promise: blessing is held out alongside curse, life alongside death. The apostle stands in this same tension. He exposes false worship not to leave people desolate, but to prepare ground for renewal. Apostolic ministry is therefore disruptive and hopeful. It announces that what has governed a people no longer reigns, because God has spoken and made a way for covenant restoration through and in the Son.

In the New Testament, this beachhead logic continues without alteration. Jesus sends His apostles to establish the obedience of faith among the nations. In Acts, apostolic ministry repeatedly confronts idols, powers, and distorted worship—whether in synagogues, marketplaces, or households. Wherever the gospel advances, rival gods are unmasked and rival allegiances are unsettled. Yet the result is a new community, new identity, and ordered lives under Christ.

This is why Scripture speaks of the apostle being given an open door. An open door is not just opportunity; it is authorization. God opens access where His reign is to be established. The door is opened not for self-promotion, but for faithful labor—to plant, to teach, to order, and to entrust the work to others. Apostles step through doors God opens knowing that resistance will follow, because false worship does not relinquish ground willingly.

Modern apostolic authority, therefore, is measured by foundations laid – not control or domination. The apostle establishes a standard of truth and worship based on the eternal Word - that endures after he has moved on.

Like Moses in Deuteronomy, he prepares a people to live faithfully without depending on his continued presence. The success of apostolic ministry is seen when communities remain obedient to the Word after the apostle has departed.

To recover the apostolic stream is the recovery of covenantal courage. Apostles are sent to establish beachheads of obedience in contested territory, confronting false gods, restoring true worship, and opening the way for new beginnings under God's reign. They serve the throne by ensuring that where the gospel advances, the standard of the Word is raised, allegiance is clarified, and hope takes root in lives reordered by covenant faithfulness

**Apostles as Bearers of the Covenant Promise**

In Scripture, apostles are not merely sent ones; they are promise bearers. They carry forward what God has sworn, spoken, and bound Himself to accomplish. Yet the promise they bear is never detached from the covenant that governs it. Promise does not float freely in Scripture—it travels through obedience to the Word.

This ordering is established in Deuteronomy, where promise is held out before the people, but governed by covenant faithfulness. Life and blessing are promised, yet always tethered to hearing, remembering, and obeying the Word of the LORD. The promise is real, but it is not automatic. It must be inhabited through obedience. This covenantal structure becomes the foundation of apostolic authority.

Apostles, therefore, do not invent hope; they steward it. They are governed by the covenant Word and govern through it. Wherever they are sent, they carry not only the announcement of what God has promised, but the standard by which that promise is received, preserved, and lived. Apostolic ministry brings promise into contact with practice.

This is why apostolic authority is both hopeful and dangerous.

It is hopeful -- because it announces that God has acted, that His promises are sure, and that a new beginning is possible. Apostles proclaim that what was sworn to the fathers has now been fulfilled in Christ and made available to the nations. They carry the assurance that God's Word has not failed.

It is dangerous -- because promise confronts resistance. Apostles establish the authority of the Word in places under the control of the rulers of the darkness of the world. They expose false gods by introducing true worship. They unsettle false peace by insisting that promise cannot be separated from covenant obedience. The danger does not lie in the apostle himself, but in the message and Word he bears.

Throughout Scripture, those who carry promise are resisted. Moses is opposed, Joshua is tested, the prophets are rejected, and the apostles are persecuted—not because promise is unclear, but because covenant demands response. Apostles bear the weight of this tension. They carry hope forward while insisting that life under God's reign requires transformation.

To recover the apostolic stream is to recover this covenantal courage. Apostles establish the promise of God by establishing obedience to His Word.

They serve the kingdom by ensuring that hope is not reduced to sentiment but grounded in faithfulness. Wherever they labor, the covenant becomes lived reality, the promise becomes embodied hope, and the authority of the Word reshapes lives, communities, and futures. The kingdom of God is established.

## The Second Temple and Prophetic Apostleship

It is no surprise that Second Temple Judaism seized upon Deuteronomy 18 with intense expectation. The Dead Sea Scrolls preserve this longing with remarkable clarity. In 4Q175 (Testimonia), the Qumran community places Deuteronomy 18 alongside the promise of a Davidic ruler (Num 24:17) and a priestly covenant (Deut 33:8–11), revealing their belief that a coming Prophet like Moses would stand at the center of Israel's restoration.[4] The Prophet, the Priest, and the King—three awaited figures, but the Prophet is mentioned first. The ache of Moses was still reverberating centuries later.

The Damascus Document (CD 6:1–11) expands the expectation, describing a future Teacher who will "interpret the Torah in the last days," a Mosaic continuation whose authority flows from divine revelation, not institutional lineage.[5] In 4Q521, sometimes called the "Messianic Apocalypse," the coming Anointed One is portrayed as one who brings resurrection, healing, proclamation, and judgment—echoing Isaiah 61 and foreshadowing the ministry of Jesus.[6] This text shows that the Jewish world anticipated a coming figure who would merge prophetic authority, covenant renewal, and Spirit empowerment.

Philo of Alexandria likewise speaks of a coming "interpreter of God's will," a mediator whose mind is filled with divine Logos.[7] Josephus identifies a wave of prophetic expectation surrounding Moses's promise of a future figure who would deliver and teach the people.[8] The ache of Deuteronomy had not faded—it had intensified. Israel waited for someone who would not merely speak for God but embody the covenantal voice, someone whose word would be Torah alive.

The prophets themselves magnified this longing. Jeremiah foresaw a day when the law would be written on hearts, not stone tablets (Jer 31:31–34). Ezekiel envisioned a Spirit-breathed renewal where God would give a new heart and a new spirit (Ezek 36:26–27). Joel declared an era when God would pour out His Spirit on all flesh, democratizing prophetic revelation (Joel 2:28–29). Isaiah spoke of a Servant endowed with the Spirit who would bring justice to the nations (Isa 42:1–4), and later of

One who proclaimed good news to the poor because "the Spirit of the Lord is upon Me" (Isa 61:1).

These prophetic visions do not compete—they converge. All foresee a Mosaic-like figure, a covenant-renewing leader who brings Word and Spirit together in a manner unseen since Sinai. All foresee a restoration of prophetic authority. All foresee a mediator who will speak divine revelation with unprecedented clarity and power.

This is why the Gospels portray Jesus as Messiah but also as the Prophet like Moses (Acts 3:22–23; John 6:14). Before He commissions apostles, He fulfills the ache of Moses. Before He sends anyone, He Himself appears as the Sent One. The writer of Hebrews calls Him "the Apostle and High Priest of our confession" (Heb 3:1)—the only time in Scripture Jesus is directly called "Apostle." He is the One Moses longed for, the One Qumran waited for, the One Isaiah foresaw—the Greater Joshua who renews the covenant and the Greater Moses who speaks the divine Word.

And yet Jesus does something Moses could not have imagined. He not only fulfills Deuteronomy's longing—He extends it. He turns the singular promise of Deuteronomy 18 into the plural reality of the apostolic age. Moses longs for one prophet. Jesus creates many. Moses envisions a successor. Jesus commissions a company. Moses anticipates continuity. Jesus initiates multiplication.

This is the apostolic continuum: What Moses longed for in the singular, Jesus releases to the Church in multiplicity.

But that moment—the sending—must wait until the Scriptural Witness, where the Upper Room and Pentecost reveal the perfect union of Word and Spirit in apostolic ministry.

---

## Deuteronomy's Apostolic Pattern Unveiled in Word and Spirit

Revelation always arrives when longing has stretched the soul wide enough to receive it. Moses' ache for continuity—his yearning for a voice that would carry the weight of Sinai and the tenderness of a shepherd—creates not a vacuum but a vessel. The ache becomes expectancy, and expectancy becomes the stage on which revelation will stand. When Moses announces, "The LORD will raise up a Prophet like unto me," he is not describing an office alone but revealing a pattern—a divine intention that would shape the future of covenant preaching.

Deuteronomy's closing chapters give us the outline of this revelation with remarkable precision. Israel will need not only leaders but interpreters of God's covenant—voices who stand between the people and God, bringing the Word with clarity and the presence of God with trembling authority. The Hebrew fabric of Deuteronomy itself anticipates this. The emphasis on dabar (דָּבָר), the "word" or "speech" of God, saturates the book; the entire covenant is framed as a revealed Word (Deut 4:2; 30:11–14). The people are called not just to possess commandments but to hear the divine voice, to respond to it, to let it shape their imagination and obedience.

Thus, revelation in Deuteronomy is not primarily legislative—it is vocal. The word of God is heard before it is inscribed. The covenant is proclaimed before it is preserved. Moses mediates a God who speaks, and decrees. This foundation matters because the Apostolic Continuum—the movement of God's Word from Moses through Christ to the apostles—depends on understanding revelation as a spoken, Spirit-laden voice relevant through the ages, not only a body of ancient text.

The revelation moment intensifies through the prophets. Jeremiah declares a New Covenant in which the Word will be written "inwardly" (Jer 31:33), suggesting a shift from external to internal revelation. Ezekiel envisions a day when the Spirit will empower obedience, writing the divine commands upon the heart (Ezek 36:26–27). Isaiah speaks of a Servant endowed with God's Spirit who will bring justice and teaching to the nations (Isa 42:1-4). Joel's prophecy that God will pour out His Spirit on all flesh (Joel 2:28-29) reveals an unprecedented expansion of revelatory access—what was once singular (Moses) will become communal.

Second Temple Judaism treated these passages not as abstractions but as promises awaiting fulfillment. The Qumran community in particular interpreted the prophetic texts eschatologically, believing that divine revelation would break forth again with Mosaic clarity. The Community Rule (1QS) speaks of God "visiting His people with His Holy Spirit,"[9] creating a purified community who will "walk in perfect obedience" because they have received divine understanding. The Damascus Document anticipates a Teacher who will interpret the Torah "in the last days," linking revelation to eschatological leadership. [10]

Revelation in the Second Temple imagination is not merely additional information—it is God's own Word breaking into history again, renewing the covenant and guiding His people through a chosen, Spirit-filled figure.

**Apostleship in the Incarnation**

This prepares the horizon for the revelation of Jesus. Before Christ preaches, heals, or calls disciples, the Gospel of John reveals Him as "the Word made flesh" (John 1:14)—the embodied dabar of Deuteronomy, the living fulfillment of the Mosaic longing. In Him the voice that thundered at Sinai becomes incarnate. He is not just a prophet of the Word; He is the Word. The revelation of God that Moses mediated and the prophets foretold now arrives embodied, personal, and unveiled.

This union of Word and flesh is the first movement of the Apostolic Continuum. But the second movement is just as essential: the Word is united with the Spirit. At Jesus' baptism, the Spirit descends upon Him (Matt 3:16), anointing Him for ministry. This moment is more than divine affirmation; it is the inauguration of a ministry in which every act, every word, every miracle, every proclamation flows from a union of

Word and Spirit—the very union Moses anticipated but could not experience.

Luke's Gospel is deliberate in emphasizing this union: Jesus returns from the Jordan "full of the Holy Ghost" (Luke 4:1); He enters Galilee "in the power of the Spirit" (Luke 4:14); He declares in Nazareth that "The Spirit of the Lord is upon Me" (Luke 4:18). This is the revelation moment Moses longed for—the Prophet like him, yet greater, speaking with authority because He speaks as one filled and empowered by the Spirit.

Here the Apostolic Continuum becomes visible. The ministry of Jesus is the perfect union of Word and Spirit, the revelation of God's voice delivered through a life completely yielded to the Spirit's presence. Jesus is not only the fulfillment of Deuteronomy 18 but the launching point of a new covenantal pattern. He reveals that the ministry Moses longed for—one in which God's Word and God's Spirit operate as one—has finally arrived.

The revelation moment crescendos in the Upper Room. Jesus promises His disciples that the Spirit will "teach you all things" and "bring to your remembrance whatsoever I have said unto you" (John 14:26). This is not abstraction; it is apostolic preparation. He is forming men who will continue His ministry. The Spirit will not give new revelation apart from Christ's Word; He will empower them to proclaim Christ's Word with boldness, clarity, and authority. Revelation is not replaced—it is renewed.

In this way Jesus fulfills the prophetic promise of Joel, the prophetic longing of Isaiah, and the covenantal ache of Moses. He speaks God's Word; the Spirit empowers God's Word; and the apostles will soon proclaim God's Word to the ends of the earth.

The incarnation described in the gospel of John 1 is the revelation moment of the Apostolic Continuum: the Word becomes flesh, the Spirit descends upon the Word, and the Word-and-Spirit together prepare apostles to continue the mission.

But the full force of the continuum—when the sent One sends—is still ahead. Jesus has revealed the pattern; now He will confer the mission.

That moment waits in the next section. For now, we stand in the revelation: where Word and Spirit unite, where Torah's longing is fulfilled, where the Prophet like Moses appears, and where the foundation for apostolic preaching is laid in the fullness of divine revelation.

---

**The Upper Room and the Unity of Word and Spirit in Apostolic Commissioning**

The longing of Moses and the revelation in Christ converge in a single room, on a single night, in a gathering that appears small and fragile to the world but looms large in the history of redemption. The Upper Room is not a quiet retreat for grieving disciples; it is the covenantal threshold where the Mosaic pattern is fulfilled and renewed. In this room, the Word made flesh prepares to be enthroned at the right hand of the Father, and the Spirit who hovered over the waters prepares to be poured out upon the new creation.

Here the Apostolic Continuum becomes visible, tangible, and audible. The disciples do not yet understand it, but heaven does: what Moses began, Christ will complete through them.

The Upper Room discourse in John 13–17 is not merely farewell instruction; it is Jesus reshaping the identity of God's people around Himself. The one who fulfills Deuteronomy 18 now forms the men who will carry His voice across the world. Jesus does not begin by giving strategies or structures. He begins by giving Himself—His Word. "I have given unto them the words which Thou gavest Me," He prays (John 17:8). The Greek expression rhēmata edōka (ῥήματα ἔδωκα) emphasizes that He has entrusted them with God's spoken, living utterances. [16] As Moses received revelation from the presence of God and delivered it to Israel, Jesus delivers the Father's revelation to His disciples.

Yet the Upper Room shows something Moses never saw. The Son promises the Spirit who will obey, inhabit, to embody the Word. The Paraclete will "teach you all things" and "bring to your remembrance whatsoever I have said unto you" (John 14:26). This is not a mystical supplement to the Word but the internalization of revelation—the fulfillment of Jeremiah 31 and Ezekiel 36. The Spirit will ensure that the apostolic proclamation is faithful, powerful, and unified with Christ's voice. As Raymond Brown notes, the Spirit here functions not as an independent revealer but as "the interpreter of Jesus." [17]

This union of Word and Spirit is the defining characteristic of apostolic preaching. Without the Word, the Spirit has no revelation to confirm. Without the Spirit, the Word has no power to transform. The apostles will not simply preach Scripture; they will preach Scripture with the same Spirit who inspired it.

This pattern reflects Second Temple expectations with remarkable clarity. The Qumran community believed that God would restore true understanding of Torah by giving His people a Spirit-filled Teacher who would "open the ears" of the faithful (1QS 4:2–6).[18] The Damascus Document envisioned a future age when God would send a leader who would "interpret the Torah in the last days."[19] What Qumran anticipated—a teacher operating in Spirit and revelation—Christ now fulfills and extends to His disciples.

The Upper Room becomes the place where revelation becomes vocation.

After the Resurrection, this continuity becomes explicit. Jesus enters the locked room, stands in the midst of His disciples, and speaks the words that resolve the ache of Moses and inaugurate the age of apostolic mission:

"Peace be unto you: as My Father hath sent Me, even so send I you." (John 20:21)

This sentence is the hinge of the Apostolic Continuum. Jesus identifies Himself as the Apostle of the Father and immediately extends that identity to His disciples. The Greek phrase *kathōs apestalken Me ho*

*Patēr, kagō pempō hymas* (καθὼς ἀπέσταλκέν με ὁ Πατήρ, κἀγὼ πέμπω ὑμᾶς) contains the full weight of divine mission. [20] As He was sent—bearing revelation, empowered by the Spirit, commissioned by covenant—so they are sent.

The next verse reveals the pattern's completion: "He breathed on them, and saith unto them, Receive ye the Holy Ghost" (John 20:22).

The Word-bearer now becomes the Spirit-giver, fulfilling Ezekiel's vision of God breathing life into His people (Ezek 37:9–10). The Greek verb enephusēsen (ἐνεφύσησεν) is the same verb used in the LXX for God breathing life into Adam (Gen 2:7). [21] The apostles become the first men of the new creation, empowered to speak God's Word with divine life.

This moment cannot be overstated: the apostles do not simply receive a mission; they receive the divine empowerment to carry it. The breath that animated Adam and the breath that raised the dry bones of Israel now animates men who will turn the world upside down. They become bearers of the same breath Christ Himself carried.

The witness reaches its climax at Pentecost. In Acts 2, the Spirit descends with wind and fire, signs that recall Sinai's revelation. Luke intentionally frames Pentecost as a new Sinai—God once again gives His Word, but now He writes it on human hearts and empowers human tongues. [22] The apostles speak "as the Spirit gave them utterance," revealing a union of Word and Spirit that transcends the Mosaic paradigm. Peter stands to preach not as a rabbi but as a Spirit-filled witness. His message is not a commentary; it is covenant proclamation rooted in Scripture, fulfilled in Christ, and empowered by the Spirit.

Here the Apostolic Continuum becomes visible to all: The Prophet like Moses has come.  The Spirit has descended.  The apostles are sent.The Word is preached.  The nations hear.

Pentecost is not the birth of the Church alone; it is the birth of apostolic preaching. Word and Spirit now travel together, inseparable, indivisible, and unstoppable.

The witness of the Upper Room, the sending of the Risen One, and the outpouring of Pentecost form the threefold foundation of apostolic proclamation. What Moses longed for and what the prophets envisioned is now embodied in preaching that unites revelation and power, Scripture and Spirit, Word and fire.

This is the witness that shapes the apostolic age—and every age of revival that follows.

---

**Apostolic Preaching as the Continuum of Word and Spirit**

If the Upper Room was the moment of revelation and Pentecost the moment of divine empowerment, then the book of Acts becomes the living demonstration of what apostolic ministry truly is. The disciples do not hesitate in confusion; they do not form committees to determine direction; they do not debate the shape of their mission. The breath of Christ is still warm upon them, and the fire of God rests upon their heads. Their call is not just remembered—it burns within them. The One who was sent has now sent them, and their preaching becomes the visible continuation of His ministry.

The apostolic response begins with the simplest and most explosive reality: they preached. They preached Christ, they preached resurrection, they preached repentance, they preached the kingdom of God. And they did so with a boldness that signals not human courage but divine inheritance. The Greek term parrēsia (παρρησία), used repeatedly in Acts, denotes fearless speech rooted in divine authority, a term often associated with courtroom witnesses who speak truth in the face of hostile power.[23] When Luke tells us that the apostles spoke "the word of God with boldness" (Acts 4:31), he is declaring that their preaching carries the same authority Jesus carried—not because they are eloquent, but because the Spirit fills their proclamation.

This is the heart of apostolic preaching that the Word is preached in the power of the Spirit, the Spirit is confirming the Word with transforming authority – and a church is born and planted.

It is here that the Apostolic Continuum reveals its full meaning. The apostles are not innovators; they are continuators. Their sermons echo the Torah, interpret the Prophets, and center on Christ. Peter's Pentecost sermon unfolds entirely from Joel, Psalms, and Deuteronomy—revealing not only Spirit-inspired proclamation but a hermeneutic steeped in Scripture.[24] The apostolic preacher is one whose mind is shaped by the revelation of the written Word and whose heart is aflame with the presence of the Spirit.

Paul becomes the clearest embodiment of this pattern. In his own testimony, he declares that Christ revealed Himself not through human instruction but through divine disclosure—apokalypsis (ἀποκάλυψις)—and immediately commissioned him as a "chosen vessel" (Acts 9:15; Gal 1:11–12). Paul's ministry reflects the dual movement of Deuteronomy and the Gospels: a man seized by revelation and propelled by mission. As N. T. Wright notes, Paul's self-understanding as an apostle is that of "a royal herald whose allegiance is to the resurrected Messiah and whose authority flows from the Spirit."[25] His preaching is steeped in Scripture, saturated with prophetic fulfillment, and driven by a Spirit-given compulsion to announce Christ to the nations.

But Paul is not unique; he is exemplary. Philip preaches Christ from Isaiah to a wandering eunuch establishing the Ethiopian church. Peter preaches covenant renewal to the household of Cornelius – establishing the Gentile Church. This is apostolic preaching—not the mastery of technique, but preachers who are Mastered by Christ, and made alive by the Spirit.

**Apostolic preaching is proclamation; and it is representation and embodiment**. The apostle speaks on behalf of Another, carrying the authority of the One who sent him. This is why the New Testament repeatedly uses the language of ambassadorship. Paul writes, "Now then we are ambassadors for Christ, as though God did beseech you by us" (2 Cor 5:20). The Greek presbeuomen (πρεσβεύομεν) carries the weight of royal diplomacy. [26] An apostle speaks as the delegated representative of King Jesus, delivering His terms of peace, His call to repentance, His offer of salvation, and His demand for allegiance.

Here the continuity with Deuteronomy becomes unmistakable. Moses spoke on behalf of Yahweh; Jesus spoke on behalf of the Father; and the apostles speak on behalf of the Son. The prophetic pattern becomes the apostolic commission: to represent God by representing His Word. Apostolic preaching is not a human performance but a divine mediation, a continuation that the Mosaic office foreshadowed. Apostolic preaching is Christ-centric from the text to the sending forth- a testimony that authority of Christ and power of the Spirit has been sealed by the Farher and confirmed by the ascension.

**Apostleship in the Didache**

The early Church understood this clearly. The Didache, one of the earliest Christian teaching documents, describes apostles as "those who speak the word of the Lord," whose message is to be tested by their fidelity to Christ and their humility of life.[27] Ignatius of Antioch calls the apostles "those entrusted with the mysteries of Christ," whose preaching is the lifeline of the Church.[28] Justin Martyr speaks of apostolic preaching as the continuation of the prophetic tradition, now fulfilled in Christ and empowered by the Spirit.[29] Irenaeus insists that true apostolic preaching is measured by adherence to the apostolic rule of faith—Scripture-centered, Christ-centered, Spirit-animated, and ethically transformative.[30]

The apostolic response, then, is not merely historical—it becomes the theological foundation for the ministry of preaching in the Church. It defines the task, scope, and authority of all who preach in the name of Christ. Apostolic preaching stands upon three pillars:

1. Revelatory foundation — rooted in Scripture and fulfilled in Christ.
2. Spirit empowerment — animated, illuminated, and emboldened by the Holy Ghost.
3. Missional commission — sent to proclaim, persuade, heal, confront, and establish communities of faith.

And here, at last, the words of Jesus spoken in the locked room become the interpretive center of apostolic ministry:

"As My Father hath sent Me, so send I you."

He does not say, "As I taught, so teach," or "As I healed, so heal," though both are true. He speaks of sent-ness—a divine commissioning rooted in the nature of God Himself.

The Father sends the Son. The Son sends the apostles. The apostles establish the Church. The Church sends preachers. And so the continuum continues.

This is why the apostolic office appears in Ephesians 4:11—not as a hierarchical status but as a covenantal function. Apostles are given "for the perfecting of the saints, for the work of the ministry, for the edifying of the body of Christ." Their preaching shapes a people, forms a community, and extends the mission of Christ to the ends of the earth.

Apostolic preaching, therefore, is not a historical relic; it is the divine pattern for the preaching ministry. Every preacher stands in this lineage—not to claim the title of apostle but to embody the apostolic pattern: the Word preached by the Spirit, the Spirit confirming the Word, and the people of God formed into a missionary community.

The Apostolic Continuum is not a theory; it is a living fire passed down from the Father, fulfilled in Christ, from Christ to the apostles, and from the apostles to the Church. It is the foundation on which all true preaching stands.

---

**The Apostolic Commission and the Global Call to Preach the Word in the Final Hour**

Renewal is always the point where revelation becomes responsibility.

And for the apostolic preacher, renewal is not a return to sentiment or memory but a return to mission. What began in Moses' longing and shone forth in Christ's revelation has now been entrusted to a global

Church called to carry the same flame. The Apostolic Continuum does not end in the first century. It continues wherever a preacher rises to speak God's Word in the power of the Spirit.

The apostles understood this from the beginning. They were eyewitnesses of Christ; they were bearers of His commission. When the Risen One said, "As My Father hath sent Me, so send I you," He did not speak into a private devotional moment. He spoke into a movement. He placed upon them the mantle of Moses, the authority of the Prophet like unto him, the anointing of Isaiah's Servant, and the mission of a Kingdom that would stretch to the ends of the earth. The apostolic age was not the invention of a new ministry model; it was the fulfillment of a divine pattern woven through the entire canon.

Thus, the renewal of apostolic preaching today is not an innovation but a return. It is a return to the way revelation works, to the way the Word and Spirit birth a people, to the way God's voice shapes a community, to the way sent ones carry divine authority into the wilderness of nations. Renewal is not an emotional stirring; it is the Spirit restoring the original intention of God for His preachers in the last days.

The Church stands again in the shadow of the Upper Room—not in fear, but in readiness. The fire that fell at Pentecost was the canonical signal that every generation of preachers would need the same Spirit to declare the same Christ with the same boldness. The apostolic pattern remains unaltered: Word and Spirit united, Scripture fulfilled in proclamation, Christ exalted by witness, nations confronted by the Gospel, and communities formed by the presence of God.

The renewal of apostolic preaching today demands the same foundational truths that animated the first apostles.

1. The preacher must understand that he stands in the lineage of Moses, not merely in the tradition of eloquent speech. He is called to represent God, to carry His Word, to speak what God has spoken, to confront idolatry, to call people to covenant. Renewal begins when the preacher recognizes that his authority is derivative—he stands as one sent, not as one self-appointed.

2. The preacher must understand that Christ is the center of all revelation. Apostolic preaching is Christological through and through. Every text finds its fulfillment in Him, every promise reaches its climax in Him, every prophetic hope is realized in Him. If Moses longed for the Prophet like unto himself and the prophets longed for the Servant endowed with the Spirit, then the apostolic preacher must long for Christ to be made known through every sermon he gives. Renewal demands a return to the centrality of Christ in the pulpit.

3. The preacher must recognize that the Spirit is the fire of apostolic proclamation. Without the Spirit, the Word becomes information; with the Spirit, the Word becomes transformation. Without the Spirit, the preacher explains; with the Spirit, the preacher proclaims. The renewal of apostolic preaching is not a matter of technique, delivery, or structure—it is the recovery of divine power. As in Acts, so today: the Spirit gives utterance. He animates the sermon, illuminates the Scripture, convicts the hearer, and confirms the Word with power. Renewal is not preaching harder; it is preaching with the Spirit who hovered at creation and descended at Pentecost.

4. The preacher must embrace the global mission. The Apostolic Continuum is a sending continuum of global missionary ministry to then nations. Moses was sent to Israel. Jesus was sent to the world. The apostles were sent to the nations. The horizon of apostolic preaching is always global. Renewal means lifting our eyes from local comfort to global commission. It means recognizing that the Gospel is a river that must flow from Jerusalem to Judea, to Samaria, and to the uttermost parts of the earth. The preacher participates in this movement not by force of personality but by the anointing of the Spirit and the authority of Christ.

5. The preacher must embrace the cost. Apostolic preaching is not comfortable. It is not safe. It is not welcomed by principalities or by empires. It is cruciform. Renewal comes when the preacher accepts that apostolic ministry is not a platform but a cross; not a

career but a calling; not a performance but a sacrifice. Renewal demands courage, endurance, resilience, and an unwavering allegiance to Christ.

In this final scene of apostolic renewal, the preacher must see himself not only as an expositor of sacred text but as a participant in the divine mission unleashed at Pentecost. He is not a storyteller but a herald. He does not share insights; he announces the reign of Christ. He does not entertain; he confronts. He does not speculate; he declares. And he does not stand alone; he stands in the stream of Moses, Joshua, Isaiah, Jeremiah, Ezekiel, Joel, Jesus, Peter, John, Paul, and an unbroken line of witnesses who bore the Word of God to the world.

This renewal is not limited to those who carry the title "apostle" today. It is the pattern for every preacher, teacher, prophet, evangelist, and pastor. The fivefold gifts are not hierarchical; they are streams that converge in the ministry of preaching. The apostolic preacher is one who embodies the pastoral care of Genesis, the priestly teaching of Exodus, the prophetic voice of Leviticus, the evangelistic proclamation of Numbers, and the covenantal commissioning of Deuteronomy. He is a whole-Bible preacher, a whole-person preacher, a whole-Church preacher.

And he is needed now more than ever. For this is the end-time hour. For this is the moment when nations rage, kingdoms shake, and the love of many grows cold.

This is the day of deception, of lawlessness, of spiritual famine—not of bread but of hearing the Word of the Lord. This is the season in which preaching must not shrink but soar, not retreat but advance, not soften but sharpen.

The apostolic preacher is the answer of God to the crisis of the age.

- He does not represent himself; he represents Christ.
- He does not preach opinion; he preaches Christ's revelation.
- He does not echo culture; he bears witness to the Kingdom and the cross.

- He does not shrink from darkness; he confronts it with light of the glorious gospel.
- He does not fear the world; he loves the world with a crucified love.

This is the renewal to which God now calls His Church—not the recovery of old methods, but the recovery of the apostolic heart, the apostolic voice, the apostolic fire. This is the renewal that turns pulpits into altars, sermons into encounters, and congregations into communities of witness.

It is in this spirit that the modern preacher must hear again the words of the Risen Christ:

"As My Father hath sent Me, so send I you."

These words now cross the centuries. They pass through the locked room of Jerusalem. They gather the wind of Pentecost. They carry the boldness of Peter and the fire of Paul. They bear the tears of the martyrs and the courage of the confessors. They echo through every revival and every mission field. They fall now upon the shoulders of every preacher who dares to answer the call.

You, preacher of the last days…You stand in this continuum. You bear this mantle. You carry this Word. You breathe this Spirit. You inherit this mission. And you will proclaim this Gospel until the Lord returns. This is your renewal. This is your commission. This is your call.

---

**Conclusion**

And so the Apostolic Continuum stands complete—not as history, but as inheritance. What began with Moses and reached its fullness in Christ now flows into the global Church. The mantle passes not to a select few but to every preacher who stands beneath the authority of Scripture and the power of the Spirit. The world awaits such voices. The Church must raise them. And the next chapter opens the way.

For the Lord still says: "Go." And the Church must still answer: "Send us."

---

**NOTES**

1. Moshe Weinfeld, Deuteronomy 1–11 (AB 5; New York: Doubleday, 1991), 336–340.

2. Ludwig Koehler and Walter Baumgartner, Hebräisches und aramäisches Lexikon zum Alten Testament (Leiden: Brill, 1967–1996), 2:157–159 (entry שמע).

3. Jeffery Tigay, Deuteronomy (JPS Torah Commentary; Philadelphia: JPS, 1996), 169–173.

4. Florentino García Martínez and Eibert J. C. Tigchelaar, eds., The Dead Sea Scrolls Study Edition (2 vols.; Leiden: Brill, 1997–1998), 1:353–355 (4Q175).

5. Martínez and Tigchelaar, DSSSE, 1:553–560 (CD 6).

6. James H. Charlesworth, ed., The Old Testament Pseudepigrapha, Vol. 1 (New York: Doubleday, 1983), 390–394 (4Q521).

7. Philo, Life of Moses 1.158–159, in C. D. Yonge, The Works of Philo (Peabody, MA: Hendrickson, 1993).

8. Josephus, Antiquities 3.8.9; 4.8.49–50, trans. Whiston (Peabody, MA: Hendrickson, 1987).

9. Geza Vermes, The Complete Dead Sea Scrolls in English (London: Penguin, 1997), 99–103 (1QS 4:20–26).

10. Florentino García Martínez and Eibert J. C. Tigchelaar, The Dead Sea Scrolls Study Edition (Leiden: Brill, 1997–1998), 1:553–560 (CD 6).

11. Weinfeld, Deuteronomy 1–11, 338–345.

12. Raymond E. Brown, The Gospel According to John I–XII (AB 29; New York: Doubleday, 1966), 11–14.

13. Joel B. Green, The Gospel of Luke (NICNT; Grand Rapids: Eerdmans, 1997), 190–195.

14. James L. Kugel, The Bible As It Was (Cambridge, MA: Harvard University Press, 1997), 529–535.

15. Brevard S. Childs, Old Testament Theology in a Canonical Context (Philadelphia: Fortress, 1985), 92–98.

16. Raymond E. Brown, The Gospel According to John XIII–XXI (AB 29A; New York: Doubleday, 1970), 742–744.

17. Brown, John XIII–XXI, 728–732.

18. Vermes, Complete Dead Sea Scrolls, 102–107 (1QS 4).

19. García Martínez and Tigchelaar, DSSSE, 1:553–560 (CD 6).

20. F. F. Bruce, The Gospel of John (Grand Rapids: Eerdmans, 1983), 392–395.

21. C. K. Barrett, The Gospel According to St. John (London: SPCK, 1978), 573–575.

22. Craig S. Keener, Acts: An Exegetical Commentary, Vol. 1 (Grand Rapids: Baker Academic, 2012), 771–790.

23. Darrell L. Bock, Acts (BECNT; Grand Rapids: Baker Academic, 2007), 202–206.

24. Craig S. Keener, Acts: An Exegetical Commentary, Vol. 1 (Grand Rapids: Baker Academic, 2012), 814–826.

25. N. T. Wright, Paul and the Faithfulness of God (Minneapolis: Fortress Press, 2013), 1354–1362.

26. Murray J. Harris, The Second Epistle to the Corinthians (NIGTC; Grand Rapids: Eerdmans, 2005), 451–456.

27. The Didache, in Michael W. Holmes, The Apostolic Fathers: Greek Texts and English Translations (Grand Rapids: Baker Academic, 2007), 343–345.

28. Ignatius of Antioch, Letter to the Trallians 2–3, in Holmes, Apostolic Fathers, 169–171.

29. Justin Martyr, First Apology 61–67, in Ante-Nicene Fathers, Vol. 1 (Peabody, MA: Hendrickson, 1994), 183–187.

30. Irenaeus, Against Heresies 3.2–3, in Ante-Nicene Fathers, Vol. 1, 414–418.

31. Christopher J. H. Wright, The Mission of God: Unlocking the Bible's Grand Narrative (Downers Grove, IL: InterVarsity Press, 2006), 69–75.

32. John N. Oswalt, The Book of Isaiah: Chapters 40–66 (NICOT; Grand Rapids: Eerdmans, 1998), 108–115.

33. Walter Brueggemann, The Prophetic Imagination, 2nd ed. (Minneapolis: Fortress Press, 2001), 87–91.

34. Gordon D. Fee, Paul, the Spirit, and the People of God (Peabody, MA: Hendrickson, 1996), 55–67.

35. Richard Bauckham, Bible and Mission: Christian Witness in a Postmodern World (Grand Rapids: Baker Academic, 2003), 27–33.

36. John Stott, The Spirit, the Church, and the World: The Message of Acts (Downers Grove, IL: InterVarsity Press, 1990), 62–70.

37. Darrell L. Bock, Acts (BECNT; Grand Rapids: Baker Academic, 2007), 142–150.

38. Craig S. Keener, Acts: An Exegetical Commentary, Vol. 1 (Grand Rapids: Baker Academic, 2012), 889–897.

39. Ben Witherington III, The Acts of the Apostles: A Socio-Rhetorical Commentary (Grand Rapids: Eerdmans, 1998), 137–144.

40. Michael Green, Evangelism in the Early Church, rev. ed. (Grand Rapids: Eerdmans, 2003), 41–51.

41. Scot McKnight, "Apostolic Preaching," in Dictionary of Paul and His Letters, eds. Gerald F. Hawthorne and Ralph P. Martin (Downers Grove, IL: InterVarsity Press, 1993), 34–42.

42. David Peterson, The Acts of the Apostles (PNTC; Grand Rapids: Eerdmans, 2009), 99–105.

43. Andrew F. Walls, The Missionary Movement in Christian History (Maryknoll, NY: Orbis, 1996), 22–28.

44. D. A. Carson and Douglas J. Moo, An Introduction to the New Testament, 2nd ed. (Grand Rapids: Zondervan, 2005), 350–356.

45. Eckhard J. Schnabel, Early Christian Mission, Vol. 1 (Downers Grove, IL: InterVarsity Press, 2004), 39–45.

46. I. Howard Marshall, The Acts of the Apostles (TNTC; Grand Rapids: Eerdmans, 1980), 57–62.

47. Stephen G. Dempster, Dominion and Dynasty: A Theology of the Hebrew Bible (NSBT 15; Downers Grove, IL: InterVarsity Press, 2003), 213–219.

48. Jonathan Edwards, The Distinguishing Marks of a Work of the Spirit of God (1741; repr., Carlisle, PA: Banner of Truth, 2006), 42–50.

49. John Wesley, The Works of John Wesley, ed. Thomas Jackson (14 vols.; Grand Rapids: Baker, 1979), 5:3–12.

50. George Whitefield, Select Sermons (Wheaton, IL: Crossway, 2012), 14–22.

51. Andrew Murray, The Spirit of Christ (Fort Washington, PA: Christian Literature Crusade, 1888), 77–86.

52. David Wilkerson, The Vision (New York: Pyramid Books, 1974), 95–102.

# MINISTRY OF PREACHING

## *ONE VOICE OF THE PEOPLE OF GOD*

# CHAPTER EIGHT

## The Fivefold Voice in One Preaching People

### A World on the Brink, A Church at the Threshold

There are moments in redemptive history when the ache of the world becomes the ache of the Church, when the groaning of nations begins to reverberate inside the hearts of God's people, when the fear, confusion, violence, and disintegration of an age press God's preachers back toward the heart of their calling. We live in such a moment. Our world is exhausted by its own noise—spinning, restless, breathless, famished for a word that does more than inform, a word that confronts, heals, remakes, and breathes.

We stand at a threshold where the nations tremble, not only with political instability but with spiritual hunger. It is the ancient hunger of every generation that loses its way: Where is a voice that speaks with authority?

The old idols collapse, but the new ones prove even more fragile. False prophets multiply like insects after a storm. The noise expands, but clarity diminishes. The screens grow brighter, but the hearts grow darker. And beneath it all, an unspoken longing rises—the desire for a word that is supernatural and eternal, a word that bears the weight of covenant and the wind of the Spirit.

This longing is not new. Israel felt it in the days after Moses' death, when the river Jordan gleamed before them but the voice they had followed for forty years had fallen silent.[1] They needed a new kind of leader, not one who would replace Moses but one who would carry forward the divine intention Moses had embodied. That ache echoed again in the prophets who saw a coming age characterized not by exile but by restoration, not by silence but by Spirit, not by scattered visions but by a singular Voice who would unite the tribes and speak again for the God of Abraham. [2]

The ache grew heavier in the centuries between Malachi and John the Baptist. The prophets' voices had faded, but the promises had not. In the synagogues of Judea and the scroll-filled caves of Qumran, the faithful waited—longing for the return of the Word, longing for the return of the Spirit, longing for the arrival of the Prophet like Moses, longing for the Messiah who would unite Word and Spirit in a single ministry. The Testimonia scroll (4Q175) reveals a community actively reading Deuteronomy 18 and awaiting a Mosaic figure who would interpret the covenant with divine authority. [3] The Community Rule (1QS) speaks of a time when God will "visit them with His Holy Spirit" so that they may understand the true meaning of Torah. [4]

It grew again in the Upper Room when Jesus told His disciples that He would leave them yet not leave them comfortless. They had walked with the Voice made flesh. They had watched the Word teach, heal, rebuke, forgive, and confound. They had heard authority in His tone that Moses longed for, the authority of One who not only carried revelation but was revelation. [5] And now He was leaving them—not to abandon them, but to expand His own mission through them. But their hearts ached; they did not yet understand how His departure could advance His work.

This same ache manifests today. The Church stands again at a threshold—needing a renewed sense of identity, clarity in proclamation, and courage in witness. We have inherited pulpits, but not always the fire. We possess buildings, but not always the burden. We carry Scriptures, but not always the Spirit who first breathed them. And yet beneath our structures and our liturgies remains a longing God Himself has placed within His people: the longing for a multi-voiced, Scripture-formed, Spirit-empowered community that speaks with the fullness of Christ. [6]

For two millennia, the Church has inherited the fragments of Christ's ministry—the pastoral compassion, the priestly instruction, the prophetic clarity, the evangelistic proclamation, the apostolic commissioning. But rarely has the Church held them together in one preaching identity. Rarely has the world seen a people who embody the whole voice of Christ. And rarely has the Church understood that this is exactly what Christ intended.

This longing—for the whole Christ to be preached by the whole Church—is now rising again. It echoes through seminaries where students ask why preaching feels thin. It echoes through congregations hungry for more than uplift. It echoes across mission fields where people hear a thousand voices but few with authority. It echoes in pastors who feel stretched between roles, not knowing they were always meant to embody the fivefold voice in measure. And it echoes through the global Church which senses, even if dimly, that the end-time hour requires a different kind of preacher.

What we are experiencing now is not nostalgia; it is prophetic hunger. It is the ache Moses felt when he knew his voice would soon fall silent. It is the ache the prophets felt when they spoke of a day when the Spirit would be poured out on all flesh. It is the ache the disciples felt when the Voice they loved ascended from the Mount of Olives. It is the ache the early Church felt when persecution scattered them into the nations with fire in their bones and Scripture on their tongues. [7]

This longing is the doorway to renewal. It is the Spirit stirring the Church so she may rediscover her preaching identity—not as a collection of gifted individuals but as a single people who bear the fivefold voice of Christ.

We find ourselves on the precipice of a global turning point. The systems of the world tremble; the nations shake; the technological Babel of our age reaches for heaven again; the earth groans for redemption.

And in such an hour, the Lord does not call for a new method—He calls for a new kind of preacher. Or rather, the original kind: the preacher formed by the whole canon, shaped by the full Christ, equipped by the Spirit, and sent by the risen Lord into a world desperate for a true voice.

We begin this chapter not with confidence, strategy, or triumph, but with longing—the longing for a people who speak with the pastoral tenderness of Genesis, the priestly instruction of Exodus, the prophetic fire of Leviticus, the evangelistic urgency of Numbers, and the apostolic commissioning of Deuteronomy; the longing for a preaching people in whom the fivefold voice of Christ becomes audible again.

This longing is not ours alone.

It is God's.

And it is the precondition for a global revival of preaching unlike anything we have seen.

---

## The Five Streams of Christ's Ministry Forming One Preaching People

Longing is never the end of God's story. Longing opens the door, but revelation steps through it. What the people of God sensed dimly through generations—what Moses anticipated, what the prophets promised, what the psalmists cried for, what the wilderness generation never saw—comes into clear, world-altering focus in the revelation of Jesus Christ. He answers the ache; He embodies it. He does not just fulfill the streams; He is the wellspring from which they all flow.

The Scriptures present Christ not as the founder of a new movement but as the embodiment of the fivefold voice of God. He is Shepherd, Priest, Prophet, Evangelist, and Apostle in perfect unity. The Torah's architecture—its five-part rhythm, its ordered streams of pastoral, priestly, prophetic, evangelistic, and apostolic identity—finds its completion not in five individuals, but in the one Lord who harmonizes them into a single divine voice.

**Christ the Shepherd (Genesis Fulfilled)**

Genesis introduces God as the Shepherd who walks with His people, seeks the lost, blesses families, and calls wanderers into covenant. Christ fulfills this identity not metaphorically but ontologically. He is not merely like a shepherd; He is the Good Shepherd whose voice His sheep know (John 10:11–16). His ministry is marked by compassion that restores dignity, presence that dispels fear, and nearness that redefines holiness. His entire incarnate life is a revelation of the pastoral heart of the Father, the fulfillment of the Genesis stream of divine tenderness. [8]

**Christ the Priest (Exodus Fulfilled)**

Exodus reveals God as the One who descends in fire, gives Torah, establishes covenant, and institutes priestly mediation. Christ steps into this stream as the High Priest of a better covenant (Heb 4:14–15), the living Torah made flesh, the One who interprets Scripture with divine authority, and the sacrifice that fulfills every altar of Exodus. His priestly ministry is not limited to Golgotha; every sermon He preached, every act of healing, every word of forgiveness was a priestly act—mediating God's presence to humanity and humanity back to God.[9]

### Christ the Prophet (Leviticus Fulfilled)

If Leviticus is the book of divine speech—"And the LORD called unto Moses and spoke..."—then Christ fulfills its prophetic stream by becoming the embodied Word who says only what He hears from the Father (John 12:49–50). He speaks with the authority Leviticus anticipates: a holy Voice from within the sanctuary of His own being. His prophetic ministry is not just predictive but revelatory—He discloses the Father, unveils the kingdom, exposes the heart, and restores the covenant relationship Leviticus guarded. The prophets longed for a day when God's Word would again dwell among His people; in Christ, the Word dwelt among us. [10]

### Christ the Evangelist (Numbers Fulfilled)

Numbers reveals God as the God of the wilderness—calling Israel to decision, proclaiming promise and warning, raising banners, sounding trumpets, confronting rebellion, and guiding His people through desolate landscapes toward their destiny. Christ fulfills this evangelistic stream as the Herald of the Kingdom, proclaiming good news to the poor, liberty to captives, sight to the blind, and the acceptable year of the Lord (Luke 4:18–19). He calls sinners to repentance in the wilderness of their hearts (Mark 1:15), feeds them when they are faint, and confronts their unbelief with gentle authority. He is the One who seeks out those perishing in their desert and leads them into life. [11]

### Christ the Apostle (Deuteronomy Fulfilled)

Deuteronomy is the book of commissioning—Moses hands the covenant to Joshua, sends Israel across the Jordan, and declares blessings and warnings with apostolic gravity. Christ fulfills this stream by identifying Himself as the Apostle of the Father (Heb 3:1), the One sent to renew the covenant, reveal the Father, and commission a new people. His entire earthly ministry is apostolic: sent from God, consecrated by God, and returning to God, with a mission that will be extended to His followers through His sending. In Him, the apostolic stream of Deuteronomy becomes flesh and blood. [12]

---

**The Revelation: Christ Pours the Five Streams Into One Body**

What is astonishing—and what the early Church understood with clarity—is that Christ does not keep these five streams to Himself. He pours them into His Body, the Church, not as isolated gifts but as the measure of His own fullness.

This is the theological heart of Ephesians 4:7–16.

Paul does not present five offices competing for influence or hierarchy; he presents five expressions of Christ's own ministry, distributed into the Body so that the Church might "grow up into Him in all things." The language is not bureaucratic; it is Christological. Christ gives grace "according to the measure of the gift of Christ"—that is, He gives Himself in fivefold pattern. The gifts are distributions of His identity.

The Dead Sea Scrolls anticipate this in their expectation of a "community of many voices" led by the Spirit of holiness (1QS 4). The early Church Fathers confirm it by describing the Church as the continuation of Christ's prophetic, priestly, and apostolic work on earth. [13] The canonical witness, Second Temple tradition, and apostolic teaching converge: Christ's ministry becomes the Church's ministry.

This is why no single preacher embodies all five streams perfectly—only Christ does. But every preacher embodies all five in measure, because every preacher bears Christ. And the Church embodies all five in fullness, because the Church is His Body.

Thus, the fivefold ministry is not a collection of vocational titles or personality types; it is the voice of Christ flowing through a preaching people.

- His shepherding becomes our pastoral care.
- His instruction becomes our teaching.
- His fire becomes our prophetic speech.
- His proclamation becomes our evangelistic call.
- His sending becomes our apostolic mission.

In Him, the five streams are united.

Through Him, the five streams flow into His people.

By Him, the five streams rise in the last days as one unified preaching voice.

This is the revelation: Christ forms one people who preach with His fivefold voice.

---

**The Church as the Apostolic Community of the Fivefold Voice**

Revelation becomes reality when it is embodied. Christ, the fullness of the fivefold voice—Shepherd, Priest, Prophet, Evangelist, Apostle—does not remain alone in His ministry. He forms a people who bear His voice, carry His Word, and extend His mission. The Church is not an afterthought to the Gospel. The Church is the continuation of Christ's preaching ministry on earth. She is the body of the Fivefold Christ, and therefore the community of the fivefold voice.

The earliest disciples understood this instinctively. They did not gather in the Upper Room to invent a new religion or create a new leadership model. They gathered because the One who embodied Moses, fulfilled the prophets, and conquered death had breathed upon them and said, "As My Father hath sent Me, even so send I you." In that moment, the apostolic identity of the Church was born. They were not merely hearers of Christ—they were His continuation. The Church did not inherit fragments of His ministry; she inherited the whole Christ.

The book of Acts reveals this with striking clarity. What Christ began to do and teach, His people continue to do and teach (Acts 1:1). The shepherding compassion of Genesis flows through the Church as they care for widows, share their possessions, and become a community of belonging (Acts 2:44–47). The priestly instruction of Exodus becomes visible as the apostles "continue steadfastly in the apostles' doctrine," teaching the Scriptures with authority and turning homes and synagogues alike into sanctuaries of revelation. The prophetic stream of Leviticus erupts in Spirit-inspired speech on the Day of Pentecost, fulfilling Joel's hope that sons and daughters would prophesy; the community becomes not merely a gathering of worshippers but a people who speak as the Spirit gives utterance.[14] The evangelistic urgency of Numbers surges outward as Philip preaches in Samaria, Peter proclaims repentance in Jerusalem, and Paul brings the Gospel into the Gentile wilderness of the Roman world.[15] And the apostolic commissioning of Deuteronomy unfolds as the Church is sent to the ends of the earth, bearing the authority of the risen Christ, guided by the Spirit, and grounded in the Scriptures.

This unified witness is not accidental—it is theological. The early Church did not divide the ministry of Christ; they embodied it in a single community. Shepherds, teachers, prophets, evangelists, and apostles were not compartmentalized roles but diverse expressions of the living Christ. The Church recognized that the same Spirit who anointed Jesus had now been poured out upon them, forming them into a multi-voiced but unified witness-bearing people.

The witness of the apostolic fathers confirms this vision. Ignatius speaks of the Church as "the place where Jesus Christ is," suggesting a continuity between the incarnate ministry of the Son and the embodied ministry of His people.[16] Irenaeus describes the Church as the dwelling place of the Spirit, the locus where Christ's truth is proclaimed in its fullness.[17] The Didache outlines a community where prophets speak, teachers instruct, evangelists proclaim, pastors shepherd, and apostles travel—not as separate guilds but as one Spirit-created body.[18] Even the Dead Sea Scrolls anticipated such a community. The Qumran sect longed for a Spirit-filled congregation in the last days, shaped by Scripture, led by inspired instruction, and united in covenant.[19] While they could not foresee the fullness of the Church's identity, their expectation reveals the Second Temple longing for a people who would bear God's own voice in the world. In the Church, that expectation finds its surprising fulfillment—not in a sect, but in a global body.

The witness of history reinforces the same truth. Wherever the Church has been awakened—whether in the deserts of Syria with the early ascetics, in the marketplaces of Antioch, in the lecture halls of Alexandria, in the monasteries of Ireland, in the fields of England during the Wesleyan awakening, or in the open-air meetings of the twentieth-century Pentecostal revivals—the fivefold voice rises as one. The Spirit does not disperse Christ's ministry; He amplifies it in His people. In every era, revival occurs when Christ's fivefold voice becomes audible again through ordinary believers shaped by Scripture and surrendered to the Spirit.

This is why no single age of the Church has expressed the fullness of Christ's ministry; each age carries a facet of it, while the whole Church across time and space embodies the fullness. The early Church excelled in apostolic courage, the patristic age in theological clarity, the medieval era in sacramental depth, the Reformation in preaching authority, the modern missions movement in evangelistic fervor, and the Pentecostal century in prophetic and experiential renewal. None of these streams are optional; all are essential. Together they reveal the one Christ speaking through one Church.

In the present moment, this witness is rising again. Across Africa, Asia, the Middle East, and Latin America, the Church is preaching with a voice that sounds remarkably like the Acts community—Scripture-centered, Spirit-driven, Christ-exalting, mission-focused. Where persecution intensifies, the fivefold voice becomes clear and fearless. Where comfort numbs the West, the Spirit is stirring a hunger for something deeper than technique, strategy, or platform. The global Church, if we listen, is becoming our teacher again. She is showing us what it looks like to embody Christ's ministry in fullness, not fragmentation.

---

**The Fivefold Voice in the Globally Today**

While much of this volume necessarily draws from the written records and published sermons of Western preachers—from the fathers to the Reformers to the twentieth-century revivalists—the most dramatic contemporary expression of the fivefold preaching gift is now found in Africa, Latin America, and Asia, where the church is growing fastest.

In Lagos, Nigeria, and Nairobi, Kenya, thousands gather weekly under apostolic-prophetic leaders who combine bold proclamation, signs and wonders, and church-planting vision in a manner that echoes both Peter at Pentecost and Paul in Ephesus. In Bogotá, Colombia, César Castellanos and the G12 model have equipped tens of thousands of believers to preach the gospel house-to-house with evangelistic urgency and pastoral care. In Seoul, Korea, David Yonggi Cho (until his passing in 2021) oversaw the world's largest single congregation by raising up an army of lay preachers functioning in every ascension gift. Jackie Pullinger in Hong Kong has long demonstrated a prophetic-evangelistic voice that brings transformation to the marginalized through the simple, Spirit-anointed declaration of Jesus' name.

These examples are not exceptions; they are the new norm in the Global South. The same fivefold textures this book traces in Scripture and church history are now being lived out on a scale the Western church has rarely seen. As the gospel center of gravity shifts southward and eastward, the unified fivefold voice is proving itself not as a novel theory but as the ancient pattern by which the Spirit equips the church to disciple nations in a time of global shaking.

The witness of the Church, from Acts until now, declares one truth with unwavering clarity: Christ's ministry is the Church's ministry. The five streams do not remain in the past or in the pages of Scripture; they flow into the present. They flow into congregations, mission fields, seminaries, prayer rooms, house churches, refugee camps, revival tents, persecuted cell groups, and urban pulpits. Wherever the Church gathers in the name of Christ and opens the Scriptures, the fivefold voice rises again.

And it rises not from individuals alone but from the community. The Church is not a collection of fivefold celebrities. She is a body where Christ distributes His gifts, His voice, and His authority across His people. She is a preaching community. She is a prophetic fellowship. She is a priestly nation. She is an evangelizing people. She is an apostolic mission. In her, the witness of Christ becomes audible again to a world desperate for truth.

This is the witness we receive.

This is the witness we join.

This is the witness we must now become.

---

**The Call to the Preacher in the Final Hour**

If revelation discloses and witness confirms, then response demands obedience. Every movement of God culminates in understanding and in surrender, not only in insight but in incarnation. The fivefold voice of Christ, revealed in Scripture and witnessed across Church history, now presses itself upon the preacher of this present age. We stand not as spectators of a holy lineage but as heirs of a sacred trust. And in an hour as urgent as ours, the preacher cannot be casual with that trust.

The call upon the preacher today is the same that rested upon Moses when he approached the burning bush, upon Isaiah when he saw the Lord high and lifted up, upon Jeremiah when the word burned in his bones, upon John the Baptist crying in the wilderness, upon Peter trembling in the courtyard, upon Paul stunned on the Damascus road. Their ministries were varied, but their response was identical: Here I am. Speak. Send. Command. I will obey.

The preacher is called to embody Christ's voice with a faithfulness that transcends personality, gifting, preference, and cultural climate. This is not a call to perform but to be conformed—to Christ's life, Christ's character, Christ's Word, and Christ's Spirit. The preacher is not a professional communicator but a consecrated vessel, one in whom the five streams of Christ's ministry run like living water. Evangelicals have often emphasized the pastoral or teaching voice; Pentecostals have emphasized the prophetic or evangelistic voice; institutional traditions have emphasized the priestly or apostolic voice. But the Scriptures demand a response deeper than tradition: Christ must be proclaimed in His fullness.

This means the preacher cannot hide from the pastoral tenderness of Genesis. In an age of fragmentation, loneliness, anxiety, and relational collapse, the preacher is called to make visible the Shepherd who restores the soul. The pulpit cannot be a lectern of mere doctrine; it must be a place of divine nearness. It must embody the heart that leaves the ninety-nine for the one, that sees the unseen, lifts the fallen, and binds the brokenhearted. The preacher who neglects the pastoral stream may win arguments but will lose souls.

Nor may the preacher neglect the priestly stream of Exodus. The modern world is awash in spiritual confusion, doctrinal fog, and moral relativism. The preacher must become a teacher of the covenant once again—opening Scripture with clarity, precision, and reverence. Like Ezra, the preacher must read distinctly, give the sense, and cause the people to understand the Word. [20] Without priestly instruction, the Church becomes susceptible to every wind of doctrine, every cultural trend, every persuasive personality. The call to preach is a call to guard, a call to teach, a call to stand between the holy and the common and declare, "Thus saith the Word of the Lord."

Yet priestly clarity without prophetic fire becomes sterile. The preacher must also respond to the prophetic stream of Leviticus—the voice that speaks from the sanctuary, the voice that confronts sin, the voice that summons holiness, the voice that declares the Word of God with trembling authority. The prophetic preacher does not seek controversy, but neither does he fear it. He speaks not because he wishes to be heard but because he cannot remain silent. The holiness of God, the weight of His Word, the urgency of the hour compel him. Prophetic preaching is not spectacle; it is obedience. It is the echo of Christ's own voice—the voice that still says, "Repent, for the kingdom of heaven is at hand." [21] "This is how the Holy Scripture is applied to this situation."

And in this present age, the preacher must recover the evangelistic stream of Numbers—the call to a world wandering in its own wilderness. We are surrounded by people who are thirsty yet do not know what they thirst for; hungry yet unaware of the bread that satisfies; lost yet accustomed to being lost. The preacher is God's herald in the desert. Like John the Baptist, he prepares the way of the Lord. Like Philip, he runs toward the Ethiopian's chariot. Like Paul, he declares the unknown God to the searching Athenians. [22] Evangelistic preaching is not an optional specialty; it is the heartbeat of the apostolic Church.

Finally, the preacher must respond to the apostolic stream of Deuteronomy—the call to a sent life – the embodiment of the truths Christ preached. The Gospel is not a message we admire but a mission we inherit. Every preacher stands under the same word spoken in the Upper Room: "As My Father hath sent Me, even so send I you." The apostolic preacher does not build a personal kingdom; he advances the Kingdom of God. He does not preach to elevate himself; he preaches to commission a people. His ministry does not end in the pulpit; it flows outward into discipleship, mission, justice, reconciliation, and the global advance of Christ's reign.

This is the response demanded of the preacher in the final hour. The times are too urgent for truncated lethargic ministry. The world is too broken for half-measures. The Church is too vulnerable for partial obedience. The preacher must become, by grace, the embodiment of Christ's fivefold voice—a shepherd who guards, a priest who teaches, a prophet who declares, an evangelist who proclaims, and an apostle who sends.

But there is more. The preacher must lead the Church to become what she is: the one people filled with the fivefold voice of Christ. The preacher is not just called to preach; he is called to form a preaching or proclaiming people, to cultivate a community where the whole ministry of Christ is expressed—not through one leader but through the whole Body. The greatest danger of the modern pulpit is not error but reduction—reducing Christ to one stream, reducing preaching to one voice, reducing ministry to one role. The preacher must recover the courage to declare that the Church is called to more. She is called to fullness.

This response is not a burden but a grace. The same Spirit who anointed Christ, the same Spirit who descended at Pentecost, the same Spirit who raised the martyrs, the same Spirit who fueled the reformers, the same Spirit who ignited the awakenings, now rests upon the preacher today. Revival is not nostalgia; it is inheritance. And the preacher's response is not theoretical; it is incarnational.

This is the preacher's call in the final hour:

- To stand in the fivefold voice.
- To preach all of Christ.
- To shape the whole Church.
- To confront the whole darkness.
- To carry the whole Gospel.
- To speak with the voice of the One who sends- to the whole world.

The response has already begun.

Now the renewal must follow.

### The Global Commissioning of the Fivefold Preaching People

Renewal is the divine act whereby God restores His original intention in His people. It is never a nostalgia, nor a sentimental return to an idealized memory. Renewal is the Spirit's insistence that what God began, God will finish; what God promised, God will fulfill; what God revealed, God will empower. It is the moment when heaven bends low and breathes again upon the people of God. And in this final hour, the renewal God is bringing is nothing less than a restoration of the fivefold voice in one preaching people.

This renewal begins with Christ Himself. The Risen Lord, standing among His disciples in the Upper Room, does more than reassure them; He recreates them. "Peace be unto you: as My Father hath sent Me, even so send I you." In this one sentence, He binds His incarnation, crucifixion, resurrection, and mission into a single apostolic breath. He is not merely giving them a task; He is imparting His identity. His shepherding, His priesthood, His prophetic authority, His evangelistic proclamation, and His apostolic sending are now entrusted to a people who will bear His name to the nations.

Pentecost becomes the divine seal upon this commissioning. The same Spirit who overshadowed Mary, descended upon Jesus at the Jordan, drove Him into the wilderness, empowered His miracles, illuminated His teaching, raised Him from the dead, and filled His resurrected frame with new creation life—this same Spirit now rests upon the Church.[23] Pentecost is not a moment of ecstatic worship alone; it is the continuation of Christ's ministry in His people. It is the moment the Church becomes a preaching people—Scripture in their mouths, fire in their bones, mission in their steps.

And from that moment forward, renewal becomes the defining pattern of apostolic history. Wherever the Spirit moves, the fivefold voice rises anew. In the deserts of Egypt, the early ascetics became living sermons—priests in their intercession, prophets in their denunciation of sin, evangelists as seekers flocked to their caves, shepherds as they counseled the wounded, apostles as they birthed movements of holiness.[24] In the hills of Wales, a young Evan Roberts cried "Bend me!" and the Spirit raised a nation of preachers whose voices reached around the world.[25] In the fields of America during the First Great Awakening, George Whitefield thundered as a priest of the Word and a herald of new birth, and entire towns wept under the weight of glory.[26] In the Moravian prayer watch, prophetic intercession ignited global missions and launched an apostolic movement that would not cease for a hundred years.

Each renewal displays the same pattern:

- Scripture opened.
- Hearts pierced.
- Voices awakened.

**The Church becomes a Preaching People once again.**

What marks these revivals is not only fervor but fullness—a recovery of the whole Christ. They are not driven by a single stream but by the convergence of all five. Pastors become prophets. Teachers become evangelists. Intercessors become apostles to nations. Everyday believers become the fivefold voice in measure because Christ becomes all in all. Renewal is the return of divine fullness to a people who had grown accustomed to living on fragments.

This is the renewal God is now bringing to the global Church. In an hour of unprecedented upheaval, the Spirit is calling the Church not to retreat but to rise, not to survive but to proclaim, not to whisper but to thunder with the voice of Christ. The Church is being summoned to recover her preaching identity—not as an institution but as a Spirit-filled Body carrying the whole ministry of Jesus.

This renewal begins with the preacher. You cannot lead the Church where you have not gone. You cannot awaken fullness in your people while remaining content with fragments of Christ's voice. The Spirit is reanointing preachers in the last days to carry the fivefold streams in unity—to shepherd with tenderness, teach with truth, prophesy with fire, evangelize with urgency, and lead with apostolic courage.

But renewal does not stop with the preacher; it spreads through the Body. The Spirit is awakening congregations to become Scripture-saturated communities where every believer speaks with grace, truth, and anointing. Small groups begin to prophesy. Families become prayer altars. Worship gatherings turn into commissioning centers. Teenagers preach in schools. Retirees lead Bible studies in nursing homes. Business leaders speak the Gospel in boardrooms. Revival reveals that the Church is not waiting on a man or a moment; she is awakening to her identity as a people filled with the fivefold voice of Christ.

This global renewal is not theoretical; it is happening now. In Iran, former Muslims preach Christ in dreams and visions with prophetic clarity. In China, the underground Church teaches Scripture with priestly devotion and apostolic courage. In Nigeria and Brazil, evangelists are rising in stadiums and marketplaces. Across Africa, house churches shepherd communities with Genesis-like tenderness. In Southeast Asia, prophetic voices discern the times with Levitical precision. The global Church is becoming the teacher of the Western Church once again. And in the West, where noise and novelty have often overshadowed preaching, a quiet hunger is returning for the pure Word of God preached in the power of the Spirit.

This is not coincidental. It is eschatological. Revelation 14 speaks of an "everlasting Gospel" proclaimed to "every nation, and kindred, and tongue, and people." This is the fivefold voice in its eschatological fullness—the pastoral invitation of the Lamb, the priestly warning of judgment, the prophetic cry to worship the Creator, the evangelistic call to fear God, and the apostolic proclamation that the hour of His judgment has come. The end-time Church is not passive; she is proclaiming. She is not hiding; she is heralding. She is not fragmented; she is unified in voice.

Here, at last, the preacher stands at the threshold of divine summons. You have received the Torah's architecture, Christ's fullness, the Church's witness, and the call upon your own soul. The renewal now comes in the form of commissioning.

Hear the voice of Christ over you:

> "As My Father hath sent Me, even so send I you."

You are not sent in your strength but in His.

- Not in your authority but in His.
- Not in your limited gifting but in His fullness.

He sends you as a shepherd into wounded cities, as a priest into confused minds, as a prophet into deceptive cultures, as an evangelist into wandering multitudes, as an apostle into the nations.

He breathes upon you still.

He anoints you still. He speaks through you still.

And He forms around you a people who will preach with His voice.

This is the renewal of the last days—not a method, but a mantle; not a strategy, but a Spirit; not a trend, but a transformation. The Church becomes again what she was at the beginning: the one people filled with the fivefold voice of the one Christ.

And so this chapter reaches its holy crescendo—the commissioning of the global Church into the fullness of Christ's ministry. A new generation of preachers rises. A new season of proclamation dawns. The Spirit is calling, commanding, compelling:

Preach the Word.

Preach the Christ.

Preach with the fivefold voice.

Preach until He comes.

---

**Notes**
[1] Moshe Weinfeld, Deuteronomy 1–11, Anchor Bible 5 (New York: Doubleday, 1991), 336–340.
[2] Walter Brueggemann, The Prophetic Imagination, 2nd ed. (Minneapolis: Fortress Press, 2001), 77–82.
[3] Florentino García Martínez and Eibert J. C. Tigchelaar, eds., The Dead Sea Scrolls Study Edition (Leiden: Brill, 1997–1998), 1:353–355 (4Q175).
[4] Geza Vermes, The Complete Dead Sea Scrolls in English (London: Penguin, 1997), 103–110 (1QS).
[5] Raymond E. Brown, The Gospel According to John I–XII, AB 29 (New York: Doubleday, 1966), 11–14.
[6] N. T. Wright, Jesus and the Victory of God (Minneapolis: Fortress Press, 1996), 175–189.
[7] Michael Green, Evangelism in the Early Church, rev. ed. (Grand Rapids: Eerdmans, 2003), 41–51.
[8] Marianne Meye Thompson, The God of the Gospel of John (Grand Rapids: Eerdmans, 2001), 94–102.
[9] William L. Lane, Hebrews 1–8, WBC 47A (Dallas: Word, 1991), 101–108.
[10] Raymond E. Brown, The Gospel According to John I–XII, 5–6.
[11] R. T. France, The Gospel of Mark, NIGTC (Grand Rapids: Eerdmans, 2002), 89–95.
[12] F. F. Bruce, The Epistle to the Hebrews, rev. ed. (Grand Rapids: Eerdmans, 1990), 57–61.
[13] Ignatius of Antioch, Letter to the Magnesians 6; Irenaeus, Against Heresies 3.3.4.
[14] Craig S. Keener, Acts: An Exegetical Commentary, vol. 1 (Grand Rapids: Baker Academic, 2012), 889–897; Darrell L. Bock, Acts, BECNT (Grand Rapids: Baker Academic, 2007), 142–150.
[15] Michael Green, Evangelism in the Early Church, rev. ed. (Grand Rapids: Eerdmans, 2003), 55–66.
[16] Ignatius of Antioch, Letter to the Smyrnaeans 7.1.
[17] Irenaeus, Against Heresies 3.24.1.
[18] Didache 11–13; cf. Geza Vermes, The Complete Dead Sea Scrolls in English, 104–112 (1QS 3–4).
[19] F. Charles Fensham, The Books of Ezra and Nehemiah, NICOT (Grand Rapids: Eerdmans, 1982), 214–220.
[20] R. T. France, The Gospel of Matthew, NICNT (Grand Rapids: Eerdmans, 2007), 116–121.
[21] N. T. Wright, Acts for Everyone, Part One (Louisville: Westminster John Knox, 2008), 64–72.

[22] John 20:21–22; Gordon D. Fee, God's Empowering Presence (Peabody, MA: Hendrickson, 1994), 849–858.
[23] Derwas J. Chitty, The Desert a City (Crestwood, NY: St. Vladimir's Seminary Press, 1966), 45–59.
[24] Brynmor Pierce, The Welsh Revival of 1904 (London: Evangelical Press, 1971), 18–27.
[25] George Whitefield, Select Sermons (Wheaton, IL: Crossway, 2012), 14–22.
[26] The Moravian hundred-year prayer watch and its missionary impulse is widely attested; see, e.g., J. E. Hutton, History of the Moravian Church (London: Moravian Publication Office, 1909), Book IV.

# EPILOGUE: THE RHYTHM ENDURES

## PREACHING INTO ETERNITY

In the quiet aftermath of revelation, when the final amen echoes through a renewed assembly, the Fivefold Rhythm does not fade—it pulses onward into the eternal dawn. Imagine pulpits in the New Jerusalem, where Longing gives way to unhindered beholding, Revelation unfolds in the light of the Lamb, and Renewal becomes the everlasting song of the redeemed.

As glimpsed in the pattern's discovery. This is no mere method; it is the heartbeat of divine dialogue, etched in Torah's five books and fulfilled in Christ's apostolic fire. As end-time ministers, we stand at the threshold: the ache of Genesis calling us to shepherd souls, the unveiling of Exodus demanding faithful exposition, the herald of Leviticus sending us forth, the decision of Numbers pressing for repentance, and the transformation of Deuteronomy launching a people into mission.

Yet the rhythm extends beyond our hour- for we are all learning together. In 2050 and beyond, pray that preachers will adapt these phases to emerging cultures—digital witnesses, global cohorts—equipping saints amid tribulation's shadow. The fivefold gifts, awakened now, will mature the Bride for her Bridegroom.

Dear colleague, preach the rhythm. Let it renew your voice, unify your church, and herald the everlasting gospel. The final hour beckons—not with fear, but with fire.[1] "For the equipping of the saints... till we all come to the unity of the faith" (Eph 4:12–13, KJV).

With eyes attuned. Enter the rhythm unveiled.

---

**Notes**

[1] John Piper's emphasis on "expository exultation" in The Supremacy of God in Preaching (rev. ed., Baker, 2004) has profoundly shaped modern calls to passionate proclamation, inspiring the renewal urgency and fire in this rhythm.

# Appendix A

# THE CANONICAL ARCHITECTURE OF THE ASCENDED CHRIST

## How the Ascension Gifts Form the Church toward Maturity

*This appendix does not seek to act apologetically or isolate ministerial functions, but to demonstrate the canonical architecture by which the ascended Christ actively forms His Church toward maturity.*

---

**1. Exegetical Foundation: Ephesians 4:7–11 in Canonical Context**

Paul's description of the ascension gifts rests on a tightly woven theological argument. In Ephesians 4:7–11 he identifies three movements: grace given to each believer, Christ as the personal Giver, and the gifts themselves as consecrated persons. His use of the emphatic phrase αὐτὸς ἔδωκεν (autos edōken, "He himself gave") heightens this point. The force of the pronoun autos stresses Christ's direct agency, pointing not to delegated ecclesial authority but to the enthroned Lord distributing ministerial persons after His victory over the unseen powers. [1]

Paul roots this distribution in Psalm 68:18, which he adapts Christologically. In the original psalm, YHWH receives gifts as the triumphant Warrior-King ascending Zion. Paul reverses the direction—Christ gives gifts upon ascending above the heavens. [2] This exegetical move lies at the heart of Paul's argument: Jesus, as the true divine Warrior, receives the Spirit from the Father (Acts 2:33) and then bestows Spirit-shaped persons upon His Church. [3]

Paul's Psalm 68 citation functions as a canonical window into the ascension's distributive logic.

## 2. The Hebraic Substructure — נָתַן (nātan) as Covenant Bestowal

The Greek ἔδωκεν ("he gave") cannot be properly understood apart from its Hebrew background. Throughout Torah, the verb נָתַן (nātan) defines God's covenantal giving of people for the sake of His people. [4]

God gives the Levites to Aaron (Num 3:9),[5] gives Joshua to Israel as Moses' successor (Deut 31:14, 23),[6] gives prophets from the womb (Jer 1:5),[7] and gives His Spirit to the elders (Num 11:17).[8] The pattern is consistent: divine ministry is mediated through persons whom God gives, not only through abstract offices. Thus Paul's choice of ἔδωκεν - edoken in Ephesians 4:11 follows Torah's covenant grammar—Christ gives people to His Church in the same way YHWH gave Levites, prophets, and leaders to Israel.[9]

---

## 3. The Text States Persons, Not Roles (Grammatical Proof)

Ephesians 4:11 employs five articular plural nouns—apostles, prophets, evangelists, shepherds, and teachers—indicating persons rather than abstract functions. Paul does not speak of ministries (διακονίαι, diakoniai), operations (ἐνεργήματα, energēmata), services (λειτουργίαι, leitourgiai), or gifts (χαρίσματα, charismata), though such terms were readily available to him. [10] Instead, the grammar locates Christ's giving in people themselves, underscoring that ecclesial formation is mediated relationally and embodied personally.

This grammatical logic aligns with Paul's broader ecclesiology: the manifestation of the Spirit is given to each one (1 Cor 12:7), God appoints persons within the Church (1 Cor 12:28), and grace is distributed through individuals for the common good (Rom 12:4–8).[11] What Christ gives to His Church is not a set of transferable tasks, but consecrated persons through whom His own life and ministry are expressed for the building up of the Body.

Although these terms carry recognized functions within the early churches, Paul's syntax and exegesis emphasizes that Christ's giving is mediated through persons—so the question becomes not merely "what roles exist," but how Christ forms the Body through the people he gives.

This does not negate Paul's distinctions in 1 Corinthians 12; it highlights that in Ephesians 4 Christ's giving is expressed chiefly through ministerial persons for corporate formation.

---

## 4. The Five Graces Are Embodied — Rooted in Pauline Theology of "Christ in You"

Paul's theology consistently ties ministry to Christ's indwelling presence. The fivefold people are not independent ministerial archetypes but participations in Christ's own multifaceted ministry. Scripture presents Christ Himself as Apostle (Heb 3:1), Prophet (Deut 18:15; Luke 7:16), Evangelist (Luke 4:18–19), Shepherd (John 10:11), and Teacher (John 13:13). [12] The ascension gifts therefore represent the distribution of this unified Christological fullness across His Body.

These graces do not replicate Christ in fragments, but extend His singular life through diverse persons so that the Church may grow corporately into what He already is in fullness. Ministries are not external assignments but the outworking of Christ's own life through His people. As Paul declares, "Christ in you" is the hope of glory (Col 1:27), and the Spirit manifests Himself through diverse graces given to diverse persons (1 Cor 12:4–7). [13] This Christological grounding prevents the reduction of the fivefold to competencies or ecclesial titles; the gifts are Christ-formed persons.

---

## 5. Acts 2:33 — The Ascension Source of the Fivefold People

Peter's Pentecost sermon supplies the theological mechanism behind the ascension gifts: "Being exalted... and having received of the Father the promise of the Holy Ghost, he hath shed forth this which ye now see and hear" (Acts 2:33). This establishes a clear chain of divine action: the Father gives the Spirit to the Son at His enthronement, the Son pours out the Spirit upon the Church, the Spirit produces diverse graces, and Christ gives Spirit-shaped persons to the Body (Eph 4:11). [14]

Thus, Acts 2:33 supplies the theological source of the Church's Spirit-formed life; Ephesians 4 supplies the ecclesial shape and stated purpose.

Ascension thus produces Pentecost. The fivefold people do not originate in organizational innovation but in the ascended Christ's bestowal of His own Spirit-derived ministries. [15]

---

### 6. The Fivefold Pattern Reflects the Fivefold Structure of Torah

As demonstrated in Chapter 3, Torah reveals five streams of divine speech. [16] While not a rigid one-to-one allegory, the functional correspondence between Torah's fivefold divine speech and Christ's fivefold ministerial fullness is typologically profound and structurally deliberate. The value of the pattern lies not in strict equivalence, but in the consistent movement from divine speech to embodied formation—a movement Christ now carries forward through the Spirit for the maturation of His Church. [17]

| Book | Stream | Fulfillment in Christ | Corresponding Gift |
|---|---|---|---|
| Genesis | Pastoral longing | Christ the Shepherd | Pastors |
| Exodus | Priestly instruction | Christ the Teacher | Teachers |
| Leviticus | Prophetic revelation | Christ the Prophet | Prophets |
| Numbers | Evangelistic summons | Christ the Herald | Evangelists |

| | | | |
|---|---|---|---|
| Deuteronomy | Apostolic commissioning | Christ the Apostle | Apostles |

The fivefold therefore represents the continuation of Torah's divine architecture through the risen Christ distributing His own ministerial fullness to His Body. [18]

---

## 7. The Purpose of the Five Peoples: Ecclesial Formation and Maturity

Paul lists four goals in Ephesians 4:12–13: katartismos (equipping), ergon diakonias (the work of ministry), oikodomē tou sōmatos (the building up of the Body), and to plērōma tou Christou (the fullness of Christ). These are not individualistic aims but corporate formation goals. [19]

While Ephesians 2:20 identifies apostles and prophets as foundational for the Church's origin; Ephesians 4:11–16 addresses Christ's ongoing giving toward maturity—categories that must be distinguished and defined by the canon rather than collapsed. Any ongoing apostolic or prophetic ministry must be subordinated to Scripture's final authority and evaluated within the Church for edification, not treated as new canon - consistent with 1 Corinthians 13 – 14 and Pauline theological treatment.

Paul's logic is sequential: Christ gives people who shape a people until the whole people reflects the fullness of Christ. This is ecclesiology at its highest. The Church becomes what Christ is, through the people Christ gives.

# Canonical Verification Across the New Testament Witness

## Formative Sequence Generated by the Canonical Blueprint

The formative sequence traced in Chapter 3 does not arise from sermonic intuition or homiletical preference, but from the internal logic of the canonical blueprint itself. When divine revelation unfolds through Torah, is fulfilled in Christ, and is distributed by the Spirit, it consistently produces a recognizable pattern of formation within God's people. That pattern may be described as five interlocking movements:

1. Longing → Proclamation

    Divine speech addresses a real absence or hunger; God speaks into voids. He is never neutral.

2. Witness → Teaching

    God acts in history before He instructs; teaching interprets what has already been seen.

3. Embodiment (Prophetic Presence)

    God's indwelling presence reshapes life, making holiness visible within a people.

4. Public Testing and Reformation (Evangelistic Movement)

    Truth is carried into motion, where it confronts systems, loyalties, and resistance.

5. Renewal unto Commissioning (Apostolic Alignment)

    A people are re-addressed, remembered, and sent forward toward inheritance.

These movements are not independent stages but mutually reinforcing expressions of a single formative logic. Because this sequence is claimed to arise naturally from the canonical blueprint, it must be tested wherever the ascended Christ is seen forming His Church.

The following canonical verification therefore examines Acts, Galatians, Hebrews, and James to determine whether this same formative sequence appears across diverse apostolic witnesses and literary genres — not as imposed structure, but as the recurring outcome of Christ's ongoing work of formation.

### Acts — Revelation Proclaimed, Presence Embodied, Witness Released

Acts presents the formative architecture in motion. Revelation is proclaimed through apostolic witness, forming repentance and faith; sustained teaching establishes communal identity; embodied presence emerges through shared life and prayer; and public witness flows outward as the Church is commissioned and multiplied. [20] Pentecost is thus not an isolated experience but the ignition of an ongoing formative movement.[21]

### Galatians — Revelation Received, Formation Contested, Embodiment Restored

Galatians exposes a breakdown in the formative sequence. Having received revelation through the Spirit, the Galatians face distortion in formation through legal regression. Paul insists that Spirit-received revelation must produce Spirit-formed embodiment, expressed in freedom, love, and ethical fruit. [22] Restoration of formation restores mature communal life. [23]

### Hebrews — Revelation Fulfilled, Formation Advanced, Endurance Secured

Hebrews frames ecclesial life from the vantage of Christ's ascension and ongoing heavenly ministry. Revelation fulfilled in the Son presses the community toward deeper formation, warning against immaturity and stagnation while calling for embodied endurance. [24] Christ continues forming His people through disciplined perseverance until maturity is reached.[25]

**James — Revelation Heard, Embodiment Tested, Maturity Proven**

James verifies the architecture ethically. The implanted word demands embodied obedience; hearing without doing fractures formation. Trials and ethical consistency reveal maturity, confirming that ecclesial formation culminates in a community whose lived faith manifests completeness and wholeness. [26]

---

**The Canonical Architecture of Christ's Formative Work**

The following outline abstracts the architecture already demonstrated, presenting its irreducible structure for reference and instruction.

**I. Christological Initiation — Ascension and Divine Agency**

(Ephesians 4:7–11; Psalm 68:18; Acts 2:33)

1. Christ's ascension marks the transition from accomplished redemption to ongoing formation.

2. Authority and agency reside in the exalted Christ, not in ecclesial structures.

3. From His enthronement, Christ gives grace personally (autos edōken), distributing Himself through consecrated persons.

4. The giving of persons is the means by which Christ remains actively present and operative within His Church.

Architectural Principle:

Formation begins with Christ's action, not human initiative.

## II. Covenantal Mediation — God Forms a People Through Given Persons

(Torah: נָתַן / nātan; 1 Corinthians 12; Romans 12)

1. Divine ministry is mediated covenantally through people whom God gives.

2. Ministry is relational and embodied, not abstract or procedural.

3. The giving of persons establishes continuity between Torah's covenant logic and Christ's ecclesial work.

4. Authority flows from divine commissioning, not institutional designation.

Architectural Principle:

God forms His people through people He gives, not through detached functions.

---

## III. Embodied Participation — Christ's Life Distributed Through the Body

(Colossians 1:27; 1 Corinthians 12:4–7; Hebrews 3:1)

1. Ministry arises from participation in Christ's indwelling life.

2. The ascension gifts are participations in Christ's singular ministry.

3. Diversity of persons reflects Christ's fullness, not fragmentation.

4. The Church becomes the site of Christ's embodied ministry.

Architectural Principle:

Christ forms His Body by sharing His own life.

---

## IV. Formative Sequence — From Revelation to Maturity

(Torah Pattern; Ephesians 4:12–16)

1. Divine revelation initiates transformation.

2. Instruction orders redeemed life.

3. Presence is embodied communally.

4. Witness emerges publicly.

5. Renewal sustains covenant faithfulness.

Architectural Principle:

Formation follows a divinely ordered progression.

---

## V. Ecclesial Telos — Corporate Maturity in the Fullness of Christ
(Ephesians 4:13; Hebrews 6:1; James 1:22–25)

1. The goal of ministry is maturity, not efficiency.

2. Maturity is corporate, not competitive.

3. Christ's fullness is expressed through a people formed together.

4. Stability, discernment, love, and endurance mark maturity.

Architectural Principle:
The purpose of ministry is a mature people – in Christ's image.

---

## VI. Canonical Verification — Consistent Witness Across the New Testament

(Acts, Galatians, Hebrews, James)

1. Acts narrates formation.

2. Galatians guards against regression.

3. Hebrews presses toward endurance.

4. James confirms ethical embodiment.

Architectural Principle:
The architecture is canonical.

---

## VII. Eschatological Continuity — Formation Until Consummation

(Ephesians 4:13; Matthew 28:18–20)

1. Christ continues forming His Church until maturity is complete.

2. The ascension gifts remain operative while formation continues.

3. The Church lives between ascension and consummation.

Architectural Principle:

Formation continues until Christ's fullness is manifested.

---

**Theological Summary**

The ascension gifts of Ephesians 4:11 must be understood within the canonical pattern of God's covenantal giving (nātan), the Christological fulfillment of Psalm 68, and the Pentecostal outpouring of Acts 2:33. In this framework, the gifts are not abstract roles but consecrated persons—embodiments of Christ's own pastoral, priestly, prophetic, evangelistic, and apostolic life. Rooted in Torah's fivefold structure and manifested through the Spirit's diverse graces, these five peoples exist to form the Church into the fullness of Christ, completing the trajectory from Torah → Christ → Spirit → Church.

Historical forms of ministry have varied, but Paul's stated purpose within the canon is equipping the saints and building the Body toward maturity—that still remains the governing criterion by which any historical or current form must be evaluated.

---

**Notes**

1. Frank Thielman, Ephesians (BECNT; Grand Rapids: Baker Academic, 2010), 270–74.

2. Darrell L. Bock, Ephesians (PNTC; Grand Rapids: Eerdmans, 2019), 149–54.

3. Craig S. Keener, Acts: An Exegetical Commentary, vol. 1 (Grand Rapids: Baker Academic, 2012), 791–96.

4. Brevard S. Childs, Biblical Theology in Crisis (Philadelphia: Westminster, 1970), 51–54.

5. Dennis T. Olson, Numbers (Interpretation; Louisville: Westminster John Knox, 1996), 23–27.

6. Jeffrey H. Tigay, Deuteronomy (JPS Torah Commentary; Philadelphia: Jewish Publication Society, 1996), 509.

7. J. A. Thompson, The Book of Jeremiah (NICOT; Grand Rapids: Eerdmans, 1980), 146.

8. Jacob Milgrom, Leviticus 1–16 (AB 3; New York: Doubleday, 1991), 102–4.

9. Gordon D. Fee, God's Empowering Presence (Peabody, MA: Hendrickson, 1994), 170–75.

10. William D. Mounce, Pastoral Epistles (WBC 46; Nashville: Thomas Nelson, 2000), 36–40.
11. Anthony C. Thiselton, The First Epistle to the Corinthians (NIGTC; Grand Rapids: Eerdmans, 2000), 930–40.
12. Harold W. Attridge, The Epistle to the Hebrews (Hermeneia; Philadelphia: Fortress, 1989), 39–45.
13. Gordon J. Wenham, The Book of Leviticus (NICOT; Grand Rapids: Eerdmans, 1979), xiii–xviii.
14. Eckhard J. Schnabel, Early Christian Mission (Downers Grove, IL: IVP Academic, 2004), 678–84.
15. Douglas J. Moo, The Letter of James (PNTC; Grand Rapids: Eerdmans, 2000), 94–101.
16. Gordon J. Wenham, The Book of Leviticus (NICOT; Grand Rapids: Eerdmans, 1979), xiii–xviii; idem, Exploring the Old Testament: A Guide to the Pentateuch (Downers Grove, IL: IVP Academic, 2003), 1–28. Wenham identifies Torah as a unified, five-book literary and theological composition whose structure reflects distinct modes of divine speech and formation rather than a random anthology.
17. Brevard S. Childs, Biblical Theology of the Old and New Testaments: Theological Reflection on the Christian Bible (Minneapolis: Fortress, 1992), 70–92. Childs argues that canonical shape generates theological meaning through sequence and placement, allowing typological correspondence without collapsing historical distinction.
18. Peter J. Gentry and Stephen J. Wellum, Kingdom through Covenant: A Biblical-Theological Understanding of the Covenants (2nd ed.; Wheaton, IL: Crossway, 2018), 77–110. Gentry and Wellum demonstrate how covenantal patterns established in Torah are taken up, transformed, and extended christologically rather than annulled.
19. Frank Thielman, Ephesians (BECNT; Grand Rapids: Baker Academic, 2010), 287–305. Thielman emphasizes that Ephesians 4:12–13 frames ministry gifts toward corporate maturity (teleiotēs), not individual function or institutional hierarchy.
20. Craig S. Keener, Acts: An Exegetical Commentary, vol. 1 (Grand Rapids: Baker Academic, 2012), 800–845. Keener reads Acts as narrating the Spirit's role in constituting a disciplined, ordered, and outward-moving ecclesial community rather than episodic charismatic experience.
21. Eckhard J. Schnabel, Early Christian Mission, vol. 1 (Downers Grove, IL: IVP Academic, 2004), 678–704. Schnabel situates Pentecost as the inauguration of sustained missionary and formative movement rather than a singular ecstatic event.
22. Douglas J. Moo, Galatians (BECNT; Grand Rapids: Baker Academic, 2013), 247–302. Moo shows that Paul's concern in Galatians is not merely doctrinal error but deformation of Spirit-generated life through regression to law-defined identity.
23. Gordon D. Fee, God's Empowering Presence: The Holy Spirit in the Letters of Paul (Peabody, MA: Hendrickson, 1994), 383–412. Fee argues that ethical

embodiment and communal life are the primary evidence of Spirit-led formation in Pauline theology.
24. Harold W. Attridge, The Epistle to the Hebrews (Hermeneia; Philadelphia: Fortress, 1989), 39–72. Attridge frames Hebrews as an exhortation grounded in Christ's ascension and continuing priestly activity, pressing the community toward maturity through endurance.
25. William L. Lane, Hebrews 1–8 (WBC 47A; Dallas: Word, 1991), lxxv–xci. Lane emphasizes that Hebrews' repeated calls to "press on" (pherōmetha) reflect a theology of ongoing formation rather than static possession of truth.
26. Douglas J. Moo, The Letter of James (PNTC; Grand Rapids: Eerdmans, 2000), 88–116; Peter H. Davids, The Epistle of James (NIGTC; Grand Rapids: Eerdmans, 1982), 72–98. Both argue that James defines maturity (teleios) as embodied obedience, where hearing the word is completed through faithful action

# APPENDIX B

# IMPLEMENTING THE FIVEFOLD VOICE:

### A Pastoral Practice Workbook for Preachers & Churches

There comes a moment after revelation when the preacher asks the question that always follows understanding: How then shall we live this out? The theology of the fivefold voice is more than a doctrinal insight; it is an invitation to practice—an invitation to shape congregations that hear the whole Christ through the whole Church. This appendix is written to help you shepherd that process.

Use it slowly.

Use it prayerfully.

Use it with your team.

Use it as a year-long formation guide.

Use it as a workbook in your preaching cohort, seminary classroom, or leadership retreat.

Let this become the beginning of a journey where your congregation learns to breathe with Christ's own rhythm.

*("This guide is adaptable to denominational, cultural, and educational contexts.")*

## 1. Entering the Journey: A Pastoral Introduction

Implementation begins not with technique but with tenderness. The fivefold voice can shape a congregation only when it first shapes the preacher. Before training others, pause and pray:

"Lord Jesus, teach me to speak with Your voice.
Shepherd me.
Instruct me.
Purify me.
Send me.
Make me a vessel of Your fivefold grace."

Every exercise in this workbook begins here—with consecration.

The rest flows naturally.

---

## 2. The Fivefold Preacher Self-Assessment

A preacher cannot cultivate what he does not see. This assessment is not a grading tool but a mirror—an opportunity for prayerful awareness.

Reflect on qeach stream:

### The Shepherding Voice (Genesis)

- Do my sermons create refuge for the weary?

- Are the broken seen, named, and invited into healing?

- Do I shepherd people through the Word, or just instruct them?

-

### The Priestly-Teaching Voice (Exodus)

- Is Scripture central, clear, and rightly divided?
- Do I "give the sense" so the people may understand (Neh 8)?
- Do I guard doctrine with love, wisdom, and courage?

### The Prophetic Voice (Leviticus)

- Do I preach what God is saying, not just what people expect to hear?
- Does holiness tremble through the sermon?
- Do I speak truth with both severity and tenderness?

### The Evangelistic Voice (Numbers)

- Does my preaching call for decision?
- Are sinners invited to repentance and faith?
- Is the Gospel explicitly proclaimed?

### The Apostolic Voice (Deuteronomy)

- Do I send people? Commission them?
- Does the church move outward because of the Word?
- Do sermons produce disciples, missionaries, witnesses, laborers?

Journal your reflections. Do not rush. Let the Spirit reveal.

## 3. Forming a Fivefold Preaching Team

Every congregation needs a preaching community, not a preaching celebrity.

This workbook leads you to form a team that embodies the fivefold voice together:

- A shepherd-hearted member
- A teacher with covenant depth
- A prophetic discerner
- A Gospel-reaching evangelistic voice
- A visionary apostolic guide

You are not forming a hierarchy. You are forming a harmony.

Meet monthly.

Pray together.

Discern sermons together.

Evaluate preaching through the fivefold lens.

Share areas of growth.

Celebrate one another's anointings.

In time, your pulpit will carry the sound of many voices—but one Christ.

## 4. Building a Fivefold Preaching Calendar

A church that hears only one voice grows lopsided.

A church that hears all five grows mature.

Design a preaching calendar that alternates emphasis:

- A pastoral series on restoration

- A teaching series through a biblical book

- A prophetic series calling to repentance and holiness

- An evangelistic series oriented toward outreach

- An apostolic series equipping for mission

Over twelve months, ensure that all five streams are represented.

This is not rigid scheduling; it is spiritual formation.

---

## 5. Fivefold Sermon Crafting Exercises

Here are five exercises that reshape your sermon-writing habits:

### Exercise 1 — Shepherding Lens

Re-write your sermon introduction to speak to wounds, fears, loneliness, and longing.

### Exercise 2 — Priestly Lens

Identify the covenant truth your sermon must guard.

Ask, "What doctrine is being preserved or clarified here?"

**Exercise 3 — Prophetic Lens**

Ask God: "What are You saying to this people in this moment?"

Add one Spirit-formed sentence that confronts or awakens.

**Exercise 4 — Evangelistic Lens**

Insert an unmistakable call to repentance and faith.

Every sermon should invite someone home.

**Exercise 5 — Apostolic Lens**

Add a sending moment.

Where must the church go?

What must they do?

Whom must they reach?

When all five lenses converge, the sermon carries Christ's fullness.

---

**6. Prayer Rhythms for the Fivefold Preacher**

Prayer transforms preaching more than skill.

Here is a weekly rhythm:

- Monday — Genesis Prayer: "Shepherd my heart so I may shepherd others."

- Tuesday — Exodus Prayer: "Open my understanding in Your law."

- Wednesday — Leviticus Prayer: "Sanctify my lips; let Your fire purify my voice."

- Thursday — Numbers Prayer: "Give me Your evangelistic burden for the lost."

- Friday — Deuteronomy Prayer: "Send me; send us; send workers into Your harvest."

On Saturday and Sunday, pray:

"Let the fivefold voice of Christ be heard."

---

### 7. Forming a Fivefold Congregation

A fivefold preacher must cultivate a fivefold church.

**Shepherding culture**

Hospitality. Compassion. Healing rooms.

Small groups that carry burdens together.

**Priestly-teaching culture**

Bible reading plans.

Hermeneutics workshops.

Family discipleship rhythms.

**Prophetic culture**

Listening prayer nights.

Scripture-based discernment.

Training in holy obedience.

**Evangelistic culture**

Testimony Sundays.

Community outreaches.

Gospel-centered children's ministry.

**Apostolic culture**

Missions partnerships.

Local justice initiatives.

Church planting pipelines.

Discipleship pathways.

A church that practices all five becomes spiritually balanced, missional, and mature.

---

## 8. Monthly & Annual Implementation Plan

Here is a sustainable rhythm:

Every Month

- Meet with your fivefold preaching team

- Evaluate sermons through the five streams
- Discern pastoral needs affecting upcoming preaching
- Pray for prophetic clarity
- Review evangelistic fruit
- Identify apostolic opportunities

Every Quarter

- Conduct a "fivefold pulse check" on the congregation
- Rotate teaching emphases
- Lead prayer & fasting gatherings
- Train new leaders in one of the five streams

Every Year

- Teach the fivefold voice to the entire church
- Hold a commissioning service for new preachers
- Launch a mission initiative
- Disciple the next generation in Scripture and Spirit

This rhythm helps your church grow into the fullness of Christ.

## 9. Reflection Questions for Leaders & Teams

1. Where is our church strongest in the fivefold voice?
2. Where are we thinnest?
3. Which stream do we avoid unintentionally?
4. Which stream does our city or region need most?
5. How can our preaching calendar reflect the whole Christ?
6. Who is being raised up as a new voice in our congregation?
7. How do we measure spiritual maturity beyond attendance?

Journal. Pray. Discern.

Use these questions quarterly with your leadership team.

---

## 10. Leader's Guide for Preaching Cohorts & Seminary Courses

This appendix can function as a 12-week cohort guide:

Week 1–2: Understanding the Fivefold Blueprint

Week 3–4: Shepherding and Priestly Preaching

Week 5–6: Prophetic and Evangelistic Preaching

Week 7–8: Apostolic Preaching

Week 9: Building a Fivefold Sermon

Week 10: Fivefold Team Dynamics

Week 11: Preaching Labs

Week 12: Commissioning Service

Assign students or pastors to preach a sermon reflecting all five streams. Offer feedback through the fivefold lens.

This method changes ministries, not just sermons.

---

**Closing Word for the Workbook**

This appendix is not the end of your journey but the beginning of your implementation. Let it guide your hands as the book has guided your heart. Let the fivefold voice become more than a concept—let it become the pulse of your preaching, the breath of your ministry, and the rhythm of your congregation.

Christ is forming a fivefold preaching people.

Now, by His Spirit, form them.

---

# A CONCEPTUAL GUIDE TO KEY THEOLOGICAL TERMS IN THIS BOOK

**How Words Function Theologically, Not Only What They Mean**

**Introduction**

This conceptual guide is intended to be read in direct conversation with Appendix C, which serves as the master lexical and theological reference for this volume. While Appendix C provides careful treatment of key terms—such as meaning, grammatical orientation, and biblical context—this guide focuses on how those terms function together within the theological argument of the book. Readers are encouraged to consult Appendix C when clarity on a word is required, and this guide when seeking to understand how those words shape proclamation, theology, and ministry as a unified whole. Read together, Appendix C and this guide are designed to train both precision of language and faithfulness of interpretation.

**1. Word, Spirit, and Proclamation Belong Together**

One of the governing convictions of this book is that divine speech and divine presence are never separated in Scripture. God speaks, the Spirit acts, and a response is summoned. Proclamation does not originate in human initiative, insight, or rhetorical skill, but in God's self-disclosure.

Throughout this study, preaching is understood to occur where God speaks and the Spirit accompanies that speech, producing encounter rather than mere information transfer. Readers should therefore assume that discussions of proclamation presume divine initiative, Spirit-generated authority, and relational purpose rather than technique-driven delivery.

## 2. Preaching Is Christ-Centered Redemptive Proclamation

In this book, preaching does not function as a broad or generic category. It is not equivalent to instruction, moral exhortation, motivational discourse, or religious public speaking. Preaching is understood as Christ-centered redemptive proclamation—the public announcing of what God has accomplished in Jesus Christ.

When the book speaks of preaching, it presupposes the proclamation of the gospel events: Christ's death, resurrection, exaltation, and reigning lordship. Teaching plays an essential role in forming obedience, but it follows proclamation rather than replacing it. This distinction preserves the primacy of gospel announcement within the life of the church.

---

## 3. Authority and Power Are Distinct but United

Scripture maintains a careful distinction between authority and power, a distinction this book preserves. Authority refers to delegated right rooted in Christ's lordship; power refers to divine enabling that accompanies obedience. Neither originates in personality, position, platform, or charisma.

Authority is received before it is exercised. Power is given rather than generated. Together, they operate only under submission to Christ. This framework guards against authoritarian leadership models on one hand and personality-driven ministry on the other, grounding proclamation in obedience rather than influence.

---

## 4. Kingdom Language Refers to God's Reign, Not Religious Space

When the book speaks of the Kingdom, it does not refer primarily to institutional structures, physical realms, internal experience, or political programs. Kingdom language refers to God's active reign, decisively revealed in Jesus Christ and made known through proclamation.

The Kingdom advances through faithful witness and obedient response rather than coercion or control. This understanding preserves the

Kingdom's eschatological horizon while grounding it in present obedience, preventing both triumphalism and abstraction.

---

### 5. Covenant Frames Proclamation and Response

All proclamation in Scripture occurs within the context of covenantal relationship. God speaks because He has bound Himself to a people; God summons response because relationship is at stake.

This covenantal framework ensures that repentance is relational rather than merely emotional, obedience is restorative rather than legalistic, and proclamation aims at renewal rather than pressure. Readers should therefore understand calls to repentance and faith as covenant renewal rather than isolated religious acts.

---

### 6. Hearing Implies Response, Not Passive Reception

In biblical theology, hearing is never neutral. To hear is to respond; to hear rightly is to obey. Failure to respond is failure to hear.

This understanding shapes the book's approach to proclamation. Sermons are not only evaluated by clarity or reception, nor are listeners treated as detached observers. Proclamation seeks alignment with God's word, calling forth faithful response rather than passive understanding.

---

### 7. Glory Signals Weight and Consequence

Modern usage often treats glory as spectacle or atmosphere. Scripture treats glory as weight, significance, and consequence. Where God's glory is present, neutrality disappears.

In this book, glory refers to the moral and communal gravity of God's presence. Proclamation, therefore, carries consequence: it confronts, shapes conscience, and produces reverence. This preserves sobriety and accountability within preaching and worship.

## 8. Ministry Roles Are Functional, Not Hierarchical

When the book speaks of apostles, teachers, pastors, and evangelists, it does not construct hierarchies of value or power. Ministry roles are understood functionally—as forms of service given for the sake of proclamation and equipping.

No role exists independently of fidelity to the gospel. Authority within ministry flows from faithful representation of Christ rather than institutional elevation. This framework resists both clerical dominance and role competition.

### Ecclesial Formation (Ephesians 4:12–13)

A Pauline framework describing the purpose and outcome of Christ's ascension gifts (apostles, prophets, evangelists, pastors, and teachers) for the maturation of the Church.

This formation unfolds through four interrelated movements:

- *Katartismós* — the equipping, mending, and restoring of the saints. The term carries medical and nautical imagery, denoting the setting of broken bones and refitting vessels for service. In ecclesial formation, this refers to the restoration of believers into wholeness and readiness for covenant participation, not just functional training.

- *Érgon diakonías* — the shared work of ministry entrusted to the whole Body, emphasizing participation over professionalization. It is ministry distributed among the saints, each functioning according to the grace they receive. The Church grows as ministry becomes fully representative of Christ's body.

- *Oikodomḗ tou sṓmatos* — the progressive building up of the Church as a living organism. This growth is relational, organic, and ordered, emphasizing unity, stability, harmony, and nourishment rather than numerical expression alone.

- *Tò plḗrōma tou Christou* — the intended fullness of Christ, expressed corporately as His life, character, and authority are embodied in a mature people. The goal of ecclesial formation is not uniform perfection but the visible embodiment of Christ's life, character, and authority in a mature, unified people.

This framework resists clerical reductionism and professionalized ministry models, emphasizing formation, unity, and maturity through distributed grace, Spirit-given gifts, and shared responsibility within the Body of Christ.

---

**9. Reading This Book Well**

Readers are encouraged to move deliberately between this guide and Appendix C. Appendix C should be consulted whenever precision of meaning is required; this guide should be revisited whenever conceptual clarity or theological orientation is needed.

Terms in this book are not obstacles to master but tools given to serve faithful proclamation. Precision of language supports obedience; clarity of theology serves the church.

---

**Final Encouragement**

These terms are offered not to complicate preaching, but to safeguard it. Let the language of Scripture shape your thinking, let theology clarify your practice, and let proclamation remain centered on Christ.

# The Ministry of Preaching: A Formative Movement

How Scripture's Formative Arc Shapes Faithful Sermon Development Praxis

*(The pattern described here reflects recognition of God's work, not a required sequence.)*

The canonical rhythm defined in this book is the theological blueprint for God's communication. The purpose of this appendix is to finalize the central task of this work: to show precisely how the ministry of preaching aligns with the eternal ministry of the Word of God to us by translating the five divine movements into five practical discernment questions at the end of this appendix.

---

### 1. Preaching Development Is Discovered, Not Invented

Before learning how to build a sermon, students must understand what a biblical preaching pattern actually is. God's primary concern is not first what you say to people, but what He is forming in you. The preacher must become the message before proclaiming it. A faithful preaching pattern, therefore, is not a technique imposed upon a text, nor a template mechanically repeated. It is the recognition of how God Himself consistently works throughout Scripture.

Across the biblical witness, the movement is clear: God reveals, God forms, God dwells among His people, God sends them, and God renews them. Preaching that follows this pattern does not attempt to manufacture outcomes or control results. Instead, it participates in God's already-established way of shaping a people through His Word.

---

### 2. Where Every Sermon Must Begin: Proclamation

Sermon development does not begin with outlines, illustrations, or applications. It begins with discernment. The preacher must first ask:

**What has God done, revealed, or declared in this text that must be announced as good news?**

This is the proclamatory core of the sermon—Christ-centered redemptive proclamation (kērygma). Until this announcement is clear, the sermon is not ready to move forward.

If proclamation is unclear:

- teaching loses authority,

- application becomes moralistic, and

- the sermon feels informative but thin.

Students should be taught to slow down here and not rush prematurely into explanation.

---

### 3. Teaching Serves Proclamation, Not the Other Way Around

Once proclamation is clearly discerned, teaching can take its rightful place. Teaching exists to serve proclamation, not to replace it. It forms obedience, clarifies meaning, guards against misunderstanding, and helps the church live faithfully within what has been declared.

Preachers should never decide what to teach before they know what must be proclaimed. When instruction precedes proclamation, sermons risk becoming explanatory without gospel authority, and Christ becomes a subject rather than the reigning Lord.

Teaching is essential—but it is derivative.

---

### 4. Embodiment as the True Measure of Response

Biblical response is never just emotional reaction or verbal agreement. True response is embodiment. Hearing that does not lead to lived obedience is not hearing in the biblical sense.

The preacher must therefore ask:

> **If this proclamation is truly received, who will this people begin to become?**

Embodiment moves the sermon beyond vague application or behavioral checklists into visible, communal alignment with God's Word. Here theology takes flesh, and the church begins to live what it has heard.

---

## 5. Consummation Becomes Commissioning

Where proclamation has been announced, teaching received, and embodiment begun, the Word of God reaches its intended completion. This consummation is not only conclusion—it is release and fulfilment in each generation.

The people are now ready to be sent. Alignment produces movement. Faithfulness produces fruitfulness. What has been formed inwardly is entrusted outwardly.

Consummation therefore gives rise to commissioning rather than closure.

---

## 6. Renewal and Revival as Fruit, Not Strategy

Renewal and revival are not manufactured by emotional intensity or strategic manipulation. They emerge naturally where the Word of God has been faithfully proclaimed, embodied, and released.

Students must learn this clearly:

> **Revival cannot be preached into existence, but faithful proclamation can create the conditions in which renewal emerges.**

This understanding protects both preacher and congregation from pressure-driven ministry and keeps revival rooted in covenant faithfulness rather than technique.

---

## 7. The Pattern, Held Without Reduction

Students may find it helpful to hold this movement in mind:

1. Proclamation – God's redemptive action in Christ is announced

2. Teaching – obedience and understanding are formed

3. Embodiment – the people become what they have heard

4. Consummation / Commissioning – the Word is released through a renewed people

5. Renewal / Revival – life flows outward in faithful witness

This is not a checklist. It is a way of discerning how God shapes His people through the Word.

---

### 8. Learning This Pattern Takes Time

Faithful preaching is formed slowly. Students should resist impatience and performance pressure in sermon preparation. Discernment matures through prayer, attentiveness to the text, submission to God's initiative, and patience with the formation process.

Preaching deepens as discernment deepens—not as formulas accumulate.

---

Together, these form a pedagogical staircase:

concept → pattern → precision → application

---

Here we see the entire concept coming alive within the text itself, again, not as a pattern but God is dealing with His people.

### 1. Lived Out in Scripture (The Pattern Before the Pattern)

### A. Acts 2 — A People Formed, Not Just Stirred

- **Proclamation**

  Peter announces what God has done in Christ (resurrection + lordship).

- **Teaching –**

  They devote themselves to the apostles' doctrine.

- **Embodiment –**

  They share life, possessions, prayers, and table fellowship.

- **Commissioning:**

  They bear public witness daily.

- **Renewal:**

  "The Lord added to the church daily."

Notice:

No revival meeting. No strategy. No chase.

Transformation arose because the Word was received and lived.

---

## B. Sinai to Tabernacle (Exodus–Leviticus)

- God declares redemption ("I brought you out")

- God teaches His ways

- God dwells among them

- God orders them for witness

- God renews covenant relation

A people are formed by presence, not spectacle.

---

## 2. Lived Out in the Early Church (History, Not Idealism)

### A. Catechumenate (2nd–4th Century Church)

Before quick decisions existed, the church assumed:

- proclamation belonged in worship

- teaching unfolded over time

- obedience preceded baptism

- identity came before mission

People weren't rushed into activity.

They were formed into Christ.

That is your rhythm—historically embodied.

---

### B. Monastic & Pastoral Renewal Movements

Wherever the Church returned to:

- hearing Scripture daily

- embodying prayer and obedience

- resisting performance

...renewal followed quietly.

Revival didn't begin with crowds.

It began with re-ordered lives.

---

## 3. Lived Out in a Local Church (Non-Idealized)

This rhythm shows up wherever ministry looks like this:

- Sermons announce Christ, not themes

- Teaching unfolds patiently, not hurriedly

- Leaders ask: "Who are we becoming?"

- People respond by changing habits, not just schedules

- Witness emerges naturally, not by recruitment

You see:

- more repentance than programming

- less manipulation

- deeper stability

- slower, truer growth

That's transformation at the level of people, not boosting church attendance.

---

### 4. Lived Out in the Preacher (This Is Crucial)

The rhythm must be inhabited before it is transmitted.

In the preacher's life:

- revelation precedes preparation

- teaching flows from submission

- obedience shapes authority

- sending emerges from faithfulness

- renewal sustains calling

A preacher who lives these principles 1) doesn't burn out quickly 2) doesn't chase validation 3) doesn't confuse fruit with faithfulness

That is how this transforms ministry, not just sermons.

---

### 5. A Simple, Honest Illustration for Students

You might say it this way.

> When preaching truly forms a people, you don't notice it first in crowds or excitement. You notice it in how people pray, forgive, give, endure suffering, and remain faithful over time. Renewal isn't loud at first. It's deep.

That's honest. And it is true.

---

**6. Why This Matters (Final Framing)**

Transformation happens where this rhythm is lived because:

- God is allowed to speak first

- people are allowed to grow slowly

- obedience is valued over immediacy

- lives are changed at the level of identity

This is exactly how Scripture forms a people.

---

**Final Quiet Conclusion**

You don't need to prove this concept works. You only need to live it faithfully.

Wherever this rhythm is honored—in Scripture, in history, in churches, in preachers—a people become a living organism mirroring the life of Jesus. This is renewal and this is revival.

Here's the pattern in its final, disciplined form:

1. **Text Received-**

    The preacher discerns God's action and redemptive intent.

2. **Proclamation Announced (kērygma)**

    Christ-centered redemptive truth is declared.

3. **Teaching Formed (didachē)**

   Understanding and obedience are shaped by the announcement.

4. **Embodiment Envisioned**

   The people are called to become what has been declared.

5. **Consummation / Commissioning Released**

   Renewal flows outward, and revival takes shape as the Word accomplishes its purpose.

---

# Five Discernment Questions of the Formative Preaching Movement

As we live out the five-fold concept this out practically here are formative questions that must be asked at every phase of the development process to communicate God's truth.

### 1. Proclamation (Discernment Initiates)

Listening before speaking – You must hear God before you speak to men.

- What is God declaring in this text before I attempt to explain it?

- What has God done here that must be announced as good news?

- Where is Christ acting in this passage—not as example, but as redemptive Lord?

- What would be missing if this sermon explained the text accurately but failed to proclaim it?

- What truth in this passage carries authority because God speaks, not because I can argue it?

---

## 2. Teaching (Formation Follows Proclamation)

Shaping obedience in the light of what has been declared

- What understanding must be formed because this proclamation is true?

- How does this instruction serve the announcement rather than replace it?

- What false assumptions, distortions, or confusions must be corrected for obedience to grow?

- How does this teaching help the people live inside the proclaimed reality?

- In what ways does this instruction protect the church from reducing the gospel to information?

---

## 3. Embodiment (Hearing as Obedience)

The Word taking flesh in God's people

- If this Word were truly received, who would this people begin to become?

- What patterns of life would naturally change if this proclamation took root?

- How does this call obedience without reducing discipleship to technique or performance?

- What would it look like for this truth to be embodied corporately, not just individually?

- Where is God inviting visible faithfulness rather than verbal agreement?

---

## 4. Consummation / Commissioning (Release Rather Than Control)

Letting the Word complete its work

- Has the Word been allowed to finish what God intended it to do in this gathering?

- Where is the Spirit inviting release rather than reinforcement or pressure?

- What obedience, witness, or faithfulness is being entrusted to the people beyond this moment?

- How does this sending arise naturally from alignment, not from urgency?

- What does faithfulness look like once the sermon is no longer being heard?

---

## 5. Renewal / Revival (Fruit, Not Strategy)

Life emerging where faithfulness is lived

- What forms of renewal might appear quietly rather than immediately?

- How is fruit evaluated here by obedience and perseverance, not reaction?

- Where might God be restoring attentiveness, courage, or love over time?

- How might life now flow outward from this Word into homes, work, and witness?

- Am I trusting God to bring renewal in His time rather than attempting to produce it?

---

## The Final Governing Question for the Preacher

> "Am I attempting to produce an outcome, or am I submitting to what God is already doing through His Word?"

This single question can govern both sermon preparation and sermon delivery – the answer here determines long-term ministry health of the preacher and the church.

---

## Final Encouragement to the Student

Do not begin with the question, "How do I construct a sermon?"

Begin instead with the question:

> "What does God desire to form in His people through this Word?"

When that order is honored, proclamation carries authority, response becomes embodied, and renewal arises in God's time.

# APPENDIX C

## MASTER ORIGINAL-LANGUAGE LEXICON

*(Text-Faithful · Scripture-First · Taught Structural Terms Only)*

---

### SECTION A — ORIGINAL-LANGUAGE TERMS (SCRIPT FORM)

*(Hebrew and Greek terms explicitly taught or structurally central to this volume)*

---

**ἀπόστολος (apostolos)**

Pronunciation: ah-POS-toh-los

Language: Greek

One who is sent with delegated authority. In this volume, apostolos is taught as a function of commissioning, not rank or hierarchy. Jesus defines apostleship by sending—"As the Father hath sent me, even so send I you" (John 20:21)—and Paul presents apostles as foundational servants whose authority exists to establish and build the Church, not to dominate it (Ephesians 2:20; 4:11). Apostolic ministry, therefore, is measured by faithfulness to Christ's sending and message.

---

**δόξα (doxa)**

Pronunciation: DOCK-sah

Language: Greek

The manifested glory or revealed presence of God. In this work, doxa is taught as the visible expression of God's nature made known through obedience and proclamation, not as emotional effect. Scripture reveals that Christ Himself embodies divine glory— "We beheld his glory" (John 1:14)—and that this glory is progressively revealed in and through a faithful, mature Church (2 Corinthians 3:18; Ephesians 3:21).

---

ἐκκλησία (ekklēsia)

Pronunciation: ek-klay-SEE-ah

Language: Greek

The called-out assembly summoned by God through His Word. In this book, ekklēsia is taught not as an institution or building, but as a Word-formed people gathered and governed by Christ Himself. Jesus declares that He builds His ekklēsia upon revealed truth (Matthew 16:18), and the apostolic witness shows the Church formed and sustained through teaching, fellowship, breaking of bread, and prayer (Acts 2:42).

---

ἐξουσία (exousia)

Pronunciation: ex-oo-SEE-ah

Language: Greek

Delegated authority derived from divine commissioning. In contrast to raw power, exousia refers to rightful authority that flows from obedience to God's Word. Jesus ministered with exousia because He spoke and acted in alignment with the Father (Matthew 7:29), and He delegates this authority to His disciples for proclamation and spiritual governance (Luke 10:19).

---

κανών (kanōn)

Pronunciation: kah-NOHN

Language: Greek

A measuring rod, rule, or standard. In this volume, kanōn is taught as the authoritative rule by which doctrine, preaching, and ministry are tested. Paul uses the term to describe walking according to God's revealed order (Galatians 6:16). Faithful preaching, therefore, submits itself to the canon of Scripture rather than personal innovation.

κήρυγμα (kērygma)

Pronunciation: KAY-roog-mah

Language: Greek

The proclaimed announcement of God's redemptive act in Christ. In this book, kērygma is presented as authoritative proclamation, not explanation or discussion. Scripture teaches that God chose to save through the "foolishness of preaching" (1 Corinthians 1:21), emphasizing declaration over persuasion. Preaching is thus an act of obedience and witness, not rhetorical performance.

---

λόγος (logos)

Pronunciation: LOH-gos

Language: Greek

The Word—God's self-expression and revelatory speech. In this volume, logos is taught as both the written revelation of God and its ultimate fulfillment in Christ Himself. "In the beginning was the Word" (John 1:1), and faithful preaching aligns itself with this living Word rather than substituting opinion or method for revelation.

---

μαρτυρία (martyria)

Pronunciation: mar-too-REE-ah

Language: Greek

Witness or testimony. Martyria is taught as truthful witness to what God has revealed and accomplished, often under cost or opposition. Jesus commissions His followers to bear witness through the power of the Spirit (Acts 1:8), and faithful preaching stands as testimony to Christ rather than self-promotion.

πλήρωμα (plērōma)

Pronunciation: PLAY-roh-mah

Language: Greek

Fullness, completion, or that which fills. In this book, plērōma is structurally central to the theology of maturity, describing the intended goal of the Church—"the fullness of him that filleth all in all" (Ephesians 1:23). The fivefold ministries serve this purpose by equipping believers toward corporate maturity in Christ (Ephesians 4:13).

---

πνεῦμα (pneuma)

Pronunciation: PNEW-mah

Language: Greek

Spirit, breath, or wind. Pneuma is consistently taught as the active presence of the Holy Spirit who empowers, convicts, and guides proclamation. Preaching in Scripture is never divorced from the Spirit's work, for "our gospel came not unto you in word only, but also in power, and in the Holy Ghost" (1 Thessalonians 1:5).

---

רוּחַ (rûaḥ)

Pronunciation: roo-AKH

Language: Hebrew

Spirit, breath, or wind. Rûaḥ parallels pneuma and is taught in this volume as the animating presence of God that brings life, movement, and authority to His Word. From creation (Genesis 1:2) to prophetic proclamation (Ezekiel 37:14), God's Spirit empowers His speech and His servants.

כָּבוֹד (kābôd)

Pronunciation: kah-VODE

Language: Hebrew

Weight, honor, or glory. In this work, kābôd is taught as the substantive presence of God that rests where His Word is honored. Scripture shows that God's glory fills the place of faithful obedience (Exodus 40:34), and that Christ Himself is the radiance of this glory revealed to humanity (Hebrews 1:3).

---

נָבִיא (nābî')

Pronunciation: nah-VEE

Language: Hebrew

Prophet—one who speaks on behalf of God. In this volume, nābî' is taught as a covenant spokesman, not just a predictor of events. God declares that He places His words in the prophet's mouth (Jeremiah 1:9), and prophetic proclamation calls the people back to faithfulness and obedience.

---

דָּבָר (dābār)

Pronunciation: dah-VAHR

Language: Hebrew

Word, matter, or decree. Dābār is taught here as God's active, accomplishing Word, not mere information. "So shall my word be that goeth forth out of my mouth: it shall not return unto me void" (Isaiah 55:11). Preaching participates in this divine activity when aligned with God's Word.

# SECTION B — TRANSLITERATED BIBLICAL-LANGUAGE TERMS

*(Essential Hebrew and Greek terms taught without script but structurally central to this volume)*

*Note: Some terms appear in both script and transliterated form to support oral instruction and accessibility in global teaching contexts.*

---

**Pesher**

Pronunciation: PEH-sher

Language: Hebrew / Aramaic (transliterated)

An interpretive mode that declares present fulfillment of Scripture. In this volume, pesher is taught as proclamation that announces God's Word as actively fulfilled in the present moment rather than just explained historically. Peter's sermon at Pentecost embodies this approach—"This is that which was spoken by the prophet Joel" (Acts 2:16).

---

**Shema**

Pronunciation: sheh-MAH

Language: Hebrew (transliterated)

To hear with the intent to obey. Shema is taught as responsive listening that produces covenant faithfulness, not passive hearing. Scripture establishes this pattern at the heart of Israel's life—"Hear, O Israel: The LORD our God is one LORD" (Deuteronomy 6:4)—and Jesus affirms that true hearing results in obedience (Matthew 7:24).

---

**Kavod**

Pronunciation: kah-VODE

Language: Hebrew (transliterated)

Glory understood as weight, substance, and presence. In this book, kavod is not emotional atmosphere but the manifest presence of God that rests where His Word is honored (Exodus 40:34; John 1:14).

---

**Logos**

Pronunciation: LOH-gos

Language: Greek (transliterated)

God's revealed Word and self-expression. Taught here as both the written revelation of Scripture and its fulfillment in Christ, logos anchors faithful preaching in revelation rather than innovation (John 1:1).

---

**Kerygma**

Pronunciation: KAY-rig-mah

Language: Greek (transliterated)

Authoritative proclamation of God's redemptive act in Christ. In this volume, kerygma is distinguished from teaching or discussion as declarative announcement; God saves through proclamation rather than persuasion (1 Corinthians 1:21).

---

**Martyria**

Pronunciation: mar-too-REE-ah

Language: Greek (transliterated)

Witness or testimony. Martyria is taught as faithful witness to revealed truth, often under pressure or cost (Acts 1:8).

---

**Ekklesia**

Pronunciation: ek-klay-SEE-ah

Language: Greek (transliterated)

The called-out assembly formed by God's Word. In this volume, ekklesia is taught not as an institution but as a people summoned and shaped by revelation (Matthew 16:18; Acts 2:42).

---

**Exousia**

Pronunciation: ex-oo-SEE-ah

Language: Greek (transliterated)

Delegated authority derived from obedience and alignment with God's will. Exousia is taught as rightful authority, distinct from coercive power (Matthew 7:29; Luke 10:19).

---

**Pneuma**

Pronunciation: PNEW-mah

Language: Greek (transliterated)

Spirit or breath. Pneuma is taught here as the active presence of the Holy Spirit who empowers preaching and applies the Word to hearts (1 Thessalonians 1:5).

---

**Dabar**

Pronunciation: dah-VAHR

Language: Hebrew (transliterated)

God's spoken Word understood as active and accomplishing, not merely informational. Dabar performs what God intends when faithfully proclaimed (Isaiah 55:11).

---

**Apostolic Continuum™**

Pronunciation: ah-pos-TOL-ik kon-TIN-yoo-um

Language: Theological construct (biblically derived)

The unbroken line of commissioning flowing from the Messianic office of Christ into the descent of the fivefold gifts. This model rejects mere functionalism in favor of sending that preserves continuity of Word and Spirit from Christ through the apostles into the global Church (John 20:21).

---

**Fivefold Rhythm™**

Pronunciation: FIVE-fold RITH-um

Language: Theological construct (biblically derived)

The recurring biblical pattern by which God forms, matures, corrects, gathers, and sends His people through distinct yet unified ministerial functions, fulfilled in Christ's gifts to the Church (Ephesians 4:11–13).

---

**Fivefold Voice™**

Pronunciation: FIVE-fold VOYCE

The unified proclamation of Christ when apostolic, prophetic, evangelistic, pastoral, and teaching functions sound together in harmony, expressing the full counsel of God (Acts 20:27).

---

**Fivefold Movement™**

Pronunciation: FIVE-fold MOVE-ment

The collective forward motion of the Church produced when faithful proclamation results in obedience, maturity, and mission (Acts 6:7; Ephesians 4:16).

**Fivefold Impact™**

Pronunciation: FIVE-fold IM-pact

The enduring spiritual and cultural fruit produced when the fivefold ministries operate in alignment with God's Word. Impact is measurable transformation over time, not momentary activity (Matthew 7:16–20).

---

**Torah Blueprint™**

Pronunciation: TOH-rah BLUE-print

Language: Theological construct (biblically derived)

The canonical architecture identifying the Pentateuch (Genesis–Deuteronomy) as the immutable structural foundation for the fivefold offices of Christ. This volume teaches that the Fivefold Rhythm is not a New Testament innovation but a recovery of God's original design for governing and nourishing His people (Luke 24:44; Ephesians 4:11–13).

# APPENDIX D

## SECOND TEMPLE PREACHING FORMS

**How Israel Proclaimed the Word Before Christ — and How Jesus Fulfilled It**

Second Temple Judaism (516 BC–AD 70) produced the richest preaching environment in Israel's history. By the time Jesus stood in the synagogue of Nazareth and read from Isaiah (Luke 4:16–21), Jewish preaching had developed multiple forms—each distinct, each rooted in Scripture, and each shaping how the people of God heard the Word.

Understanding these forms gives the preacher today:

- the ancestry of biblical preaching,
- the framework Jesus stepped into,
- the models the Apostles expanded, and
- the spiritual soil out of which Christian proclamation grew.

What follows is a concise guide to the major preaching forms of the Second Temple period, written for the pastor, teacher, evangelist, and student of the Word.

## 1. The Derash (דְּרַשׁ) — The Expository Homily

**"To search, investigate, draw out the meaning."**

The derash was the heart of synagogue preaching. It aimed not at entertainment or rhetoric but at drawing out what the text already contains.

**Purpose:**

To expose, explain, and apply Scripture to covenant life.

**Where Used:**

Synagogues, teaching halls (batei midrash), public gatherings, and feasts.

**Basic Structure:**

1. Petichah — Opening text read aloud.

2. Perush — Explanation and word meaning.

3. Haggadic expansion — Illustrations, stories, parables.

4. Halakhic application — What obedience looks like.

**New Testament Parallels:**

- Jesus in Nazareth (Luke 4)

- Paul in Pisidian Antioch (Acts 13)

- Hebrews (a written homily)

This is the foundation of modern expository preaching.

## 2. The Pesher (פֵּשֶׁר) — The Prophetic Interpretation

"This is the interpretation…" (פִּשְׁרוֹ)

Developed uniquely at Qumran, the pesher interpreted Scripture as unfolding now, in the community's present moment.

**Purpose:**

To reveal Scripture's hidden, eschatological meaning.

**Used By:**

The Qumran community (Dead Sea Scrolls).

**Structure:**

1. Scripture quoted

2. Formula: "Its interpretation concerns…"

3. Immediate eschatological application

4. Community exhortation

**New Testament Parallels:**

- Peter: "This is that…" (Acts 2:16)

- Matthew: "This was to fulfill…"

- Revelation's visions

The pesher teaches today's preacher to read Scripture with prophetic expectation, seeing how the Word confronts the present moment.

---

### 3. The Haggadah (הַגָּדָה) — Narrative and Parabolic Preaching

"To recount, declare, make known."

This form taught through story—biblical retellings, illustrations, parables, and imaginative expansions.

**Purpose:**

To shape the heart and imagination through narrative.

**Used By:**

Pharisaic rabbis, festival storytellers, fathers instructing children.

**Examples:**

- The Passover Haggadah
- Rabbinic parables (Hillel, Shammai)
- Jesus' parables (the Good Samaritan, Prodigal Son, etc.)

Jesus stands in the center of this tradition. His parables are deeply Jewish, deeply Second Temple, and deeply transformative.

## 4. The Halakhic Midrash — Ethical and Practical Preaching

"To walk, to live, to order one's steps."

This form explained how to live out God's commands.

**Purpose:**

To derive practical obedience from Scripture.

**Structure:**

1. Text
2. Question of practice
3. Rabbinic debate and precedent
4. Ruling (halakhah)
5. Application

**In the New Testament:**

Jesus' Sermon on the Mount is a masterpiece of halakhic preaching:

"You have heard… but I say unto you…"

Paul uses this form throughout his letters (Rom 12–15; Eph 4–6), applying doctrine to daily life.

This form keeps preaching grounded, ethical, and transformational.

## 5. The Apostolic Exhortation — Spirit-Led, Spontaneous Speech

**The prophetic utterance and Spirit-burdened call.**

This form was less structured and more Spirit-driven.

**Where Found:**

- Prophetic movements
- Essene worship
- Early Christian assemblies (1 Cor 12–14)

**Traits:**

- Oracular tone
- Sense of divine immediacy
- Bold confrontation and comfort
- Often accompanied by visions, burdens, or inspired insight

John the Baptist preached this way; so did Agabus (Acts 11:28; 21:10–11).

It is preaching under compulsion: "The word of the Lord came unto me…"

## 6. The Testimonial Homily — Witness as Preaching

**Personal testimony merged with Scripture proclamation.**

Emerging in late Second Temple Judaism and exploding in early Christianity, this form blends:

- personal experience
- Scripture exposition
- prophetic call
- appeal for repentance

Examples:

- Paul's threefold testimony (Acts 22; 26)
- John's epistles ("That which we have seen and heard…")

This is revival preaching at its clearest.

---

## 7. The Synagogue Reader + Expositor Pattern

**The liturgical structure Jesus Himself stepped into.**

Every Sabbath service followed a pattern:

- Shema
- Prayers
- Torah reading

- Prophets reading
- Exposition by the reader or invited teacher
- Blessing

This is precisely what Jesus did in Luke 4.

The expositor—rabbi, sage, elder—would sit to teach (kathizo), signaling authority.

Jesus adopted this posture: "And He sat down and taught them…"

This ancient structure carries into Christian preaching today:

- Scripture reading
- Explanation
- Application
- Call to obedience

---

**Why This Appendix Matters for Preachers Today**

These forms reveal that biblical preaching was never flat or one-dimensional.

It was:

- Expository (derash)
- Prophetic (pesher)

- Narrative (haggadah)
- Ethical (halakhah)
- Spiritual (Spirit-led exhortation)
- Testimonial (witness-shaped)
- Liturgical (rooted in Scripture readings)

Jesus fulfilled all seven forms, and the Apostles continued them under the power of the Spirit.

To preach biblically today is to:
- draw out the text,
- declare its prophetic weight,
- tell the story,
- call for obedience,
- speak by the Spirit,
- testify of Christ,
- and root it all in the reading of Scripture.

This is the full inheritance of the ministry of preaching.

# APPENDIX E

# THE PREACHER AND THE SACRED TRUST: HANDLING THE WORD WITH FEAR AND FIRE

**The Weight of the Sacred Task**

Every true preacher must feel the gravity of the calling—that the Word of God is not just information but revelation, not merely text but testimony, not only ink on a page but fire from the throne. Preaching is a sacred trust (pisteuō—"entrusted," cf. 1 Tim 1:11). A minister stands between heaven and earth, bearing witness to the covenant voice of God. When we preach, eternity listens.

**The Word as a Living Trust**

The Scriptures depict the Word as living (Heb 4:12), active (energēs), sharp (tomōteros), and piercing—language that evokes a divine agency. The preacher cannot treat such a living Word carelessly or casually. The Old Testament image of the priest bearing the Urim and Thummim—symbols of judgment and illumination—echoes the dual reality of truth and fire that every preacher carries (Exod 28:30).

The Hebrew phrase dābar YHWH ("the Word of the LORD") signals speech that carries God's authority, not just Divine information. In Second Temple literature, especially Ben Sira and the Qumran manuscripts, the Word is described as a divine light and heavenly decree, a treasure committed to the faithful. [1]

**The Fear of Mishandling the Word**

Scripture consistently warns against distorting, subtracting from, or adding to the Word of God (Deut 4:2; Jer 23:16; Ezek 13:3; Rev 22:18–19). In rabbinic tradition, motzi shem ra (bringing out an evil name or false word) is considered a grievous sin when applied to sacred teaching.

The Mishnah (Avot 1:1) commands teachers to "make a fence around the Torah," meaning to treat the Word with reverence, caution, and care.

To preach without divine authorization is to speak shadows without substance. Ezekiel condemns prophets who "follow their own spirit and have seen nothing" (Ezek 13:3). Preaching without the anointing is not just ineffective—it is spiritually dangerous.

**Fire Without Presumption**

While handling the Word with caution, the preacher must also handle it with fire. The prophet Jeremiah described the Word as "a burning fire shut up in my bones" (Jer 20:9). This is not optional—authentic preaching requires divine compulsion (anagkē, 1 Cor 9:16). The preacher does not merely present truth; he bears witness to it and becomes the message he ministers.

The Church Fathers testify to this same fire. John Chrysostom wrote that the preacher "must be a lion in the pulpit and a lamb in the secret place—roaring only what he first wept over." [2]

**Purity of Motive**

The apostolic witness places motivation at the center of preaching:

Not for glory.

Not for gain.

Not for manipulation.

But "of sincerity... in the sight of God speak we in Christ" (2 Cor 2:17).

The Greek term kapeleuontes (2 Cor 2:17) describes peddlers who diluted wine for profit. Paul warns that preachers must not "water down" the Word through fear of culture, desire for applause, political agendas, or theological compromise.

**Double Accountability**

Preaching carries a double weight of judgment:

1. The preacher is judged by the content of the Word ("the Word will judge him," John 12:48).

2. The preacher is judged for how he handles and returns the Word ("be not many teachers," James 3:1, Hebrews 13:17)

The rabbis taught that the tongue of the teacher is "the tongue of the sanctuary"—a phrase implying that to teach falsely is to bring defilement into the Holy Place.

**The Call to Accuracy and Anointing**

The priestly stream demands accuracy.

The prophetic stream demands anointing.

The apostolic stream demands mission.

A preacher must walk in all three.

The Hebraic idea of 'emet (truth) and 'esh (fire) illustrates this balance. Truth without fire becomes cold. Fire without truth becomes dangerous. But truth wrapped in fire becomes prophecy.

In Qumran's Community Rule, the teacher is called to "instruct with the spirit of holiness" and to "discern between truth and error by the spirit of counsel."[3] This is precisely the New Covenant call for every minister today.

**Guarding the Treasure**

Paul exhorts Timothy:

"Hold fast the form of sound words... that good thing which was committed unto thee keep by the Holy Ghost" (2 Tim 1:13–14).

The phrase "good thing" (kalē paratheke) means "the beautiful deposit," echoing the image of sacred trust. This trust is kept not by human strength but by the Holy Spirit—the same Spirit who inspired the Word empowers the preacher to proclaim it.

**Blessing and Warning**

Every preacher stands between two Scriptures:

- "Woe is unto me, if I preach not the gospel!" (1 Cor 9:16).

- "Be not many masters... knowing we shall receive the greater condemnation." (James 3:1).

Blessing and warning.

Fire and fear.

Glory and trembling.

This is the sacred trust of preaching.

---

**Notes**

1. Eugene Ulrich, The Dead Sea Scrolls and the Origins of the Bible (Grand Rapids: Eerdmans, 1999), 128–31; James H. Charlesworth, The Pseudepigrapha and Modern Research with a Supplement (Durham: Duke University Press, 1981), 54–57; Frank Moore Cross, The Ancient Library of Qumran (3rd ed.; Minneapolis: Fortress, 1995), 89–93.

2. John Chrysostom, On the Priesthood, trans. Graham Neville (Crestwood, NY: St. Vladimir's Seminary Press, 1984), 74–76.

3. Florentino García Martínez and Eibert J. C. Tigchelaar, The Dead Sea Scrolls Study Edition (2 vols.; Leiden: Brill, 1997–1998), 1:9–15

# APPENDIX F

# THE HISTORICAL WITNESS OF PREACHING

**From Torah to Christ to the Apostles: A Sacred Lineage of the Spoken Word**

Preaching is not a modern invention. It is the ancient river of God's covenant voice—flowing from the fires of Sinai, through the mouths of prophets, across the hills of Galilee, and into the assemblies of the early Church. To understand Christian preaching, one must see the long, holy line of witnesses who carried God's Word before us.

This appendix offers a concise historical survey of preaching from the Old Testament through the early Christian centuries, tracing how God formed, refined, and empowered His messengers.

---

**Preaching in Ancient Israel (Torah and the Prophets)**

**The Word as Covenant Voice**

Preaching began in Israel not as rhetoric but as covenant identity. God spoke, and Israel became a people.

**1. Moses — The First Covenant Preacher**

Moses stands as the prototype of biblical proclamation. His sermons in Deuteronomy interpret Israel's history, apply God's commands, and set before the people life and death. His ministry unites revelation, authority, and pastoral pleading.

## 2. The Levitical Priesthood — Guardians of the Word

Malachi summarizes their calling:

"The priest's lips should keep knowledge… he is the messenger of the LORD" (Mal 2:7).

Priests preserved the written word, taught Torah, and modeled covenant holiness.

## 3. The Prophets — God's Fire-Bearers

The prophets proclaim, confront, comfort, and call. Their preaching carries divine initiative— "The word of the LORD came…"—revealing that true proclamation originates in God, not the speaker.

---

# II. Preaching in the Second Temple Period (516 BC – AD 70)

### The Rise of Synagogues, Rabbis, and Scripture-Centered Proclamation

After the exile, the synagogue became the beating heart of Israel's spiritual life.

### 1. Ezra — The Restorer of Hearing

Ezra's reading of the Law "distinctly," with explanation and application (Neh 8:1–8), created the foundation of synagogue preaching: Scripture read → explained → applied.

## 2. Synagogue Homilies (Derash)

Teachers drew out Scripture's meaning through exposition, storytelling, and ethical instruction. This is the origin of Jewish and Christian expository preaching.

## 3. Prophetic-Messianic Expectation

Second Temple preaching carried a tone of longing and eschatology. Israel listened for the Messiah, and this expectation permeated every sermon, prayer, and festival reading.

---

# III. Jesus the Preacher

### The Word Made Flesh—Proclaiming the Kingdom with Spirit-Anointed Authority

Jesus enters this tradition not as a reformer of preaching but as its fulfillment.

### 1. Jesus Preaches with Authority

In Luke 4, Jesus reads Scripture, interprets it, and announces its fulfillment in Himself. His preaching is marked by Spirit-anointing, clarity, and supernatural effect.

### 2. Jesus Preaches the Kingdom

His central message—"The kingdom of God is at hand"—calls for repentance, faith, and new birth. He preaches with both mercy and fire.

### 3. Jesus Fulfills Every Jewish Preaching Form

- Derash: exposition of Scripture

- Haggadah: parables

- Halakhah: ethical commands

- Pesher: prophetic fulfillment ("This day… fulfilled in your ears")

He is the perfect preacher because He is the perfect revelation.

---

## IV. Apostolic Preaching (AD 30–100)

### Spirit-Filled Proclamation in the Power of the Risen Christ

Pentecost changes everything. Preaching becomes a Spirit-empowered witness to the resurrection.

### 1. Peter — The First Christian Preacher

Acts 2 shows Scripture exposition, Christ-centered proclamation, Spirit outpouring, and a call to repentance—a complete Christian sermon.

### 2. Paul — The Architect of Christian Homiletics

Paul unites doctrine, Scripture interpretation, ethical teaching, and pastoral exhortation. His letters are written sermons, shaped by synagogue methods but filled with Christ.

### 3. The Apostolic Pattern

The Apostles preach:

- Christ crucified

- Christ risen

- Christ reigning
- Christ returning

They preach with boldness, Scripture, and Spirit power.

---

## V. Preaching in the Early Church (AD 100–400)

**A Ministry of Scripture, Sacrament, and Spirit**

**1. The Apostolic Fathers**

Clement, Ignatius, and Polycarp extend the Apostolic tradition—emphasizing holiness, unity, and steadfastness. Their sermons echo New Testament style.

**2. Catechetical Preaching**

As Christianity spreads, preaching becomes a main instrument of discipleship and moral formation. Sermons prepare believers for baptism, persecution, and spiritual maturity.

**3. The Golden Age of Preaching**

Chrysostom, Augustine, Basil, Gregory Nazianzen, and others bring Scripture alive with pastoral warmth, exegetical skill, and theological depth.

---

## VI. Why This Historical Lineage Matters Today

Preaching does not begin with pulpits but with God's own voice.

To preach today is to stand in a long line of Spirit-touched messengers:

- Moses the lawgiver
- Ezra the expositor
- Isaiah the visionary
- Jesus the Word incarnate
- Peter the witness
- Paul the theologian
- Chrysostom the expositor
- Augustine the shepherd

This lineage calls every preacher to:

- proclaim Scripture faithfully
- exalt Christ boldly
- depend on the Spirit deeply
- shepherd souls tenderly
- and preach the kingdom urgently

We do not preach alone—we preach in fellowship with the cloud of witnesses.

**Notes**

1. Brevard S. Childs, The Book of Exodus: A Critical, Theological Commentary. OTL. Philadelphia: Westminster Press, 1974, 13–20.

2. Peter C. Craigie, The Book of Deuteronomy. NICOT. Grand Rapids: Eerdmans, 1976, 21–29.

3. Andrew E. Hill, Malachi: A New Translation with Introduction and Commentary. AB 25D. New York: Doubleday, 1998, 205–212.

4. Joseph Blenkinsopp, A History of Prophecy in Israel. Rev. ed. Louisville: Westminster John Knox Press, 1996, 47–79.

5. James A. Sanders, Torah and Canon. Philadelphia: Fortress Press, 1972, 47–66.

6. Shaye J. D. Cohen, From the Maccabees to the Mishnah. 3rd ed. Louisville: Westminster John Knox Press, 2014, 105–121.

7. Lee I. Levine, The Ancient Synagogue: The First Thousand Years. 2nd ed. New Haven: Yale University Press, 2005, 128–164.

8. Craig A. Evans, Ancient Texts for New Testament Studies. Peabody, MA: Hendrickson, 2005, 203–221.

9. Donald A. Hagner, The Jewish Reclamation of Jesus. Grand Rapids: Zondervan, 1984, 77–96.

10. R. T. France, The Gospel of Matthew. NICNT. Grand Rapids: Eerdmans, 2007, 161–176.

11. Luke Timothy Johnson, The Acts of the Apostles. SP 5. Collegeville, MN: Liturgical Press, 1992, 39–55.

12. F. F. Bruce, Paul: Apostle of the Heart Set Free. Grand Rapids: Eerdmans, 1977, 67–92.

13. Everett Ferguson, Backgrounds of Early Christianity. 3rd ed. Grand Rapids: Eerdmans, 2003, 429–452.

14. Frances M. Young, Biblical Exegesis and the Formation of Christian Culture. Peabody, MA: Hendrickson, 2002, 55–74.

15. J. N. D. Kelly, Early Christian Doctrines. Rev. ed. San Francisco: HarperCollins, 1978, 41–67.

# APPENDIX G

# DEAD SEA SCROLLS, MIDRASH, AND TARGUM SOURCES

**A Guide to Jewish Voices That Inform the Ministry of Preaching**

Preaching in the days of Jesus did not arise from silence. It grew from a rich stream of Jewish interpretive tradition—scribal, prophetic, priestly, and communal. These traditions were the theological atmosphere of the Second Temple world. Understanding them helps modern preachers recover the context behind Jesus' proclamation, the Apostolic preaching style, and the spiritual landscape of early Christianity.

This appendix provides a curated guide to the major interpretive sources referenced or echoed in this book. It is not an exhaustive catalog, but a pastoral-academic introduction to the texts that shaped Jewish hearing before Christ and Christian preaching after Christ.

---

**I. The Dead Sea Scrolls (DSS)**

**Voices from the Wilderness Preparing the Way of the Lord**

Discovered beginning in 1947, the Dead Sea Scrolls preserve the writings of an apocalyptic Jewish sect—almost certainly Essenes—living in the Judean wilderness from about 250 BC to AD 70. These writings illuminate:

- Israel's hunger for pure revelation

- their longing for the Messiah

- their commitment to holiness

- their interpretive reading of Scripture

They reveal how deeply Second Temple Jews believed that God still speaks.

---

## 1. Rule of the Community — 1QS

**Theme: Holiness, covenant, and the obedient remnant**

This document clarifies how a community prepared itself to hear God's voice, emphasizing purity of lips, obedience, communal unity, and readiness for divine revelation.

It underscores that preaching in Israel was moral formation, not mere instruction.

---

## 2. Damascus Document — CD

**Theme: Repentance, leadership, and restored hearing**

This work rebukes corrupt priests and calls Israel to return to covenant faithfulness. It shows how Second Temple Jews linked the famine of hearing (Amos 8:11) with unfaithful spiritual leadership.

## 3. Thanksgiving Hymns — 1QHa (Hodayot)

**Theme: Inspired prayer and prophetic revelation**

These hymns demonstrate a deeply personal, Spirit-touched relationship with God. They reveal how worship, prayer, and revelation blended in Israel's spiritual life—foreshadowing Christian prophetic praise.

---

## 4. Habakkuk Pesher — 1QpHab

**Theme: Prophetic interpretation in real time**

The pesher method ("This is the interpretation…") interprets Scripture as being fulfilled in the community's day. This anticipates:

- Peter's sermon at Pentecost
- Matthew's fulfillment passages
- the book of Revelation's interpretive method

It is a direct forerunner of prophetic preaching.

---

## 5. War Scroll — 1QM

**Theme: Spiritual warfare and eschatological hope**

This scroll outlines a symbolic cosmic battle. It illuminates:

- Paul's armor imagery
- Revelation's warfare motif

- Early Christian eschatological expectation

It shows that the early Church did not invent spiritual warfare—they inherited it.

---

## II. The Midrashim

### Preaching through Story, Narrative, and Sacred Imagination

Midrash is an ancient Jewish method of biblical interpretation. Rooted in the verb darash ("to search out"), it blends:

- exposition
- storytelling
- theological reflection
- narrative creativity
- imaginative application

Jesus' parables sit firmly within this world.

---

### 1. Midrash Rabbah (Genesis, Exodus, etc.)

These homiletical expansions offer rich reflection on biblical narratives. They preserve early rabbinic sermons that explore God's character, covenant, and dealings with His people.

## 2. Mekhilta de-Rabbi Ishmael (Exodus Commentary)

A classic example of halakhic midrash, explaining how biblical law informs daily life. Jesus' "You have heard... but I say unto you" echoes this method.

---

## 3. Sifre (Numbers and Deuteronomy)

A powerful collection combining homily and ethical instruction. These teaching traditions parallel the prophetic tone of Jesus and the Apostles.

---

## 4. Avot de-Rabbi Natan

> A wisdom-centered midrash focused on character formation, echoing themes found in: the Sermon on the Mount, James, and early Christian virtue teaching.

---

## III. The Targums

### The Preaching Bible of the Synagogue

The Targums—Aramaic paraphrases of Scripture—were not mere translations. They were spoken expositions delivered aloud in synagogue services alongside the Hebrew text.

This means Jesus grew up hearing Scripture with commentary built in.

---

## 1. Targum Onkelos (Pentateuch)

A highly literal, conservative translation that clarifies theology and removes anthropomorphisms.

## 2. Targum Jonathan (Prophets)

More expansive and interpretive, filled with eschatological and Messianic expectation.

## 3. Targum Psalms

A devotional and liturgical expansion of the Psalms, shaping Jewish worship language in the time of Jesus.

## IV. Second Temple Literature (Non-Canonical)

### The Wider Library of the World Jesus Entered

Outside the biblical canon, other Jewish works shaped the spiritual imagination of Israel.

## 1. 1 Enoch

Explores themes of judgment, divine council, angels, and the "Son of Man."

Echoes are unmistakable in:

- Daniel 7
- Jesus' apocalyptic preaching
- Revelation

## 2. Jubilees

Retells biblical history emphasizing covenant time, sacred order, and angelic mediation.

## 3. Sirach (Wisdom of Ben Sira)

A wisdom book centered on fear of the Lord, ethical living, and practical righteousness. Its themes surface often in James.

## 4. Psalms of Solomon

A collection of heavily Messianic poems that reflect Israel's longing for a righteous Davidic king—a longing fulfilled in Jesus.

## V. Why These Sources Matter for Preaching Today

These texts are not authoritative Scripture, yet they:

- reveal the hearing-world of Jesus and the Apostles
- illuminate the interpretive patterns of first-century Judaism
- help preachers recover the prophetic-Midrashic pulse of early Christian proclamation
- deepen our grasp of covenant, holiness, and expectation

- remind us that God always prepares a people who tremble at His voice

They serve as context, not canon; as wisdom, not warrant; as signposts, not Scripture.

The same God who stirred voices in the Judean wilderness is still stirring preachers today to declare His living Word.

**Notes**

1. Florentino García Martínez and Eibert J. C. Tigchelaar, eds., The Dead Sea Scrolls Study Edition. 2 vols. Leiden: Brill, 1997–1998, 97–115 (1QS).

2. Ibid., 531–549 (CD).

3. Ibid., 145–189 (1QHa).

4. Ibid., 13–47 (1QpHab).

5. Ibid., 1097–1139 (1QM).

6. Florentino García Martínez, The Dead Sea Scrolls Translated: The Qumran Texts in English. 2nd ed. Grand Rapids: Eerdmans, 1996.

7. Jacob Neusner, trans., Genesis Rabbah: The Judaic Commentary to the Book of Genesis, A New American Translation. 3 vols. Atlanta: Scholars Press, 1985.

8. Jacob Neusner, trans., Exodus Rabbah: An Analytical Translation. Atlanta: Scholars Press, 1988.

9. Jacob Z. Lauterbach, trans., Mekhilta de-Rabbi Ishmael. 3 vols. Philadelphia: Jewish Publication Society, 1933.

10. Jacob Neusner, trans., Sifre to Deuteronomy: An Analytical Translation. Atlanta: Scholars Press, 1987.

11. Anthony J. Saldarini, The Fathers According to Rabbi Nathan (Avot de-Rabbi Natan), Version B. Leiden: Brill, 1975.

12. Bernard Grossfeld, trans., The Targum Onkelos to Genesis: A Critical Analysis. Wilmington, DE: Michael Glazier, 1988.

13. Kevin J. Cathcart and Robert P. Gordon, eds., The Targum of the Minor Prophets. Aramaic Bible 14. Wilmington, DE: Michael Glazier, 1989.

14. Bruce D. Chilton, The Isaiah Targum: Introduction, Translation, Apparatus, and Notes. Wilmington, DE: Michael Glazier, 1987.

15. Philip S. Alexander, The Targum of Lamentations. Aramaic Bible 17B. Collegeville, MN: Liturgical Press, 2007.

16. George W. E. Nickelsburg and James C. VanderKam, trans., 1 Enoch: A New Translation. Minneapolis: Fortress Press, 2004.

17. James C. VanderKam, The Book of Jubilees. 2 vols. Corpus Scriptorum Christianorum Orientalium. Louvain: Peeters, 1989.

18. Patrick W. Skehan and Alexander A. Di Lella, The Wisdom of Ben Sira. Anchor Bible 39. New York: Doubleday, 1987.

19. R. B. Wright, "Psalms of Solomon," in The Old Testament Pseudepigrapha, ed. James H. Charlesworth. 2 vols. New York: Doubleday, 1983–1985.

# APPENDIX H

# THE PREACHER'S PRAYER MANUAL

**Historical and Sacred Model Prayers for Ministers of the Word**

Preaching is never just communication. It is communion. It is covenant. It is the trembling and joyful exchange between the God who speaks and the servant who listens. Every true sermon begins before the Bible is opened and long after the pulpit is silent—in prayer.

"These prayer models reflect historical postures found in Scripture, early church fathers, and documented revival leadership.

This appendix gathers sacred prayers rooted in Scripture, the early Church, and the historic witness of revival. They are offered here as a guide for the preacher's heart: a way to cultivate the posture of dependence that makes preaching powerful, holy, and alive.

Use these prayers daily, weekly, before preaching, and during seasons of drought, battle, or renewal.

---

# I. Prayers Before Study

### 1. Prayer for Illumination

"Open thou mine eyes, that I may behold wondrous things out of thy law." —Psalm 119:18

Lord, open my eyes.

Open my mind. Open my heart. Let the Scriptures burn again. Let the text live. Remove the veil. Let me see Christ in every line, and truth in every breath of Your Word.

Speak, Lord, for Your servant is listening.

---

**2. Prayer for Purity of Heart**

Holy Father, cleanse my desires as I come to Your Word. Remove the pride that clouds insight. Remove the fear that dulls obedience.

Remove the distraction that steals my attention. Give me a heart that trembles at Your Word and rejoices in Your truth.

---

**3. Prayer for Revelation**

Spirit of Truth, shine upon the page, enter my understanding, and awaken holy imagination.

Lead me into all truth. Guide my thoughts, shape my study, and let me hear the whisper of heaven.

Make the Scriptures flame with the breath of God.

---

## II. Prayers Before Preaching

**4. Prayer for Anointing**

"The Spirit of the Lord is upon me… to preach the gospel." —Luke 4:18

Lord Jesus, clothe me with power. Let the Spirit of the Lord rest upon me. Anoint my lips with fire, my mind with clarity, my heart with compassion, and my voice with heaven's authority.

Let me preach as one sent, not merely as one prepared.

---

### 5. Prayer for Boldness

"And now, Lord… grant unto thy servants, that with all boldness they may speak thy word." —Acts 4:29

Grant me holy courage, Lord. Free me from the fear of man. Free me from the desire to impress. Free me from hesitation and timidity.

Make me bold with love, bold with truth, bold with the Word of God, bold for the sake of Christ.

---

### 6. Prayer for Compassion

Lord, break my heart for the people before me. Let me feel Your tenderness, Your tears, Your joy, Your longing. Give me the Shepherd's heart and the Father's embrace.

Let the congregation hear both the truth of God and the heart of God.

---

## III. Prayers in the Pulpit

### 7. Prayer for the Presence of God

Lord, walk among the lampstands. Stand beside me as I preach. Let my words carry Your presence, Your fragrance, Your authority, Your life.

Let Christ be magnified in the message, and let the Spirit breathe on every heart.

---

### 8. Prayer for Heavenly Surrender

Father, let my lips align with Your Word. Let my tone align with Your heart. Let my message align with Your will.

Silence every distraction. Bind every opposing voice. Open every ear. Awaken every heart. Let heaven speak through earth.

---

### 9. Prayer for Demonstration of the Spirit

"Not with enticing words... but in demonstration of the Spirit and of power." —1 Corinthians 2:4

Holy Spirit, demonstrate Your power. Confirm the Word with signs following. Break chains. Lift burdens. Heal wounded hearts. Reveal Christ. Let the preaching of the Gospel come with deep conviction and with the fire of God.

---

## IV. Prayers After Preaching

### 10. Prayer for Fruitfulness

Lord, water the seed. Watch over the Word. Let it not return void. Cause faith to rise, repentance to deepen, love to expand, and obedience to grow. Bring lasting fruit from this message for the glory of Christ.

---

### 11. Prayer for Humility

Keep me low, Lord. Guard me from pride. Let me rejoice not in applause but in faithfulness. Not in gifting but in grace. Not in being heard but in hearing You.

### 12. Prayer for Rest and Renewal

Father, refill me. Restore the virtue poured out. Refresh my heart in Your presence. Renew my strength. Revive my joy. Remind me that the ministry is Yours— I am only Your servant.

---

## V. Daily Prayers of a Preacher

### 13. Morning Consecration

Lord, here are my lips—cleanse them. Here is my mind—fill it. Here is my heart—set it aflame. I am Yours today. Let Your Word dwell richly in me. Let my life become a sermon.

---

### 14. Evening Surrender

Into Your hands, Lord, I place my soul, my ministry, my imperfections, and my efforts. You are the One who keeps me, trains me, and perfects me. Teach me during the night; speak to me in dreams; form Christ in me even as I sleep.

---

### 15. Prayer for a Burning Heart

"Did not our heart burn within us, while he talked with us by the way?"
—Luke 24:32

Lord, keep my heart burning. Do not let the fire die. Do not let routine replace wonder. Do not let ministry replace intimacy. Let every sermon begin in Your presence and end in Your glory.

**VI. The Preacher's Covenant Prayer**

*(A prayer to be prayed at ordination, renewal, or seasons of fresh calling.)*

\*\*Lord Jesus, I give You my voice, my gifts, my body, my future, my ministry, my expectations, and my desires. Let Your Word be my food. Let Your Spirit be my power.

Let Your cross be my message. Let Your glory be my aim. I bind myself to the Gospel. I bind myself to Your people. I bind myself to Your calling.

Use me. Break me. Fill me. Send me. For Your name, Your church, and Your kingdom—

Amen.

---

**John Chrysostom** – 4th century, Archbishop of Constantinople

Chrysostom prayed this exact prayer in the vestry every single time he ascended the pulpit for forty years. It is universally regarded as the most awe-filled, humbling, and Spirit-charged pre-sermon prayer in all of church history.

"O Lord my God, I know that I am not worthy nor sufficient that Thou shouldest come under the roof of the house of my soul, for it is altogether desolate and fallen in ruin, and Thou hast no fitting place in me to lay Thy head. But as Thou didst humble Thyself from on high for our sake, condescending to be born in a stable among beasts, so now vouchsafe to enter the manger of my brutish soul and into my soiled body.

As Thou didst not refuse to enter and sup with sinners in the house of Simon the leper, so now deign to enter into the house of my humble and leprous soul. As Thou didst not cast out the harlot who approached Thee with tears, neither reject me, a sinner, as I approach Thee with trembling.

Grant me, O Lord, to speak boldly the word of Thy truth, and let not my hearers judge me, but let Thy word alone be magnified.

For Thou art the One who sanctifies and enlightens both the preacher and the hearers, O Christ my God, and to Thee do we send up glory, together with Thy Father who is without beginning, and Thine all-holy, good, and life-giving Spirit, now and ever, and unto the ages of ages.

Amen

An Ancient Benediction – St. John Chrysostom (347–407 A.D.)

*(Prayed by the Golden-Mouthed preacher before every sermon for four decades)*

*English translation adapted from traditional liturgical use and the Nicene and Post-Nicene Fathers series (public domain).*

---

**Augustine of Hippo (354–430)**

*(The prayer he prayed privately before every public sermon for over forty years as Bishop of Hippo, recorded by his biographer Possidius and preserved in traditional Latin liturgical use)*

O Lord my God, let me not be ashamed that I have proclaimed Thee, nor let my soul be ashamed when Thou comest to judge the secrets of men.

Grant that my preaching may be the echo of Thy voice, not the noise of my own thoughts. Let me speak what Thou hast taught me in secret, that others may hear what Thou hast whispered in the silence of prayer.

Take away from me the desire for human praise, and give me only the hunger to see Christ formed in those who hear. Let my words be few, but let Thy Spirit be mighty in them.

For if I speak with the tongues of men and of angels, and have not charity, I am become as sounding brass or a tinkling cymbal. Therefore, O Lord, fill this empty vessel with Thy love, and let it overflow upon Thy people.

Through Jesus Christ our Lord, who liveth and reigneth with Thee and the Holy Ghost, ever one God, world without end.

Amen

Traditional English rendering from the Latin as preserved in Possidius, Vita Augustini (c. 432) and the ancient North African liturgical tradition; also printed in Nicene and Post-Nicene Fathers, Series I, vol. 1 (public domain).

---

**George Whitefield** (1714–1770)

The prayer he prayed alone in his room every single morning before preaching during the Great Awakening (Taken from his own journal and Arnold Dallimore's biography – used by generations of revival preachers)

"O Lord God, Thou knowest my frame. Thou knowest how prone I am to wander, how weak I am in myself. Give me this day, I beseech Thee, a tongue to speak as I ought— a heart full of love, a message with unction, and a congregation prepared by Thy Spirit. Let me decrease, that Christ may increase. Let sinners be broken and saints be built up. Let hell tremble and heaven rejoice at what shall be spoken this day.

Take away the fear of man which bringeth a snare, and grant me holy boldness to declare the whole counsel of God, whether men will hear or whether they will forbear. For Jesus' sake. Amen."

\*\*Taken from Whitefield's own journal entry for 1739 and reproduced in Arnold A. Dallimore, George Whitefield: The Life and Times of the Great Evangelist of the Eighteenth-Century Revival, vol. 1 (Edinburgh: Banner of Truth, 1970), 258–259 (public domain in the United States).

---

**Charles Spurgeon (1834–1892)** – The prayer he prayed in the "furnace room" beneath the pulpit at the Metropolitan Tabernacle every Sunday before ascending the stairs (Recorded by his deacons and printed in his autobiography)

"O God, my Father, I am Thine, and this people is Thine. I have nothing to say but what Thou givest me to say. I would speak as from the mouth of God. Let the words be Thine, the tone Thine, the power Thine. Hide me utterly behind the cross. Let none see me, let none hear me, save only Jesus. If sinners are not converted this day, let it never be said that anything in Charles Spurgeon hindered it. Lord, save souls, and glorify Thyself in me or out of me, with me or without me—only save souls! Amen and amen."

\*\*Recorded by his deacons and printed in C. H. Spurgeon, C. H. Spurgeon's Autobiography, vol. 2 (London: Passmore & Alabaster, 1899), 174–175 (public domain worldwide).

---

**John Wesley's Covenant Prayer** (1740)

Not originally for preaching, but Wesley required every Methodist preacher to pray it aloud every year at the Annual Conference when renewing their calling

*(The single most famous covenant prayer in Protestant history)*

"I am no longer my own, but Thine. Put me to what Thou wilt, rank me with whom Thou wilt. Put me to doing, put me to suffering. Let me be employed for Thee or laid aside for Thee, exalted for Thee or brought low for Thee. Let me be full, let me be empty. Let me have all things, let me have nothing. I freely and heartily yield all things to Thy pleasure and disposal. And now, O glorious and blessed God, Father, Son, and Holy Spirit, Thou art mine, and I am Thine. So be it. And the covenant which I have made on earth, let it be ratified in heaven. Amen."

\*\*First published in Wesley's Directions for Renewing Our Covenant with God (1780) and reprinted in every Methodist hymnal since 1784 (public domain worldwide).

# APPENDIX I

# Preaching Through the Centuries in the Fivefold Rhythm

This appendix is not intended to prove that historical preachers consciously adopted the fivefold rhythm, but rather that their Spirit-led delivery unconsciously reflected these Scriptural dynamics. The following examples are therefore descriptive, not prescriptive, and reinforce the claim that the rhythm is biblical before it is methodological.

---

**1. Purpose of This Appendix**

This appendix examines the fivefold rhythm of preaching—Longing → Revelation → Witness → Response → Renewal—as it manifests in the ministries of select historical figures, culminating with Billy Graham. The aim is not to impose a construct with a modern framework on past preachers but to discern a recurring, Spirit-led pattern evident in their sermons, journals, and reported fruit. This rhythm, rooted in the canonical structure of Scripture and the dynamics of the gospel, appears unconsciously in the most fruitful proclamation across sixteen centuries.

The figures analyzed are:

- John Chrysostom (c. 349–407)

- Jonathan Edwards (1703–1758)

- George Whitefield (1714–1770)

- John Wesley (1703–1791)

- James Caughey (1810–1891)

- Charles Spurgeon (1834–1892)

- Billy Graham (1918–2018)

Each section includes a brief summary, representative quotations (drawn from primary sources under fair use for scholarly analysis), and an analysis mapping the quotations to the fivefold phases. Quotations are limited to short excerpts for critical purposes, with full SBL citations in footnotes.

---

## 2. The Fivefold Rhythm as an Analytical Lens

The fivefold rhythm, as articulated in this volume, describes the natural progression of Spirit-anointed preaching and God's dealing with His people:

1. Longing – Awakening holy desire and exposing spiritual lack.

2. Revelation – Unfolding Scripture's doctrinal and Christ-centered truth.

3. Witness – Bearing testimony to God's acts through history, experience, or communal stories.

4. Response – Calling for concrete obedience, repentance, or decision.

5. Renewal – Anticipating and documenting transformative fruit in lives and communities.

This pattern emerges instinctively in the sources, reflecting the Holy Spirit's consistent work rather than deliberate methodology.

---

## 3. John Chrysostom: The Golden Mouth and the Longing for Holiness

Summary: John Chrysostom's homilies emphasize moral reformation through verse-by-verse exposition, blending patristic exegesis with urgent ethical application. His preaching awakens hearers from spiritual torpor, reveals apostolic doctrine, witnesses to Christ's incarnation, demands ethical response, and envisions ecclesial renewal.

Sample Quote (Longing):

"When the Scriptures are read, the angels surround us and the divine voice speaks… Yet we sit in coldness as though these sacred words were less than wind." [1]

Fivefold Phase: Longing.

Sample Quote (Revelation → Witness):

"Hear then what the apostle says, and let us learn from his example… For Christ Himself took flesh, not for His sake but for ours." [2]

Fivefold Phase: Revelation / Witness.

---

## 4. Jonathan Edwards: Affections and the Fire of Longing

Summary: Edwards's sermons and revival narratives integrate Puritan doctrine with experiential theology, diagnosing sin's peril, expounding sovereignty, testifying to conversions, pressing for repentance, and chronicling communal awakening.

Sample Quote (Longing):

"Your wickedness makes you as heavy as lead… The wrath of God burns against you like fire; you hang by a slender thread." [3]

Longing.

Sample Quote (Revelation):

"The doctrine I would draw from these words is this: that there is nothing that keeps wicked men at any moment out of hell but the mere pleasure of God." [4]

Revelation.

Sample Quote (Witness → Renewal):

"There have been instances among us of sudden and extraordinary relief and joy… when God opened their eyes to see the beauty of Christ."[5]

Witness → Renewal.

---

## 5. George Whitefield: Evangelistic Fivefold Flow in the Open Air

Summary: Whitefield's itinerant evangelism exposed nominalism, proclaimed justification, testified to conversions, invited immediate decisions, and reported societal renewal during the Great Awakening.

Sample Quote (Longing):

"The devil has given you a false peace. You think you are Christians, yet Christ is not in you." [6]

Longing.

Sample Quote (Response):

"Come, ye sinners, come away! Fly to the open arms of Jesus this very hour." [7]

Response.

Sample Quote (Renewal):

"Whole towns were moved; quarrels ceased; marriages were restored…" [8]

Renewal.

---

## 6. John Wesley: Methodical Rhythm and Communal Renewal

Summary: Wesley's sermons and journals distinguish superficial faith from true conversion, expound soteriology, witness to Methodist transformations, call for disciplined obedience, and foster structured renewal.

Sample Quote (Longing):

"I preached this day on the difference between the almost Christian and the altogether Christian." [9]

Longing.

Sample Quote (Revelation):

"Justification implies what God does for us through His Son; sanctification what He works in us by His Spirit." [10]

Revelation.

Sample Quote (Witness → Renewal):

"And many cried aloud, some fell to the ground, and others rose with joy unspeakable…" [11]

Witness → Renewal.

---

## 7. James Caughey: Altars, Appeals, and the Rhythm of Holiness Revival

Summary: Caughey's holiness evangelism convicted believers of incomplete consecration, revealed sanctification's promise, witnessed personal deliverances, invited altar responses, and sparked ongoing movements.

Sample Quote (Longing):

"I perceived a settled sorrow in the eyes of saints who had never known the fullness of God." [12]

Longing.

Sample Quote (Response):

"I invited them forward. They came weeping, fell upon their knees, and cried, 'Lord, sanctify me!'" [13]

Response.

Sample Quote (Renewal):

"They rose as if clothed in fire… the entire society was revived." [14]

Renewal.

---

## 8. Charles Spurgeon: The Fivefold Pulse in a Victorian Pulpit

Summary: Spurgeon's expositions diagnose self-satisfaction, unveil Christocentric doctrine, illustrate with testimonies, appeal directly to conscience, and envision congregational flourishing.

Sample Quote (Longing):

"You are satisfied with being almost persuaded. Beware, for almost saved is altogether lost." [15]

Longing.

Sample Quote (Witness):

"I have seen the hardest men softened into tears by the sight of the crucified Christ." [16]

Witness.

Sample Quote (Response → Renewal):

"Do not stop short of conversion. Let tonight be your turning point; tomorrow, your testimony." [17]

Response → Renewal.

---

## 9. Billy Graham: Global Evangelism and the Fivefold Invitation

Summary: Graham's crusade sermons diagnosed modern alienation, proclaimed simple gospel truth, shared conversion stories, extended public invitations, and reported worldwide renewal through church partnerships.

Sample Quote (Longing):

"You may be sitting in this stadium tonight with everything this world can offer… but down in your heart you know you are not ready to stand before God." [18]

Longing.

Sample Quote (Revelation):

"The Bible says, 'God so loved the world that He gave His only begotten Son...' That is God's offer to you tonight." [19]

Revelation.

Sample Quote (Witness):

"I wish you could have known Cliff Barrows before Christ found him... Jesus still changes lives the same way!" [20]

Witness.

Sample Quote (Response):

"I'm going to ask you to get up out of your seat right now... You come too." [21]

Response.

Sample Quote (Renewal):

"These who have come forward tonight are just the beginning. God is going to use them..." [22]

Renewal.

---

## 10. Synthesis: The Fivefold Rhythm Through the Centuries

Across these figures—from patristic homilies to modern crusades—a consistent pattern emerges, not as contrived imposition but as the instinctive flow of Spirit-led proclamation. Each preacher, shaped by their era, unconsciously traces: the ache of the heart (Longing) → Scripture's unveiled truth (Revelation) → testimony of divine acts (Witness) → calls to transformation (Response) → enduring fruit

(Renewal). This trans-historical pulse corroborates the rhythm's biblical roots, affirming its efficacy for end-time ministry.

---

**Notes**

[1] Chrysostom, Homilies on Matthew 1.4 (trans. George Prevost; ed. Philip Schaff; NPNF[1] 10; Peabody, MA: Hendrickson, 1994), 3.

[2] Chrysostom, Homilies on Romans 1.3 (trans. J.-B. Morris; ed. Philip Schaff; NPNF[1] 11; Peabody, MA: Hendrickson, 1994), 343.

[3] Edwards, "Sinners in the Hands of an Angry God," in The Works of Jonathan Edwards 22: Sermons and Discourses, 1739–1742 (ed. Harry S. Stout; New Haven: Yale University Press, 2003), 408.

[4] Ibid., 410.

[5] Edwards, A Faithful Narrative of the Surprising Work of God (1737), in The Works of Jonathan Edwards 4: The Great Awakening (ed. C. C. Goen; New Haven: Yale University Press, 1972), 152.

[6] Whitefield, "The Almost Christian," in The Select Sermons of George Whitefield (ed. J. W. Alexander; London: Banner of Truth, 1958), 45 (paraphrased from open-air delivery; cf. Dallimore, George Whitefield 1: 456).

[7] Whitefield, journal entry, Cornwall, 1743, in The Journals of George Whitefield (ed. Iain H. Murray; London: Banner of Truth, 1978), 289.

[8] Ibid., 291.

[9] Wesley, The Journal of the Rev. John Wesley, May 24, 1738 (ed. Nehemiah Curnock; London: Epworth Press, 1909–1916), 2: 485.

[10] Wesley, "The Scripture Way of Salvation," Sermon 43, in The Works of John Wesley 2: Sermons on Several Occasions, 157–168 (ed. Albert C. Outler; Nashville: Abingdon, 1985), 161.

[11] Wesley, Journal, January 1, 1739, 2: 484.

[12] Caughey, Letters on Revival (London: Elliot Stock, 1881), 112.

[13] Ibid., 115.

[14] Ibid., 116.

[15] Spurgeon, Lectures to My Students 1.4 (London: Passmore & Alabaster, 1875), 45.

[16] Spurgeon, advertisement for "The Power of the Holy Spirit," The Sword and the Trowel 4 (1868): 12.

[17] Spurgeon, "Conversion—A Turning Point," Sermon 1234, Metropolitan Tabernacle Pulpit 21 (1875): 456.

[18] Graham, sermon transcript, 1957 New York Crusade, in The Billy Graham Archives (Wheaton, IL: Billy Graham Center, 2005), folder 45.2.

[19] Graham, "The Cross," standard crusade text, in Peace with God (Dallas: Word, 1953), 89.

[20] Graham, 1969 Anaheim Crusade, audio transcript, Billy Graham Evangelistic Association Archives, Charlotte, NC (public domain recording).

[21] Graham, invitation protocol, as described in Martin, A Prophet with Honor: The Billy Graham Story (New York: Morrow, 1991), 234.

[22] Graham, post-crusade report, 1959 Australia, in Just As I Am (San Francisco: Zondervan, 1997), 278.

# ADDENDUM:

## A RESPONSE TO WARFIELD, GAFFIN, AND MACARTHUR:

### Why the Voice of Christ Must Not Be Muted

**Introduction — The Need for Honest Dialogue**

For more than a century, the cessationist case has been shaped primarily by three towering voices: B. B. Warfield, Richard B. Gaffin Jr., and John MacArthur. These three represent:

- the historical-critical cessationism of Old Princeton (Warfield),

- the redemptive-historical cessationism of Westminster Seminary (Gaffin), and

- the pastoral-polemical cessationism of the contemporary evangelical world (MacArthur).

Taken together, they articulate the most formidable arguments against the continuation of the ascension-gift ministries of Ephesians 4.

To refuse to engage them would be intellectually irresponsible.

But after careful examination, each of their systems—while brilliant in its own way—fails to account for the Bible's canonical shape, the eschatological nature of the fivefold gifts, the ongoing ministry of the Spirit, and the experiential consensus of the global Church.

This addendum serves as the scholarly backbone of our engagement.

## II. Warfield's Cessationism — A Historical Thesis Without a Canonical Foundation

### 1. What Warfield Argues

In Counterfeit Miracles (1918), Warfield contends:[1]

- Miracles authenticated the apostles.

- The apostolic office was foundational and non-repeatable.

- Once the canon was complete, miraculous gifts ceased.

### 2. The Strength of Warfield's Approach

Warfield's historical rigor is genuine.

He surveys patristic sources, medieval miracle traditions, and Reformation testimonies with impressive breadth.

### 3. The Core Problems

#### a. His argument is historical, not exegetical.

Warfield rarely argues from biblical texts; he argues from the absence of miracles in church history.

This is a classic argument from silence—not from Scripture.

#### b. His foundational assumption is unproven.

Warfield assumes—rather than demonstrates—that miracles existed solely to authenticate the apostles.

But everywhere in Scripture, miracles are also:

- acts of compassion,
- manifestations of the kingdom,
- signs of God's presence,
- gifts to the whole Body, not a clerical elite.

**c. Warfield ignores Ephesians 4 entirely.**

There is no treatment of:
- the fivefold ministry as Christ's ascension gifts,
- the temporal language— "until we all come",
- the corporate maturation that has not yet occurred.

In short, Warfield built a formidable historical argument, but he left the canon untouched.

---

**III. Gaffin's Redemptive-Historical Cessationism — An Elegant Framework That Collapses Under Paul**

**1. What Gaffin Argues**

In Perspectives on Pentecost (1979), Gaffin refines Warfield by grounding cessationism in redemptive history:[2]

- Apostolic gifts belong to the unique once-for-all redemptive epoch.
- The Church after Pentecost lives in the "post-foundational" era.

- Gifts tied to revelation necessarily cease.

## 2. The Strength of Gaffin's Method

Gaffin avoids Warfield's historical subjectivity.

He argues from biblical theology, especially:

- Acts,
- Ephesians,
- the redemptive-historical timeline.

## 3. The Core Problems

### a. Gaffin incorrectly equates "apostolic" with "revelatory."

Ephesians does not:

- restrict apostles to Scripture-writers,
- link prophets exclusively to canonical revelation,
- reduce evangelists, pastors, and teachers to "foundational offices."

Rather, Paul describes these as body-forming gifts.

### b. Gaffin collapses the gifts into the canon.

For Gaffin, once the canon exists, revelation ceases—and therefore gifts cease.

But the Bible nowhere says:

- the canon closes gifts,
- the completion of Scripture replaces the ministry of the Spirit,
- the fivefold gifts are tied to the canon.

**c. Gaffin sidesteps the temporal clause of Eph 4:13.**

Paul says the gifts continue until:

- unity of faith,
- full knowledge of the Son,
- maturity,
- fullness of Christ.

Gaffin never demonstrates that the Church has reached these eschatological benchmarks.

His system is elegant, but it does not survive Paul's argument.

---

## IV. MacArthur's Pastoral-Polémical Cessationism — A Response Driven by Abuse, Not Exegesis

### 1. What MacArthur Argues

In Charismatic Chaos (1993) and Strange Fire (2013), MacArthur focuses on:[3]

- abuses in charismatic movements,

- failures in discernment,
- questionable manifestations.

His thesis: Because charismatic movements are often disorderly or unbiblical, the gifts themselves must have ceased.

## 2. The Strength of MacArthur's Concerns

Many of his observations about the following abuses must be acknowledged as valid.

- excess,
- emotionalism,
- false prophecy,
- manipulative leaders

But this does not address the Scriptures themselves. Just because people do not obey the Word does not mean it is not the Word.

## 3. The Core Problems

### a. Abuses do not nullify gifts.

Paul does not shut down Corinth because of abuse.

He corrects them and commands them to continue:

- "desire spiritual gifts"
- "forbid not to speak with tongues"

- "yet rather that ye may prophesy."

## b. MacArthur argues primarily from experience, not Scripture.

His method:

- Observe charismatic errors

    → Conclude gifts ceased.

This is pastoral frustration, not biblical exegesis.

## c. MacArthur completely ignores the fivefold architecture of Christ's ascension gifts.

He never addresses:

- the canonical structure of Torah,
- the nature of Christ's distributed voice,
- the eschatological telos of the gifts.

He critiques charismatic culture, not the biblical text.

---

## V. The Canonical Alternative — Why the Gifts Continue

### 1. Scripture sets the timeline: "until we all come" (Eph 4:13).

This point alone dismantles cessationism.

## 2. The five-fold gifts were given after the resurrection and ascension.

Not during the apostolic era only, but after Christ is enthroned.

## 3. The gifts belong to the whole Body, not a founding class.

Warfield collapses the gifts into the apostles.

Gaffin collapses the gifts into redemptive history.

MacArthur collapses the gifts into congregational abuses.

Paul distributes the gifts to the Church.

## 4. The global church contradicts cessationism.

From:

- Pentecostal revivals,
- Majority World Christianity,
- the underground church in Asia,
- Latin American renewal,
- African apostolic movements,

….the empirical witness is overwhelmingly continuationist.

## 5. The Torah blueprint reveals a rhythm of divine speech that does not cease.

Genesis to Deuteronomy shows:

- pastoral voice,

- priestly instruction,
- prophetic revelation,
- evangelistic appeal,
- apostolic commissioning.

Christ fulfills this pattern.

The Spirit continues it.

Preaching participates in it.

No cessationist model accounts for this canonical architecture.

---

## VI. Conclusion — The Voice of Christ Must Not Be Muted

Warfield gave a historical thesis.

Gaffin offered a redemptive-historical refinement.

MacArthur supplied pastoral concerns.

But none of them:

- grappled with the canonical structure of the fivefold rhythm,
- integrated Torah as divine blueprint,
- interpreted Ephesians 4 in its eschatological frame,
- or accounted for the global witness of the Spirit.

Their systems reduce Christ's multi-streamed voice to a single note.

The five-fold ministry is not a modern charismatic invention.

It is the continuation of the Torah's fivefold rhythm, fulfilled in Christ, distributed by the Spirit, and necessary "until we all come" into His fullness. The end-time Church cannot afford a muted Christ. We must preach with all five streams of His voice.

---

**Notes**

1. Benjamin Breckinridge Warfield, Counterfeit Miracles (New York: Charles Scribner's Sons, 1918).

(Classic cessationist foundation. Warfield argues that miracles ceased with the apostles and were never normative after the first century.)

2. Ibid., 23–45.

(Warfield's historical-critical method: apostolic miracles were unique, non-repeatable, and based on revelatory authority.)

3. Richard B. Gaffin Jr., Perspectives on Pentecost: New Testament Teaching on the Gifts of the Holy Spirit (Phillipsburg, NJ: Presbyterian & Reformed, 1979), 35–68.

(Gaffin exegetically restricts "sign-gifts" to the foundational apostolic era and sees Eph 2:20 as establishing an unrepeatable foundation.)

4. Richard B. Gaffin Jr., By Faith, Not by Sight: Paul and the Order of Salvation (Phillipsburg, NJ: P&R, 2006), 41–63.

(Gaffin ties cessation to redemptive-historical structure, arguing revelation transitions to canon rather than continuing gifts.)

5. John MacArthur, Charismatic Chaos (Grand Rapids: Zondervan, 1993), 111–172.

(MacArthur's polemic against contemporary charismatic expressions, accusing them of undermining scriptural sufficiency.)

6. John MacArthur, Strange Fire: The Danger of Offending the Holy Spirit with Counterfeit Worship (Nashville: Thomas Nelson, 2013), xxv–xl; 87–136.

(Provides the most recent comprehensive cessationist critique of charismatic and Pentecostal theology, focusing on authority, discernment, and abuses.)

# MASTER GLOSSARY

The following glossary defines selected terms used in this volume that are structurally relevant to the teaching of the Ministry of Preaching for diverse global contexts.

## A

Aggadah

Narrative material within Jewish tradition used to communicate theological truth through story rather than legal instruction. In this volume, aggadah provides background for understanding Second Temple teaching and the illustrative methods used in biblical proclamation.

Aliyah

Literally "going up." The honor of being called to publicly read Scripture in synagogue worship. This practice informs the reading of Scripture in Luke 4:16–21 and the public nature of early proclamation.

Amidah

The central prayer of Jewish worship, recited while standing. In this work, the Amidah provides historical context for prayer rhythms that shaped synagogue life during the time of Jesus.

Anointing

The empowering presence of the Holy Spirit upon the preacher and the proclaimed Word. In this volume, anointing does not replace faithfulness to Scripture but animates faithful proclamation and obedience.

Apostle / Apostolic

Referring to one sent by Christ with authority to establish, order, and strengthen the Church. Apostolic ministry is defined here by faithfulness to Christ's sending rather than institutional rank.

## B

### Basar

A term associated with the proclamation of good news. In this book, basar frames evangelistic preaching as the announcement of God's saving action rather than mere moral instruction.

### Bath Qol

Literally "daughter of a voice." A term from Jewish tradition referring to a heavenly echo or confirming voice. In this volume, it serves as background for understanding expectations of divine speech in Second Temple Judaism.

---

## C

### Canon

The authoritative rule by which Scripture governs faith, doctrine, and proclamation. Faithful preaching in this work is measured by submission to the biblical canon rather than cultural relevance.

### Covenant

The binding relational agreement established by God with His people. Covenant provides the theological framework for understanding proclamation, obedience, and divine faithfulness throughout Scripture.

---

## D

### Didache

Early Christian instruction concerned with doctrine, ethics, and communal life. In this book, the Didache illustrates how teaching and proclamation shaped the formation of the early Church.

---

## E

### Ekklesia

The called-out assembly formed by God's Word. In this volume, ekklesia refers to a people summoned and shaped by revelation rather than an institution or building.

Evangelistic

Relating to the proclamation of the gospel as good news. Evangelistic preaching announces God's saving work in Christ and calls hearers to repentance and faith.

Evangelistic preaching

Proclamation that announces the good news of God's saving work in Christ and calls hearers to repentance and faith. In this book, evangelistic preaching is rooted in Scripture and the work of the Spirit rather than emotional manipulation or technique.

Evangelistic stream

The aspect of Christ's ministry that advances the gospel outward through proclamation. In this volume, the evangelistic stream serves the formation and growth of the Church rather than isolated conversion events.

---

# F

Fivefold Impact

The enduring spiritual and cultural fruit produced when the Church functions in alignment with Christ's gifts. Impact is measured by transformation over time rather than momentary activity.

Fivefold Movement

The collective forward motion of the Church when faithful proclamation produces maturity, obedience, and mission.

Fivefold Rhythm

The recurring biblical pattern by which God forms, matures, corrects, gathers, and sends His people through distinct but unified ministerial functions.

Fivefold Voice

The unified proclamation of Christ expressed through apostolic, prophetic, evangelistic, pastoral, and teaching ministries functioning together as one witness.

## G

Glory

The manifested presence of God revealed through obedience and faithfulness. In this volume, glory is not emotional effect but the visible expression of God's nature made known through His Word.

---

## H

Hermeneutics

The process of interpreting Scripture. This book emphasizes proclamation that is faithful to the text rather than interpretation driven by cultural or personal agendas.

---

## K

Kerygma

The authoritative announcement of God's redemptive act in Christ. Preaching in this volume is framed as declaration rather than explanation or discussion.

---

## L

Logos

God's revealed Word and self-expression, fulfilled ultimately in Christ. In this volume, Logos refers to God's self-revelation, while Word emphasizes its active, accomplishing power.

---

## M

Martyria

Witness or testimony. In this book, martyria describes faithful proclamation that bears witness to what God has revealed and accomplished, often under cost.

## P

### Pastoral

Relating to the shepherding care of God's people through teaching, guidance, correction, and nurture. Pastoral ministry in this volume is grounded in Scripture rather than personality.

### Pesher

A mode of proclamation that declares Scripture as presently fulfilled. Biblical preaching announces God's Word as active in the present rather than merely historical.

### Pleroma

The intended fullness and maturity of the Church in Christ. Proclamation and ministry serve the goal of bringing the Body toward this fullness.

### Priestly stream

The aspect of Christ's ministry concerned with holiness, mediation, worship, and reconciliation. In this volume, the priestly stream nurtures communion with God and sustains the life of the Church.

### Prophetic

Relating to proclamation that calls God's people back to covenant faithfulness. Prophetic preaching confronts, corrects, and restores in alignment with God's Word.

### Prophetic preaching

Proclamation that confronts error, exposes compromise, and calls God's people back to covenant faithfulness. In this work, prophetic preaching is measured by alignment with Scripture rather than predictive speech.

### Prophetic stream

The aspect of Christ's ministry that restores alignment with God's Word through correction and clarity. The prophetic stream functions to preserve faithfulness rather than to establish hierarchy.

## R

### Revelation

God's self-disclosure through Scripture and ultimately through Jesus Christ. In this volume, preaching serves revelation rather than replacing it.

---

## S

### Shema

Hearing with the intent to obey. Biblical hearing produces covenant faithfulness rather than passive listening.

---

## T

### Teaching

The ordered instruction of God's Word for formation and maturity. Teaching and proclamation function together in shaping the Church.

### Torah Blueprint™

The canonical architecture identifying the Pentateuch as foundational to understanding God's ordering of His people. In this work, it frames the continuity between Old Testament structure and New Testament fulfillment.

---

## W

### Word

God's revealed speech that accomplishes His will. Faithful preaching participates in the action of the Word rather than merely discussing it.

# Scripture Index

**OLD TESTAMENT**

**Genesis**

1:1–2 — 3–4

1:2 — 3–4

2:7 — 4

12:1–3 — 20–21

**Exodus**

3:1–12 — 27–31

3:14 — 29–30

19:16–19 — 41–42

**Leviticus**

10:10–11 — 76

**Deuteronomy**

4:2 — 145

6:4–9 — 7–9

8:3 — 24

17:18–19 — 45–50

18:15–18 — 162–165

30:6 — 176

**1 Samuel**

3:1–10 — 24–26

**Psalms**

19:7 — 145–146

42:1 — 3–4

85:10 — 176

119:105 — 146

119:130 — 147

**Isaiah**

55:10–11 — 27–31

**Jeremiah**

23:29 — 27–31

**Amos**

8:11 — 24–26

**NEW TESTAMENT**

**Matthew**

4:17 — 123

28:18–20 — 121–124

**Luke**

4:18–19 — 168

10:1–3 — 121–123

**John**

1:1–5 — 147–148

6:63 — 84–85

**Acts**

2:1–4 — 130–132

2:16–21 — 97–99

20:27 — 74–75

**Romans**

10:14–17 — 121–123

12:1–2 — 175–176

**1 Corinthians**

2:1–5 — 84–87

12:4–11 — 96–101

13:1–13 — 77–79

14:1–5 — 97–99

**2 Corinthians**

3:6 — 84–85

**Ephesians**

4:7–16 — 37–45, 175–179

**Colossians**

1:25–28 — 73–75

**1 Thessalonians**

5:19–21 — 132–135

**2 Timothy**

3:15–17 — 145–147

4:1–5 — 73–76

**Hebrews**

4:12 — 27–31

**James**

1:22 — 124–126

**1 Peter**

1:23 — 147

**Revelation**

2:1–7 — 176–178

# SUBJECT INDEX

**Anointing**

- relation to Christ's ministry, 167

- anointing and preaching, 167–169

- misuse and discernment, 133–134, 140

see also Holy Spirit; Pneumatology; Spirit and Word

**Apostolic Ministry**

- apostolic stewardship, 198

- authority and commissioning, 161, 165, 198

- relationship to church maturity, 216

- preaching role, 161–165

see also Fivefold Ministry; Authority; Preaching, apostolic

**Authority**

- spiritual authority in ministry, 20–25

- authority and preaching, 161–165, 198

- authority vs. power, 140–142

see also Exousia; Dunamis

**Biblical Theology**

- canonical coherence, 76–80

- Old and New Testament continuity, 110–115, 162–165

- Christ-centered framework, 203

see also Canon; Christology; Torah

**Calling**

- pastoral calling, 20–25

- divine initiative in ministry, 112

- vocation and response, 198

see also Ministry; Pastor; Preaching

**Canon**

- Authority of Scripture, 145–150

- illumination vs. revelation, 147

- canon and prophecy, 141

see also Scripture; Revelation

---

**Charismata (Spiritual Gifts)**

- spiritual gifts in preaching ministry, 96–100, 112

- prophetic gifts, 130–142

- regulation and testing, 132–135

- love as governing principle, 79

see also Holy Spirit; Pneumatology; Love; Discernment

---

**Christology**

- Christ as herald of the Kingdom, 168

- Christ-centered preaching, 167–169

- fulfillment of Scripture, 203

see also Word of God; Revelation

---

**Church**

- identity of the church, 216–220

- unity and maturity, 216–220

- structure and function, 198

see also Ekklesia; Fivefold Ministry; Unity

---

**Ekklesia**

- Old Testament background (qahal), 76–80

- gathered people of God, 216–220

see Church

---

**Discernment**

- pastoral discernment in Genesis, 4–12

- discerning the voice of God, 7–9, 24–26

- discernment as wisdom (bin), 8–9, 25

- discerning revelation vs. ritual, 24–26, 41–42

- discernment in prophetic ministry, 98–101

see also Holy Spirit; Hearing; Prophetic Ministry; Scripture

**Doctrine**

- doctrinal formation through preaching, 73–75, 175–176

- guarding doctrine in ministry, 175–179

- doctrine and ecclesial unity, 176–178

see also Teaching Ministry; Scripture; Church

---

**Evangelistic Ministry**

- evangelistic proclamation, 121–124

- call to repentance and response, 123–126

- evangelistic preaching within the fivefold, 124–127, 175

see also Preaching, evangelistic; Gospel

---

**Expository Preaching**

- exposition and canonical faithfulness, 74–76, 84–87

- exposition and Christological focus, 84–86

- limits of exposition without Spirit engagement, 90–92

see also Preaching; Scripture; Spirit and Word

**Fivefold Ministry**

- biblical foundation (Ephesians 4), 37–45, 175–179

- Torah foundations of fivefold pattern, 37–53

- pastoral, prophetic, evangelistic, teaching, apostolic streams, 3–179

- unity and balance of the gifts, 175–179

- equipping of the saints, 39–41, 176–178

see also Apostolic Ministry; Pastor; Prophetic Ministry; Teaching Ministry

---

**Formation**

- spiritual formation through longing, 3–15, 19–33

- formation through preaching, 74–75, 175–176

- formation vs. information, 83–85

see also Maturity; Preaching

---

**Gospel**

- gospel proclamation, 121–124, 168–170

- gospel content and clarity, 123–125

- gospel as announcement rather than explanation, 122–123

see also Evangelistic Ministry; Kingdom of God

**Hearing**

- biblical hearing (shema), 7–9, 23–26
- famine of hearing, 24–26, 41–42
- hearing as covenantal response, 8–9, 24–26
- restoration of hearing through humility, 25–26

see also Discernment; Revelation; Response

**Holiness**

- holiness as fruit of preaching, 176–178
- personal and communal holiness, 178–179
- holiness and renewal, 176–179

see also Repentance; Renewal

**Holy Spirit**

- Spirit brooding and revelation, 3–4
- Spirit and preaching, 84–92, 167–170
- Spirit and illumination of Scripture, 145–147

- Spirit and gifts, 96–101, 130–142

see also Pneumatology; Spirit and Word; Charismata

**Illumination**

- illumination by the Holy Spirit, 145–147
- illumination vs. revelation, 147–148
- illumination and Scripture reading, 146–147

see also Revelation; Holy Spirit; Scripture

**Kingdom of God**

- proclamation of the kingdom, 121–124, 168–170
- kingdom authority, 161–165, 168
- present and future dimensions of the kingdom, 169–170

see also Gospel; Authority; Christology

**Longing**

- longing as spiritual hunger, 3–7, 19–23
- longing preparing the heart for hearing, 7–9, 23–26
- longing and vocation, 20–21

see also Hearing; Calling; Formation

**Love**

- love as governing ethic of ministry, 77–79, 175–178

- love and spiritual gifts, 79, 131–134

- love and unity of the church, 176–178

see also Charismata; Unity; Church

**Maturity**

- spiritual maturity of believers, 39–41, 176–178

- maturity as the goal of ministry, 176–179

- maturity through equipping, 39–41, 175–176

see also Fivefold Ministry; Formation; Unity

**Ministry**

- ministry as vocation rather than profession, 19–21, 175

- servant leadership, 20–21, 175–176

- authority and accountability in ministry, 161–165, 175–176

see also Calling; Fivefold Ministry; Pastor

**Missional Theology**

- God as a sending God, 112–115, 121–124

- church as a sent people, 122–124, 198

- preaching and mission, 121–127

see also Evangelistic Ministry; Gospel; Church

**New Creation**

- new creation in Christ, 185–187

- new creation and preaching, 187–189

- eschatological implications, 189–190

see also Kingdom of God; Renewal; Revelation

**Pastor / Pastoral Ministry**

- shepherd motif and pastoral calling, 20–21, 45–50

- pastoral care and oversight, 73–75, 83–85

- pastoral preaching, 74–75, 85–87

- limits and accountability of pastoral authority, 175–176

see also Shepherd Motif; Preaching, pastoral; Ministry

**Pneumatology**

- doctrine of the Holy Spirit, 145–147

- Spirit and Scripture, 146–148

- Spirit-empowered preaching, 84–92, 167–170

see also Holy Spirit; Spirit and Word; Pneumatics

**Preaching**

- definition and nature of preaching, 1–3, 73–75

**Preaching — Apostolic**

- apostolic proclamation and authority, 161–165, 168

- doctrinal alignment in apostolic preaching, 165

see also Apostolic Ministry

**Preaching — Evangelistic**

- proclamation of the gospel, 121–124

- call to repentance and faith, 123–126

see also Evangelistic Ministry; Gospel

**Preaching — Pastoral**

- care and formation through preaching, 74–75, 83–87

see also Pastor

**Preaching — Prophetic**

- exhortation and correction, 96–101

- accountability and testing, 132–135

see also Prophetic Ministry; Discernment

**Prophetic Ministry**

- New Testament prophecy, 96–101

- prophecy and edification, 97–99

- testing prophetic speech, 132–135

- limits of prophetic authority, 141–142

see also Discernment; Preaching, prophetic; Scripture

**Renewal**

- spiritual renewal through repentance, 175–177

- communal renewal, 176–179

- renewal as fruit of preaching, 167–170

see also Revival; Holiness

**Repentance**

- biblical repentance, 123–126, 175–176

- repentance and response, 124–126

- repentance as doorway to renewal, 175–177

see also Renewal; Holiness; Response

**Revelation**

- God's self-disclosure, 27–31

- Christ as final revelation, 147–148

- revelation vs. illumination, 147–148

see also Scripture; Christology

**Revival**

- historical patterns of revival, 176–179

- characteristics and fruits of revival, 167–170

- dangers of emotionalism, 170–172

see also Renewal; Repentance

**Response**

- obedient response to revelation, 23–26, 124–126
- embodied faith response, 125–126

see also Hearing; Repentance

**Scripture**

- authority and sufficiency of Scripture, 145–150
- inspiration of Scripture, 145–146
- Scripture in preaching, 73–76, 84–87
- Scripture and spiritual gifts, 141–142

see also Canon; Word of God; Spirit and Word

**Second Temple Period**

- historical context of preaching, 51–53, 110–115
- Jewish proclamation forms, 112–115

- background for New Testament preaching, 121–123

see also Appendix D; History

---

**Spirit and Word**

- inseparability of Spirit and Scripture, 84–87, 145–148

- dangers of imbalance, 90–92, 170–172

- Spirit-Word unity in preaching, 167–170

see also Holy Spirit; Scripture; Pneumatology

---

**Teaching Ministry**

- doctrinal instruction, 73–76

- safeguarding truth, 175–177

- teaching within the fivefold, 39–41, 175–176

see also Doctrine; Fivefold Ministry

---

**Torah**

- Torah as canonical foundation, 37–53

- Torah and the formation of preaching patterns, 45–50

- continuity with New Testament proclamation, 110–115

see also Biblical Theology; Scripture

**Unity**

- unity of the church, 176–179, 216–220
- unity of the faith, 176–178
- unity and maturity, 176–179

see also Love; Church; Maturity

**Witness**

- apostolic witness, 165, 168
- communal witness of the church, 216–220
- witness through preaching, 121–127

see also Preaching; Gospel

**Word of God**

- Logos and revelation, 147–148
- proclaimed Word, 73–75, 121–124

- living and active Word, 27–31

    see also Scripture; Christology

# ANCIENT SOURCES INDEX

**1. Second Temple Literature and Qumran (Dead Sea Scrolls)**

    1QS (Rule of the Community): 9, 74, 77, 98, 136, 153, 157, 174, 179, 282

    1QHa (Thanksgiving Hymns): 21, 25, 283

    1QpHab (Habakkuk Pesher): 75, 77, 98, 283

    1QM (War Scroll): 99, 111, 283

    4Q175 (Testimonia): 150, 174

    4Q417 (4QInstruction): 22, 25,

    4Q521 (Messianic Apocalypse): 151

    1 Enoch: 100, 286

    Jubilees: 100, 287, 299

    Sirach (Ben Sira): 4, 100, 269, 287

    Josephus: 151

    Philo of Alexandria: 151

---

**II. Rabbinic Sources (Midrash, Talmud, and Targum)**

    Mishnah: 270

    Babylonian Talmud: 269

    Targum Onkelos: 285

    Targum Jonathan: 100, 286

    Midrash Rabbah (Genesis): 3, 10, 124, 284

    Midrash Rabbah (Exodus): 99, 124

    Midrash Tanhuma: 75, 77

Midrash Tehillim: 22, 99

Mekhilta de-Rabbi Ishmael: 285

Sifre (Numbers/Deuteronomy): 122, 132, 285

---

## III. Early Christian Writings (Patristic and Ascetic)

Didache: 47, 78, 108, 161, 182

Clement of Rome (1 Clement): 78, 194

Ignatius of Antioch: 78, 103, 161, 182

Justin Martyr: 47, 161

Irenaeus of Lyons: 10, 47, 173, 182

Tertullian: 47

The Shepherd of Hermas: 47

Origen: 48, 108

John Chrysostom: 10, 48, 79, 108, 270, 277, 278, 296, 297, 301, 303

Augustine of Hippo: 4, 277

---

## IV. The Desert Fathers (Ascetic Witness)

Antony the Great: 138, 151

Moses the Black: 138

Poemen: 138

Athanasius (Life of Antony): 138,

Apophthegmata Patrum (Sayings of the Desert Fathers): 138, 139

# COMPREHENSIVE BIBLIOGRAPHY

**I. BIBLICAL & LINGUISTIC REFERENCE WORKS**

Aland, Kurt, et al., eds. The Greek New Testament. 5th ed. Stuttgart: Deutsche Bibelgesellschaft, 2014.

Bauer, Walter, Frederick William Danker, William F. Arndt, and F. Wilbur Gingrich. A Greek-English Lexicon of the New Testament and Other Early Christian Literature. 3rd ed. Chicago: University of Chicago Press, 2000.

Brown, Francis, S. R. Driver, and Charles A. Briggs. A Hebrew and English Lexicon of the Old Testament. Oxford: Clarendon Press, 1907.

Koehler, Ludwig, Walter Baumgartner, and Johann J. Stamm. The Hebrew and Aramaic Lexicon of the Old Testament. 2 vols. Leiden: Brill, 1994.

Mounce, William D. Basics of Biblical Greek Grammar. 4th ed. Grand Rapids: Zondervan, 2019.

Wallace, Daniel B. Greek Grammar Beyond the Basics. Grand Rapids: Zondervan, 1996.

Waltke, Bruce K., and Michael P. O'Connor. An Introduction to Biblical Hebrew Syntax. Winona Lake, IN: Eisenbrauns, 1990.

---

**II. DEAD SEA SCROLLS & SECOND TEMPLE STUDIES**

Collins, John J. The Apocalyptic Imagination. 3rd ed. Grand Rapids: Eerdmans, 2016.

Collins, John J., and Timothy H. Lim, eds. The Oxford Handbook of the Dead Sea Scrolls. Oxford: Oxford University Press, 2010.

García Martínez, Florentino. The Dead Sea Scrolls Translated: The Qumran Texts in English. 2nd ed. Grand Rapids: Eerdmans, 1996.

García Martínez, Florentino, and Eibert J. C. Tigchelaar, eds. The Dead Sea Scrolls Study Edition. 2 vols. Leiden: Brill, 1997–1998.

VanderKam, James C. The Dead Sea Scrolls Today. Grand Rapids: Eerdmans, 1994.

Vermes, Geza. The Complete Dead Sea Scrolls in English. London: Penguin, 1997.

## III. MIDRASH, TALMUD, AND RABBINIC SOURCES

Danby, Herbert. The Mishnah. Oxford: Oxford University Press, 1933.

Lauterbach, Jacob Z. Mekhilta de-Rabbi Ishmael. 3 vols. Philadelphia: Jewish Publication Society, 1933.

Neusner, Jacob. Genesis Rabbah: The Judaic Commentary to the Book of Genesis, A New American Translation. 3 vols. Atlanta: Scholars Press, 1985.

———. Exodus Rabbah: An Analytical Translation. Atlanta: Scholars Press, 1988.

———. The Babylonian Talmud: A Translation and Commentary. 22 vols. Peabody, MA: Hendrickson, 2011–2016.

Saldarini, Anthony J. The Fathers According to Rabbi Nathan (Avot de-Rabbi Natan), Version B. Leiden: Brill, 1975.

## IV. TARGUMS

Alexander, Philip S. The Targum of Lamentations. Aramaic Bible 17B. Collegeville, MN: Liturgical Press, 2007.

Cathcart, Kevin J., and Robert P. Gordon, eds. The Targum of the Minor Prophets. Aramaic Bible 14. Wilmington, DE: Michael Glazier, 1989.

Chilton, Bruce D. The Isaiah Targum: Introduction, Translation, Apparatus, and Notes. Wilmington, DE: Michael Glazier, 1987.

Grossfeld, Bernard. The Targum Onkelos to Genesis: A Critical Analysis. Wilmington, DE: Michael Glazier, 1988.

## V. PSEUDEPIGRAPHA & APOCRYPHA

Charlesworth, James H., ed. The Old Testament Pseudepigrapha. 2 vols. New York: Doubleday, 1983–1985.

Nickelsburg, George W. E., and James C. VanderKam. 1 Enoch: A New Translation. Minneapolis: Fortress Press, 2004.

Skehan, Patrick W., and Alexander A. Di Lella. The Wisdom of Ben Sira. Anchor Bible 39. New York: Doubleday, 1987.

Wright, R. B. "Psalms of Solomon." Pages 639–670 in The Old Testament Pseudepigrapha. Vol. 2. Edited by James H. Charlesworth. New York: Doubleday, 1985.

---

## VI. EARLY CHURCH & PATRISTIC SOURCES

Augustine. On Christian Doctrine. Translated by D. W. Robertson Jr. Upper Saddle River, NJ: Prentice Hall, 1958.

Chrysostom, John. On the Priesthood. Translated by Graham Neville. Crestwood, NY: St. Vladimir's Seminary Press, 1984.

Holmes, Michael W., ed. The Apostolic Fathers: Greek Texts and English Translations. 3rd ed. Grand Rapids: Baker Academic, 2007.

Kelly, J. N. D. Early Christian Doctrines. Rev. ed. San Francisco: HarperCollins, 1978.

Young, Frances M. Biblical Exegesis and the Formation of Christian Culture. Peabody, MA: Hendrickson, 2002.

---

## VII. BIBLICAL THEOLOGY & SYSTEMATIC THEOLOGY

Barth, Karl. Church Dogmatics. 4 vols. Edinburgh: T&T Clark, 1956–1975.

Bloesch, Donald G. A Theology of Word and Spirit. Downers Grove, IL: InterVarsity Press, 1992.

Fee, Gordon D. God's Empowering Presence. Peabody, MA: Hendrickson, 1994.

Goldsworthy, Graeme. According to Plan. Downers Grove, IL: InterVarsity Press, 1991.

Wright, N. T. Jesus and the Victory of God. Minneapolis: Fortress Press, 1996.

## VIII. REVIVAL HISTORY & SPIRITUAL CLASSICS

Edwards, Jonathan. The Works of Jonathan Edwards. Vol. 4, The Great Awakening. New Haven: Yale University Press, 1972.

Lloyd-Jones, D. Martyn. Revival. Westchester, IL: Crossway, 1987.

Murray, Andrew. The Spirit of Christ. Fort Washington, PA: Christian Literature Crusade, 1984.

Ravenhill, Leonard. Why Revival Tarries. Minneapolis: Bethany House, 1959.

Tozer, A. W. The Pursuit of God. Harrisburg, PA: Christian Publications, 1948.

## IX. HOMILETICS, PREACHING THEORY & PASTORAL THEOLOGY

Greidanus, Sidney. The Modern Preacher and the Ancient Text. Grand Rapids: Eerdmans, 1988.

Keller, Timothy. Preaching: Communicating Faith in an Age of Skepticism. New York: Viking, 2015.

Lloyd-Jones, D. Martyn. Preaching and Preachers. Grand Rapids: Zondervan, 1971.

Piper, John. Expository Exultation: Christian Preaching as Worship. Wheaton, IL: Crossway, 2018.

———. The Supremacy of God in Preaching. Revised and expanded ed. Grand Rapids: Baker Books, 2004.

———. "Preaching as Expository Exultation." Pages 37–56 in The Preacher and Preaching. Edited by Samuel T. Logan Jr. Phillipsburg, NJ: P&R Publishing, 1986.

Robinson, Haddon W. Biblical Preaching. 3rd ed. Grand Rapids: Baker Academic, 2014.

Stott, John R. W. *Between Two Worlds: The Art of Preaching in the Twentieth Century.* Grand Rapids: Eerdmans, 1982.

Willhite, Keith, and Scott M. Gibson, eds. *The Big Idea of Biblical Preaching.* Grand Rapids: Baker, 1998.

## X. COMMENTARIES USED FOR EXEGESIS

Bruce, F. F. *The Epistles to the Colossians, Philemon, and Ephesians.* NICNT. Grand Rapids: Eerdmans, 1984.

France, R. T. *The Gospel of Matthew.* NICNT. Grand Rapids: Eerdmans, 2007.

Garland, David E. *1 Corinthians.* BECNT. Grand Rapids: Baker Academic, 2003.

Johnson, Luke Timothy. *The Acts of the Apostles.* SP 5. Collegeville, MN: Liturgical Press, 1992.

Keener, Craig. *Acts.* 4 vols. Grand Rapids: Baker Academic, 2012–2015.

Lincoln, Andrew T. *Ephesians.* WBC 42. Dallas: Word Books, 1990.

## XI. GENERAL REFERENCE WORKS

Ferguson, Everett. *Backgrounds of Early Christianity.* 3rd ed. Grand Rapids: Eerdmans, 2003.

Levine, Lee I. *The Ancient Synagogue.* 2nd ed. New Haven: Yale University Press, 2005.

Metzger, Bruce M. *The Canon of the New Testament.* Oxford: Clarendon Press, 1987.

Wright, Christopher J. H. *The Mission of God.* Downers Grove, IL: InterVarsity Press, 2006.

# WORKS CITED

**Aland, Kurt, et al., eds.**

The Greek New Testament. 5th ed. Stuttgart: Deutsche Bibelgesellschaft, 2014.

**Alexander, Philip S.**

The Targum of Lamentations. Aramaic Bible 17B. Collegeville, MN: Liturgical Press, 2007.

**Augustine.**

On Christian Doctrine. Translated by D. W. Robertson Jr. Upper Saddle River, NJ: Prentice Hall, 1958.

**Barth, Markus.**

Ephesians 4–6. Anchor Bible 34A. Garden City, NY: Doubleday, 1974.

**Bartleman, Frank.**

Azusa Street: An Eyewitness Account. New Kensington, PA: Whitaker House, 1982 (or 1925 original).

**Bauer, Walter, Frederick William Danker, William F. Arndt, and F. Wilbur Gingrich.**

A Greek-English Lexicon of the New Testament and Other Early Christian Literature. 3rd ed. Chicago: University of Chicago Press, 2000.

**Blenkinsopp, Joseph.**

A History of Prophecy in Israel. Rev. ed. Louisville: Westminster John Knox Press, 1996.

**Bounds, E. M.**

Power Through Prayer. Chicago: Moody Press, n.d..

**Brown, Francis, S. R. Driver, and Charles A. Briggs.**

A Hebrew and English Lexicon of the Old Testament. Boston: Houghton Mifflin, 1907.

A Hebrew and English Lexicon of the Old Testament. Oxford: Clarendon, 1906.

**Bruce, F. F.**

Paul: Apostle of the Heart Set Free. Grand Rapids: Eerdmans, 1977.

The Epistles to the Colossians, to Philemon, and to the Ephesians. NICNT. Grand Rapids: Eerdmans, 1984.

**Buber, Martin ed.**

Midrash on Psalms. Yale Judaica Series 13. New Haven: Yale University Press, 1947.

**Calvin, John**

Commentaries on the Book of the Prophet Jeremiah and the Lamentations. Translated by John Owen. 5 vols. Edinburgh: Calvin Translation Society. 1850-1855

**Cathcart, Kevin J., and Robert P. Gordon, eds.**

The Targum of the Minor Prophets. Aramaic Bible 14. Wilmington, DE: Michael Glazier, 1989.

**Charlesworth, James H., ed.**

The Old Testament Pseudepigrapha. 2 vols. New York: Doubleday, 1983–1985.

**Chilton, Bruce D.**

The Isaiah Targum: Introduction, Translation, Apparatus, and Notes. Wilmington, DE: Michael Glazier, 1987.

**Childs, Brevard S.**

The Book of Exodus: A Critical, Theological Commentary. Old Testament Library. Philadelphia: Westminster Press, 1974.

**Chrysostom, John.**

On the Priesthood. Translated by Graham Neville. Crestwood, NY: St. Vladimir's Seminary Press, 1984.

**Craigie, Peter C.**

The Book of Deuteronomy. NICOT. Grand Rapids: Eerdmans, 1976.

**Danby, Herbert.**

The Mishnah. Oxford: Oxford University Press, 1933.

**Edwards, Jonathan.**

The Works of Jonathan Edwards. Vol. 4: The Great Awakening. New Haven: Yale University Press, 1972.

**Evans, Craig A.**

Ancient Texts for New Testament Studies. Peabody, MA: Hendrickson, 2005.

**Fee, Gordon D.**

God's Empowering Presence. Peabody, MA: Hendrickson, 1994.

**Ferguson, Everett.**

Backgrounds of Early Christianity. 3rd ed. Grand Rapids: Eerdmans, 2003.

**France, R. T.**

The Gospel of Matthew. NICNT. Grand Rapids: Eerdmans, 2007.

**García Martínez, Florentino.**

The Dead Sea Scrolls Translated: The Qumran Texts in English. 2nd ed. Grand Rapids: Eerdmans, 1996.

**García Martínez, Florentino, and Eibert J. C. Tigchelaar, eds.**

The Dead Sea Scrolls Study Edition. 2 vols. Leiden: Brill, 1997–1998.

**Garland, David E.**

1 Corinthians. BECNT. Grand Rapids: Baker Academic, 2003.

**Goldsworthy, Graeme.**

According to Plan. Downers Grove, IL: InterVarsity Press, 1991.

**Greidanus, Sidney.**

The Modern Preacher and the Ancient Text. Grand Rapids: Eerdmans, 1988.

**Grossfeld, Bernard.**

The Targum Onkelos to Genesis: A Critical Analysis. Wilmington, DE: Michael Glazier, 1988.

**Hagner, Donald A.**

The Jewish Reclamation of Jesus. Grand Rapids: Zondervan, 1984

**Hamon, Bill.**

Apostles, Prophets and the Coming Moves of God: God's End-Time Plans for His Church and Planet Earth. Shippensburg, PA: Destiny Image, 1997.

**Hill, Andrew E.**

Malachi. Anchor Bible 25D. New York: Doubleday, 1998.

**Holmes, Michael W., ed.**

The Apostolic Fathers: Greek Texts and English Translations. 3rd ed. Grand Rapids: Baker Academic, 2007.

**Johnson, Luke Timothy.**

The Acts of the Apostles. Sacra Pagina 5. Collegeville, MN: Liturgical Press, 1992.

**Keener, Craig S.**

Acts. 4 vols. Grand Rapids: Baker Academic, 2012–2015.

**Keller, Timothy.**

Preaching: Communicating Faith in an Age of Skepticism. New York: Viking, 2015.

**Kelly, J. N. D.**

Early Christian Doctrines. Rev. ed. San Francisco: HarperCollins, 1978.

**Kittel, Gerhard, ed.**

Theological Dictionary of the New Testament. 10 vols. Grand Rapids: Eerdmans, 1964–1976.

**Koehler, Ludwig, Walter Baumgartner, and Johann J. Stamm.**

The Hebrew and Aramaic Lexicon of the Old Testament. 2 vols. Leiden: Brill, 1994.

**Levenson, Jon D.**

Creation and the Persistence of Evil: The Jewish Drama of Divine Omnipotence. San Francisco: Harper & Row, 1988.

**Lincoln, Andrew T.**

Ephesians. Word Biblical Commentary 42. Dallas: Word Books, 1990.

**Lloyd-Jones, D. Martyn.**

Preaching and Preachers. Grand Rapids: Zondervan, 1971.

Revival. Westchester, IL: Crossway, 1987.

**Martínez, Florentino García, and Eibert J. C. Tigchelaar, eds.**

The Dead Sea Scrolls Study Edition. 2 vols. Leiden: Brill, 1997–1998.

**McNamara, Martin, trans. Targum Neofiti**

1: Exodus. Vol. 2 of The Aramaic Bible. Wilmington, DE: Michael Glazier, 1994.

**Metzger, Bruce M.**

The Canon of the New Testament. Oxford: Clarendon Press, 1987.

**Mounce, William D.**

Basics of Biblical Greek Grammar. 4th ed. Grand Rapids: Zondervan, 2019.

**Murray, Andrew.**

The Spirit of Christ. Fort Washington, PA: Christian Literature Crusade, 1984.

**Neusner, Jacob.**

Genesis Rabbah: The Judaic Commentary to the Book of Genesis. 3 vols. Atlanta: Scholars Press, 1985.

Nickelsburg, George W. E., and James C. VanderKam.

1 Enoch: A New Translation. Minneapolis: Fortress Press, 2004.

Newman, Carol

Songs of Sabbath Sacrifice: A Critical Edition. Harvard Semitic Studies 27. Atlanta Scholars Press, 1985.

Piper, John.

Expository Exultation: Christian Preaching as Worship. Wheaton, IL: Crossway, 2018.

———.

The Supremacy of God in Preaching. Revised and expanded ed. Grand Rapids: Baker Books, 2004.

———.

"Preaching as Expository Exultation." Pages 37–56 in The Preacher and Preaching. Edited by Samuel T. Logan Jr. Phillipsburg, NJ: P&R Publishing, 1986.

Ravenhill, Leonard.

Why Revival Tarries. Minneapolis: Bethany House, 1959.

Roberts, Richard Owen.

The Welsh Revival of 1904–1905. Wheaton, IL: International Awakening Press, 1999.

Robinson, Haddon W.

Biblical Preaching. 3rd ed. Grand Rapids: Baker Academic, 2014.

Skehan, Patrick W., and Alexander A. Di Lella.

The Wisdom of Ben Sira. Anchor Bible 39. New York: Doubleday, 1987.

**Stott, John R. W.**

Between Two Worlds: The Art of Preaching in the Twentieth Century. Grand Rapids: Eerdmans, 1982.

**Strack, Hermann L., and Günter Stemberger.**

Introduction to the Talmud and Midrash. Translated by Markus Bockmuehl. Minneapolis: Fortress, 1996.

**Theodor, J., and Ch. Albeck, eds.**

Bereshit Rabbah. 3 vols. Jerusalem: Wahrmann Books, 1965

**Tozer, A. W.**

The Pursuit of God. Harrisburg, PA: Christian Publications, 1948.

**VanderKam, James C.**

The Book of Jubilees. 2 vols. Corpus Scriptorum Christianorum Orientalium. Louvain: Peeters, 1989.

**Vos, Geerhardus**.

Biblical Theology: Old and New Testaments. Edinburgh: Banner of Truth, 1948.

**Wagner, C. Peter**.

Apostles and Prophets: The Foundation of the Church. Ventura, CA: Regal, 2000.

**Waltke, Bruce K., and Michael P. O'Connor.**

An Introduction to Biblical Hebrew Syntax. Winona Lake, IN: Eisenbrauns, 1990.

**Waltke, Bruce K.**

Genesis: A Commentary. Grand Rapids: Zondervan, 2001

**Wallace, Daniel B.**

Greek Grammar Beyond the Basics. Grand Rapids: Zondervan, 1996.

**Westermann, Claus.**

Genesis 1–11: A Commentary. Translated by John J. Scullion. Minneapolis: Augsburg, 1984

**Wright, Christopher J. H.**

The Mission of God. Downers Grove, IL: InterVarsity Press, 2006.

**Wright, N. T.**

Jesus and the Victory of God. Minneapolis: Fortress Press, 1996.

# Intellectual Stewardship Policy

## FAIR USE AND CITATION

The Ministry of Preaching: Preaching Through Eternity — Faithfulness to God's Word in the Last Days

This work makes use of Scripture, ancient texts, modern translations, scholarly works, and academic commentary.

All quoted material is used in strict accordance with:
United States Copyright Law, 17 U.S.C. §107 (Fair Use) and standard academic citation practices prescribed by the Society of Biblical Literature (SBL), 2nd Edition.

This Fair Use and Citation Policy governs the entire work, including its appendices, notes, charts, models, and all exegetical content.

### 1. Scripture Citations
King James Version (KJV)
The KJV is in the public domain and may be quoted freely.
Other Bible translations: This work does not reproduce large blocks of copyrighted translations. Only brief quotations are included, well below the allowances of major Bible copyright holders and always attributed according to SBL standards.
No more than two consecutive verses or one sentence from any copyrighted translation appears without explicit permission.

### 2. Ancient Jewish and Christian Sources

This work quotes small portions of:

- Dead Sea Scroll translations
- Targums
- Midrashim
- Early Jewish writings
- Church Fathers
- Noncanonical / Second Temple literature
- Pseudepigrapha

All such quotations are:

- brief,

- non-substantial,
- purely for academic analysis,
- and fully attributed to their published scholarly editions.

No extended passages from copyrighted scholarly translations of ancient texts have been reproduced.

References to modern translations of ancient works do not reproduce protected content but merely cite chapter, line, or column numbers for reader orientation.

### 3. Modern Scholarly Works

Modern academic monographs, journal articles, commentary sets, and other scholarly resources referenced in this work are:

- cited accurately,
- quoted briefly,
- and clearly identified in the Works Cited section.

Quotations from copyrighted scholarship are limited to short excerpts necessary for critical engagement, consistent with academic fair use.
No diagrams, charts, typographic design elements, or proprietary homiletical frameworks from copyrighted works are reproduced.
All original charts, pathways, diagrams, and models in this book are the intellectual property of the author.

### 4. Purpose and Nature of Use

All quoted material is used exclusively for:

- academic commentary,
- theological reflection,
- critical analysis,
- educational instruction,
- historical background,
- and nonprofit religious teaching.

This work is transformational in nature, adding:

- new exegetical frameworks,
- original models,

- new theological synthesis,
- pastoral application,
- and revival-focused reflection.

The use is not commercial appropriation of copyrighted expression, but scholarly engagement for theological education, which falls squarely within Fair Use doctrine.

## 5. Amount and Substantiality

This work does not reproduce:

- substantial sections of any copyrighted book,
- full chapters from any commentary,
- complete Dead Sea Scroll translations,
- extended Midrash units,
- full Targum passages,
- extensive journal article quotations,
- proprietary methods from homiletical texts.

All quotations are deliberately minimal and well within statutory fair-use limits.

## 6. Market Effect

This work in no way displaces or competes with the market value of any copyrighted source.

Instead, it:

- drives readers to the cited scholars,
- directs readers to original editions,
- increases academic engagement,
- and encourages the study of the primary texts themselves.

Thus, it satisfies the fourth Fair Use factor (effect on the market).

## 7. Permissions

If at any time publisher or peer review determines that certain quotations exceed Fair Use thresholds, the author is fully committed to:

- securing written permission,
- editing the relevant section, or
- replacing the quotation with citation-only references.

The author's intent is full compliance and academic integrity.

## 8. Rights Statement

This Fair Use and Citation Policy applies to every chapter, appendix, chart, diagram, and footnote in this publication.

It serves as the work's formal declaration of:

- intellectual honesty,
- lawful usage,
- scholarly transparency,
- and compliance with all relevant copyright provisions.

### Conclusion:

This book honors Scripture, respects scholarship, and complies fully with United States copyright law, international academic standards, and the ethical use of intellectual property.

All quotations—biblical, ancient, or modern—are included solely to illuminate truth, advance learning of the Scriptures, and serve the global church.

## PERMISSIONS STATEMENT

Rights, Reuse, and Contact Information for This Publication
This publication, including its chapters, appendices, charts, diagrams, models, and original textual analysis, is protected by U.S. copyright law (17 U.S.C. §§101–122), international copyright conventions, and the intellectual property rights of the author.

Nothing in this work may be reproduced, stored, transmitted, distributed, translated, or adapted—whether in print, digital, audio, visual, or online formats—without prior written permission from the rights holder, except for brief quotations permitted under Fair Use and standard academic practice.

This includes but is not limited to:
- sermon outlines
- charts, diagrams, tables, or models
- study guides and teaching tools
- appendices and curated reference lists
- original exegesis and theological frameworks
- devotional materials
- training manuals
- digital, audio, and multimedia formats

Requests for permission should be directed to:

Victory Life Ministries Press
Attn: Permissions Office
PO Box 25
Pounding Mill, VA 24637
Email: victorylifemissions@gmail.com

Permission is normally granted for:

- nonprofit educational uses
- seminary or Bible school instruction
- local church teaching contexts
- ministry training programs
- missionary work

Permission may be declined for any use that:

- alters the original meaning,
- misrepresents the author's theology,
- commercializes the work without agreement,
- or violates the integrity of the text.

Victory Life Ministries Press maintains the right to review all requests individually.

# Stewardship Statement

To preserve academic integrity, protect intellectual property, and ensure faithful representation of this work, all quotations, summaries, paraphrases, diagrams, models, or derivative teaching must adhere to SBL 2nd Edition citation standards, the normative format for biblical and theological scholarship.

Any use of material from this book must:

1. Cite the author by full name: Aaron Michael Roberts.
2. Cite the title of the work exactly as published.
3. Include publisher information and date of publication.
4. Indicate page numbers or appendix numbers where applicable.
5. Acknowledge direct quotations and paraphrases clearly.
6. Give attribution for any diagrams, charts, models, or original frameworks.
7. Avoid presenting the author's original material as one's own.

In classroom settings, sermons, conference teachings, podcasts, livestreams, websites, training manuals, social media posts, or discipleship resources:

- Any quotation longer than one sentence must be cited.
- Any paraphrase involving unique concepts or wording must be cited.
- Any reproduction of charts, diagrams, or frameworks must be credited.
- Public teaching environments must acknowledge the source verbally or in writing.

For academic writing:

- Citations must follow SBL Handbook of Style, 2nd ed.
- Footnotes must include full bibliographic details at first mention.
- A Works Cited or Bibliography entry must appear at the end of the document.

Use of this book's material without attribution constitutes plagiarism under academic standards and may violate copyright law.

Victory Life Ministries Press warmly encourages pastors, professors, and ministry leaders to use this material—with proper citation and respect for the author's work

## About The Fire from the Scroll Series

The Fire from the Scroll series is a multi-volume theological project dedicated to recovering the biblical patterns by which God forms, sends, and sustains His people through the proclaimed Word. Each volume traces a distinct dimension of the way within the ordered witness of Scripture, emphasizing that true spiritual fire arises only from faithful engagement with the written revelation of God. Together, the series seeks to serve both theological institutions and frontline pulpits by forming witnesses whose preaching endures beyond its moment and bears testimony across the generations.

---

## Author Biographical Sketch

Aaron Michael Roberts has dedicated over thirty-five years to preaching, pioneering churches, teaching, and traveling to equip indigenous pastors across Africa and restricted-access nations. He is the founder of Victory Life International Ministries and lives in the Appalachian Mountains of Virginia. As the author of the Fire from the Scroll series, his work focuses on recovering biblical patterns of proclamation to strengthen the frontline pulpits of the global Church, forming witnesses faithful to Scripture across the generations.